YOUNG PEOPLE AND HOUSING

Younger generations across a wide range of societies face increasing difficulties in gaining access to housing. Housing occupies a pivotal position in the transition from parental dependence to adult independence. Delayed independence has significant implications for marriage and family formation, fertility, inter- and intragenerational tensions, social mobility and social inequalities.

The social and cultural dimensions are, of course, enormously varied, with strong contrasts between Asian and Western societies in terms of intergenerational norms and practices in relation to housing. Nevertheless, younger households in China (including Hong Kong), Japan, the USA, Australasia and Europe face very similar challenges in the housing sphere. Moreover, concerns about the housing future for younger generations are gaining greater policy and popular prominence in many countries.

All the papers in *Young People and Housing* were specially commissioned for a symposium in Hong Kong that took place in summer 2011. This brought together a small group of specially invited international experts, in a round table format, to explore the specific institutional, economic and cultural factors at work in different national contexts.

Ray Forrest is Chair Professor in Housing and Urban Studies, City University of Hong Kong and Professor Emeritus of Urban Studies at the University of Bristol.

Ngai ming Yip is an Associate Professor in the Department of Public and Social Administration, City University of Hong Kong.

Housing and society series

Edited by Ray Forrest, School for Policy Studies,
University of Bristol

This series aims to situate housing within its wider social, political and economic context at both national and international level. In doing so it will draw on the full range of social science disciplines and on mainstream debate on the nature of contemporary social change. The books are intended to appeal to an international academic audience as well as to practitioners and policymakers – to be theoretically informed and policy relevant.

Young People and Housing
Transitions, trajectories and generational fractures
Edited by Ray Forrest and Ngai ming Yip

Beyond Home Ownership
Edited by Richard Ronald and Marja Elsinga

Housing Disadvantaged People?
Jane Ball

Women and Housing
Edited by Patricia Kennett and Chan Kam Wah

Affluence, Mobility and Second Home Ownership
Chris Paris

Housing, Markets and Policy
Peter Malpass and Rob Rowlands

Housing and Health in Europe
Edited by David Ormandy

The Hidden Millions
Graham Tipple & Suzanne Speak

Housing, Care and Inheritance
Misa Izuhara

Housing and Social Transition in Japan
Edited by Yosuke Hirayama and Richard Ronald

Housing Transformations
Shaping the space of 21st century living
Bridget Franklin

Housing and Social Policy
Contemporary themes and critical perspectives
Edited by Peter Somerville with Nigel Sprigings

Housing and Social Change
East-West perspectives
Edited by Ray Forrest and James Lee

Urban Poverty, Housing and Social Change in China
Ya Ping Wang

Gentrification in a Global Context
Edited by Rowland Atkinson and Gary Bridge

YOUNG PEOPLE AND HOUSING

Transitions, trajectories and generational fractures

Edited by Ray Forrest and Ngai ming Yip

Routledge
Taylor & Francis Group

LONDON AND NEW YORK

First edition published 2013
by Routledge
2 Park Square, Milton Park, Abingdon, Oxon, OX14 4RN

Simultaneously published in the USA and Canada
by Routledge
711 Third Avenue, New York, NY 10017

Routledge is an imprint of the Taylor & Francis Group, an informa business

British Library Cataloguing in Publication Data
A catalogue record for this book is available from the British Library

Library of Congress Cataloging-in-Publication Data
A catalog record has been requested for this book

ISBN13: 978-0-415-63335-2 (hbk)
ISBN13: 978-0-415-63336-9 (pbk)
ISBN13: 978-0-203-09509-6 (ebk)

Typeset in Bembo by
RefineCatch Limited, Bungay, Suffolk

MIX
Paper from
responsible sources
FSC
www.fsc.org   FSC® C004839

Printed and bound in Great Britain by the MPG Books Group

CONTENTS

FIGURES

TABLES

CONTRIBUTORS

Andrew Beer is a Professor in the School of Social Sciences, University of Adelaide. He is the Director of the Centre for Housing, Urban and Regional Planning and a geographer by background. His interests include the relationship between housing and the life course, regional economic development policies and homelessness.

Fanny Bugeja-Bloch is an Associate Professor at the University of Nanterre (Université Paris-Ouest). Her interests are in urban and consumption sociology and social stratification. She is responsible for quantitative sociology teachings. She is the author and co-author of chapters and articles on housing tenure and housing costs in France and in the United Kingdom.

Dimitris Emmanuel studied architecture and planning at NTU, Athens and undertook postgraduate work in urban geography and planning at the LSE, where he received his MSc and PhD. He has worked mainly in social and economic research and on planning and policy studies in the field of housing and urban development. He was a Head of the Research and Housing Policy Studies Unit at DEPOS, the Greek Public Corporation for Housing and Urban Planning (1979–2003). Since 2004 he has been a Research Director in the Institute for Urban and Rural Sociology at the Greek National Centre for Social Research. His recent publications include *Supply of Planned Land, Housing and Prices in Athens (1984–2004)* (Athens, NCSR).

Debbie Faulkner is a Research Fellow in the Department of Geography and Environmental Studies at the University of Adelaide. She has published widely on issues of housing and ageing, demographic processes and immigration.

Ray Forrest is Chair Professor in Housing and Urban Studies, City University of Hong Kong and Professor Emeritus of Urban Studies at the University of Bristol.

He is a founding member of the Asia-Pacific Network for Housing Research and co-editor of *Housing Studies*. He is currently involved in research on neighbourhood change in Vietnam and on the post-80s generation in Hong Kong.

Yosuke Hirayama is a Professor of Housing and Urban Studies at the Graduate School of Human Development and Environment, Kobe University, Japan, working extensively in the areas of housing and urban change, home ownership and social inequalities, as well as comparative housing policy. His work has appeared in numerous international and Japanese academic journals and he is a co-editor of *Housing and Social Transition in Japan* (Routledge). He has received academic prizes from the City Planning Institute of Japan, Architectural Institute of Japan and Tokyo Institute for Municipal Research. He is also a founding member of the Asia-Pacific Network for Housing Research.

William D. H. Li is an Associate Professor at the National Dong Hwa University, Taiwan, and is currently the visiting scholar at the Southwestern University of Finances and Economics, Chengdu, China. He is the author of *Housing in Taiwan: Agency and Structure?* (Ashgate, 1998) and currently he is undertaking research on housing, family and social policy.

Mats Lieberg is a Professor of Urban Sociology at the Department of Landscape Architecture, Swedish University of Agricultural Sciences. His special areas of expertise are urban studies and urban theory, youth culture, housing research and urban recreational studies. His current research concerns spatial and ethnographic studies of social networks, informal structures and urban encounters in public spaces.

Michelle Norris lectures at the School of Applied Social Science, University College Dublin, Ireland. She previously worked as a Director of the Centre for Housing Research, which conducts housing research and policy analysis for the Irish housing ministry and the local government sector. She has researched and published on a wide range of housing issues including: social housing management and finance, urban regeneration, state support for and regulation of private rented housing and housing inequalities across the European Union. She co-convenes the Comparative Housing Working Group of the European Network for Housing Research.

Teresio Poggio is an Executive Coordinator of the Research Laboratory of the Department of Sociology and Social Research at the University of Trento. His main research interests include housing, welfare, family and social stratification. His recent work is focused on the role of the intergenerational transmission of home ownership in the shaping of Mediterranean welfare systems and in the structuring of social inequality. He has coordinated, with Chiara Saraceno, the EQUALSOC working group *The intergenerational transmission of inequality: analytic possibilities from existing data* (2008–2010).

Nessa Winston is a Lecturer in the School of Applied Social Science, University College Dublin. Her main research interests centre on sustainable housing policies and practices in urban and rural contexts. She is currently involved in an international project funded by the EU Seventh Framework Programme on the impacts of increasing inequalities. The focus of her research is on housing and inequality from a comparative perspective. She has received a number of research grants to examine housing, urban regeneration and sustainability, and continues to pursue her interest in the development of sustainable communities from a housing perspective.

Ngai ming Yip is an Associate Professor in the Department of Public and Social Administration, City University of Hong Kong. His research covers housing policy and management, spatial segregation, urban policy and issues relating to neighbourhood and grassroots government. He is currently undertaking a project on the neighbourhood and social change in Hanoi, Vietnam. His work appears in international journals on housing and urban studies as well as China and Asian studies

Jane Zavisca is an Associate Professor of Sociology at the University of Arizona. Her research focuses on inequality and legitimacy of housing systems. Her book *Housing the New Russia* (Cornell University Press, 2012) explores the failed attempt to transplant the American model of housing markets to Russia. She is currently designing a new survey of housing mobility and inequality in Russia and working on a new manuscript on the culture of American mortgages.

Yapeng Zhu is Associate Professor at the Centre for Chinese Public Administration Research/School of Government, Sun Yat-sen University (Guangzhou, China). His research interests focus on the policy process, social security and housing policy in China. He publishes in both Chinese and English. His publications include *Housing Reform in China: Policy Innovation and Housing Inequality* (Sun Yat-Sen University Press, 2007) and articles in *The Pacific Review*, *The China Review* and *Politics and Policy.*

PREFACE

This book originated in a two-day symposium held at the City University of Hong Kong in May 2011. Eleven invited speakers presented specially prepared papers which were then discussed and debated among the small number of participants in a round table format. This arrangement, unlike the more conventional open forum conference, allowed substantial time for an exchange of views and for an intensive but relaxed exploration of the conceptual and policy issues.

The primary objective of the symposium was to bring together a small group of international experts to explore the contemporary housing experiences of younger people. Younger generations across a wide range of societies seemed to be facing increasing difficulties in gaining access to decent and appropriate housing. There seemed to be a number of interconnected factors at work, which were creating more problematic housing trajectories for younger generations – trajectories which were often in sharp contrast to those of previous, baby boomer generations. These factors included the impact of neoliberalism on housing institutions and policies, growing affordability difficulties associated with greater market dominance of housing systems, flexibility and casualization in labour markets, longer periods in full-time education, and rising debts and growing economic instability and uncertainty. The consequences of these developments was evident in an increased or renewed reliance of younger people on parental resources, delayed departure from the family home, declining marriage rates and falling levels of home ownership among younger generations.

It was recognized, however, that specific institutional, economic and cultural factors could be at work in different national contexts producing apparently similar trends. And similar patterns in housing systems could conceal quite different underlying drivers of change with both common and differentiated consequences for younger people. Moreover, social and cultural dimensions are enormously varied. There are strong contrasts between, for example, East Asian and Western societies and between southern and northern Europe in terms of intergenerational norms and practices in relation to housing. In addition, the nature and pace of economic development and social change is strikingly different between Europe and East Asia – a difference which has sharpened since the symposium. Thus, this collection encompasses the experiences of Australia, Russia, Japan, Ireland, China, Sweden, Greece, Ireland, Italy, Taiwan and Hong Kong. Following an introductory essay, the chapters are organized under three main themes: the family, demography and the transition to adulthood; housing affordability and youth housing trajectories; and economic change and generational fractures. These thematic sections are designed to convey the different emphases of the chapters rather than to suggest there are clear-cut boundaries in the discussion. There are inevitable overlaps and interconnections.

Finally, various acknowledgements and thanks are required. The Department of Public and Social Administration at the City University of Hong Kong provided the funding for the entire event. Particular thanks go to Ying Wu and Otto Lau, who took charge of all the logistical and administrative arrangements including organizing the venue, and to Heidi Ng who did an enormous amount of work transforming all the chapters into the required format and generally tidying up the script for publication. This book provides the international backcloth for the research project *Housing the Post-Eighties Generation: Attitudes, Aspirations and Future Trajectories* supported by the Hong Kong RGC (No. 9041696).

1

MAKING SENSE OF THE HOUSING TRAJECTORIES OF YOUNG PEOPLE

Ray Forrest

Introduction

Debates in housing and urban studies have often neglected, or at least underplayed, relevant theory and evidence from other research areas. Equally, an appreciation of the importance of housing and a proper understanding of housing market dynamics and shifts in housing policy are sometimes lacking in accounts of contemporary social change. A key point of contact between these different literatures is the process of transition from the parental home to independent living. Describing it as a 'process' rather than a 'moment' is a central theme of this book and in the wider literature on contemporary youth transitions. The idea that on a particular day we pack up and say goodbye forever to the parental home has never accurately captured the tentative messiness of this moment in our lives. For some it may well have been that definitive. But for others it has often been experienced as a more gradual transition, perhaps initially involving short periods away for training or work or in some cases compulsory military service. Initial forays into the housing and labour markets, and into relationships, may go wrong and necessitate a return 'home'.

Disorderly transitions and more deep-seated transformations in the nature and pattern of the shift to adulthood are also likely to be more evident in periods of rapid social and economic change. There are the direct and indirect disruptions associated with war, the consequences of rapid economic collapse and forced mass migrations. For the postwar youth of the global north, the evident changes in the transition to adulthood have generally been occasioned by less dramatic and negative events – more closely associated with ideas of the 'second demographic transition', the 'modernization' of the life course and increasing individualization. These developments are associated with a mix of less predictability in personal biographies, a greater independence of action and thought, greater differentiation in terms of aspiration and outcomes among young people themselves and a more 'episodic' conception of the transition from youth to adulthood. The common view would seem to be that the period of youth is now longer and less tidy – and that this untidiness is now more commonly experienced and is becoming more problematic.

We shall return later to the explanation for these developments, and indeed whether this represents an accurate view of this stage in the contemporary life course. At this point, however, it is appropriate initially to explore where housing fits into this picture. In general terms, the issue of housing is and has always been absolutely central to this stage in our personal biographies. Roberts (2006) stresses that there is a whole mix of interrelated factors which structure youth opportunities, including labour market changes, welfare systems and justice systems. But the transition from 'living in dwellings headed by adult seniors to ones in which young adults are the seniors' is of fundamental importance. Moreover, the 'school-to-work and family/housing transitions are always interrelated, but neither determines the other' (p.205). In more specific terms, the more recent ideological and economic climate would seem to have made access to independent housing more difficult for current younger generations. Housing analysts refer to greater problems of affordability, reduced investment in social housing and the need for higher deposits in a more risk-averse economic environment as key factors affecting the ability to leave home. The relevance of these housing market and housing policy factors to patterns of leaving home will, of course, vary substantially across time and space. For example, relatively affluent societies with mature and dominant home ownership sectors will provide a very different context for new, younger households compared to a more rapidly developing society in which traditional housing practices mix with nascent private market developments.

Housing is clearly important in the transition to adulthood. But from a housing perspective its importance should not be reduced to only issues of rent or house price levels, changes in housing policies or the impacts of housing booms and busts. It is not just about access to rental or mortgaged housing at a particular stage in the life course. Nor from a broader sociological perspective is it only about the acquisition of social status and social position. Housing is important as home, as an emotional as much as a material good (Smith and Munro, 2008), as parental home, as well as a key signifier of independence and for its symbolic role in the maturation of relationships. Housing is implicated in processes of both commitment and escape, freedom and responsibility, independence and reciprocity. In other words, we should be cautious in overemphasizing the impact of housing market discontinuities and of neglecting the housing continuities of the aspects of the transition to adulthood.

We should also be wary of describing the position of young people in any particular society at any particular moment in an undifferentiated way. There will be significant intra- as well as inter-cohort differences in relation to social trajectories and opportunities. These differences may also conflict with caricatures and dramatizations of more general changes affecting younger people. Doogan (2009) has, for example, argued that, particularly for young people, part-time work should not be seen as necessarily synonymous with insecurity and casualization. Nor should we take at face value statements about the end of the age of 'careers' and sequential progress in employment. These questions always need to be examined empirically; nor should comparisons be made with some usually unspecified era in which predictability and neat progression are assumed to have been a universal experience.

Conceptualizing the transition from youth to adulthood

There is an inevitable tendency and temptation to see things from a contemporary and ethnocentric perspective. The dominant contemporary pattern of departure from the parental home is taken as the norm. The postwar baby boomers in northern European societies may have assumed, for example, that leaving home at a relatively early age was normal. Moreover, they assumed that they had left home at an earlier age than their parents and their children would probably do the same. There is also sometimes a normative element here: an implicit view that it is intrinsically desirable to leave home at a relatively young age in order to establish an independent, adult identity and lifestyle – to grow up. Trends suggesting a shift in the opposite direction are thus often taken to be socially problematic – captured in pejorative labelling such as 'parasite singles' (Genda, 2000) or 'kippers' (kids in parents' pockets eroding retirement savings) (BBC, 2003).

The next section will address cross-national variations in patterns of leaving home. Here the focus is on two interrelated issues with regard to the more general conceptualization of the transition to adulthood. First, in what general ways has the pattern of transition changed and what are the explanations for these changes? Second, how can we best capture the different kinds of living arrangements experienced by young adults?

It is appropriate to reflect briefly on the historical evidence in this field. Much of the relevant evidence is found in narratives of family life from past centuries and in cultural rather than sociological studies. Census data do permit some longitudinal analyses, although it is often difficult to gain the precision required to make systematic comparison of patterns of leaving home over time. It is also important to stress again the importance of differentiating leaving home from living away (see, for example, Jones, 1995; Geurrero, 2001). For example, my grandfather was living away from home a year earlier than I was. He left to join the navy at 17 whereas I left for university at 18. My father, however, left home much earlier than I did. I finally left home and set up an independent household when I was 21. He started work and rented 'digs' when he was 19. There is therefore a highly uneven historical pattern in the transition to adulthood – as there is in patterns of mobility. Serving in the armed forces, or more pertinently the era of mass domestic service in European societies, involved many young people living away from home at a very early age. In this context Billari (2004) observes that 'In the central and northwestern parts of the continent [Europe], a significant percentage of young people spent a more or less prolonged period of time outside their parents' household, normally involved as rural servants or as urban workers. As a consequence, young people often left the parental household long before marriage' (p.22). Equally, the need for adult children to stay on in the domestic household and to contribute in cash or in kind was much greater in western societies in the past. Inevitably, these patterns differed between urban and rural areas and there are longstanding historical differences between Northern and Southern Europe on a number of dimensions (a point taken up by Emmanuel in this volume).

It is possible, therefore, to construct arguments that, if indeed the transition to independent living is taking longer now, then it may be the recent past which is aberrant, and we are returning to a more historically typical state of affairs in many societies. Of course, the conclusions drawn from these kinds of comparisons are fundamentally affected by the time periods being compared as well as the depth and scope of the data. Moreover, cross-cultural comparisons may produce quite different patterns – or alternatively reveal similar patterns produced by different factors. Greater complexity is also produced by intra-cohort analysis. For example, working class children may be leaving home at a young age because they enter the labour market earlier, migrate to other cities to work and qualify for access to social housing when they start a family, whereas the opposite trend may hold for middle class children who stay longer in the education system, experience periods of living away and enter the labour market much later.

Urbanization and industrialization had a major impact on family life and youth transitions in the nineteenth and early twentieth centuries in Europe and North America. Just as in China today, or in other parts of Asia or Latin America, migrants to new cities were often young single people rather than whole families. In the USA it was estimated that around 20 per cent of nineteenth-century urban households had lodgers (Modell and Harven, 1973, referred to in Thornton and Fricke, 1987, p.760). Sometimes these youth migrations for work involve dormitory living, which, as Thornton and Fricke (1987) point out, represents a significant change in living arrangements for young people. More contemporary youth migrations involving dormitory-type accommodation have been common in East Asia. As Taiwan industrialized, a study found that 'about one third of women reaching adulthood have experienced living in a work-related dormitory' (Thornton and Fricke, p.761). And China's high-speed development has involved short- and medium-term migration of generally younger people on a truly monumental scale, with many living in dormitories. Interestingly, such dormitory-type developments have often attracted concerns about youth socialization from governments uneasy about the lack of social control in such areas (Thornton and Lin, 1994).

Evidently then, one's perspective on, and experience of, the contemporary process of leaving home depends on who you are, where you are, and when you are. While proletarianization and industrialization continue to shape many parts of the world, in western societies the dominant view is that the industrial narrative has ended and the post-Fordist or post-industrial era has created greater complexity, unpredictability and variety in the transition from youth to adulthood. Biggart and Walther (2006) refer to 'yo-yo transitions', in which leaving home involves more false starts and periods of semi-dependency. 'We begin by providing an outline of the concept of de-standardization and the increasing 'yo-yo' nature of transitions as they have become less linear, more complex and also reversible' (p.41–42).

A paper written thirty years earlier, however, offers a rather different representation of the youth transition. Modell, Furstenberg and Hershberg (1976) attempt a comparison between the youth transitions of the nineteenth century and the 1970s. In doing so, they remark that, 'As is often the case, our historical image is the product of no research in particular, but is instead based on nostalgia and the need for a contrasting image to our concept of youth today' (p.7). They refer to a literature which suggested that pre-adult life courses were much less predictable 'then' than 'now': 'Early life in the nineteenth-century might be said to be disorderly. . . . Youth was not a clearly progressive and irreversible status sequence, but was variable and seemingly capricious' (p.8). Sounds familiar. Using data which are admitted to be broad brush, they conclude *inter alia* that the youth transition of the 1970s in the USA has become more integrated primarily because it is 'constrained by a set of formal institutions. The institutions with which individuals must increasingly deal call for and reward precise behaviour' (p.21). Here they are referring to schooling, occupational training and the structure of the contemporary labour market. Moreover, the nineteenth-century family had to cope with a whole range of risks and contingencies which in the twentieth century were taken over by non-familial institutions to varying degrees. This necessitated a more extended period in the family home. Basically, if the chief breadwinner was incapacitated or died, others had to step in. There was no insurance policy or welfare safety net. In sharp contrast to commentaries on youth transitions of the early twenty-first century, Modell *et al.* suggest that 'Growing up, as a process, has become briefer, more normal, bounded, and consequential – and thereby more demanding on the individual participants'(p.23).

If they are right, then at least in the USA much has changed in the last three decades, which does encompass the period of rapid service sector growth and industrial decline. Their historical account also offers a useful set of conceptual tools for analysing status transitions and could point to a more systematic approach to the housing dimensions of this stage of the life course. *Prevalence* refers to how common a particular transition is (death being universal); *timing* refers to a point at which more than half a population has experienced a transition (for example leaving home), whether it is early or late and the age at which particular groups have made the transition; *spread* refers to the time it takes for (say) a majority to make the transition. For example, how many years does it take for 80 per cent of a particular age cohort to leave home for the first time? There are, in addition, two more complex measures. Modell *et al.* conceive of *age-congruity* as the overlap of spreads. In other words, how close are the aggregate distributions of two different transition spreads (leaving home, getting a job)? Finally, to what extent are the transitions *integrated* – that is, at the individual level to what extent is one transition dependent or contingent upon another (for example accessing independent housing, getting married)?

A second set of issues relates to how best to represent the different kinds of living arrangements among young adults. We are dealing here with terms such as *dependent*, *independent* and *autonomous*. Guerrero (2001) provides a simple but effective two-way matrix to capture the different types of household situations experienced by young households. It contains two dimensions – financial and social. A young adult may be socially and financially dependent, for example living with parents with no independent source of income. At the opposite corner are those who are both socially and financially independent – left home, bought a house, got a job. But you could also be living at home and working (financially independent but socially dependent) or living away from home but still relying on your parents for money.

Social scientists may have different perspectives on the degree and significance of the changes which have impacted on this key stage in the life course, but there is agreement that it is a period in our lives when a lot is going on – and a phase in our lives which plays a critical role in shaping future trajectories in relation to household formation, household dissolution, housing and work. Rindfuss (1991) refers to it as 'demographically dense': 'By "dense" I mean that more demographic action occurs during these years than during any other stage of the life course' (p.496). Both fertility and mobility peak during this phase. Moreover, this intensity of demographic change is typically associated with limited economic and social resources – income and assets are low, as are social and cultural capital. *Cohort* effects are also notably marked for younger people. Precisely because of the demographic density of the youth–adulthood transition, any major economic or social disruption has a disproportionate impact on youth. Events such as the Great Depression, World Wars, the recent Global Financial Crisis may have impacted entire populations – what demographers refer to as *period* effects (Hillman and Marks, 2002) – but they are likely to have had the most substantial effects on the opportunity structures of young people in terms of education, housing and employment. 'The density of events during the young adult years would be even more dramatic during periods of rapid social change because young adults typically are the engines of social change' (Rindfuss, 1991, p.499). And with regard to housing, when housing market busts occur it is typically younger, newly formed homeowner households which bear the brunt of asset depreciation and the associated fallout (see, for example, Forrest, Kennett and Leather, 1999). It is the young who are disproportionately concentrated in the 'last in' category – and thus are often the first out.

In any period, young people will tend to be at the forefront of social and economic changes, in terms of both causes and consequences. And social commentators will look to the changes affecting youth as indicative of broader social discontinuities. It is probably the 1960s which are most popularly recalled as the period of dramatic social change and disruption, at least in more affluent western societies of the time. Youthful demands for far-reaching structural changes were inextricably bound up with massive shifts in lifestyles and attitudes. Retrospective analyses of this period typically offer a more cautious and considered judgement of the extent to which the social and political worlds were transformed – the extent to which the key elements of this 'new world' proved resilient or evanescent. In the post-sixties, post-Fordist, globalized world it is youth which is at the sharp end of a supposedly more episodic, fleeting and insecure social existence in which the virtual and real are becoming increasingly difficult to disentangle. The more ordered progression from youth to adult, from parental home to independent home, from school to work has supposedly given way to a much greater diversity of experiences and a less predictable sequencing of key events. Youth lifestyles and biographies have become more individualized, reflecting more complex social relations, the erosion of key social institutions and a higher sense of risk (Beck, 1992). The rapidity of social changes in the late twentieth and early twenty-first centuries has perhaps severed young people from the anchor points available to previous generations in relation to role models and life planning. This is an era of choice, projects, culture and lifestyles rather than class, structure and constraints. Here postmodern theory has gained considerable traction in relation to analyses of youth culture and youth trajectories.

In theorizing the youth transition Furlong and Cartmel (2007) offer a useful assessment of where the balance should lie between 'agency' and 'structure' in understanding the contemporary opportunity structures of young people. They reject the more extreme postmodern formulations while accommodating the conception of theorists of late modernity such as Giddens and Beck. For Furlong and Cartmel, in a more individualized society and one in which youth culture(s) have a less stark class dimension, constraints may be less evident. Individuals may place more weight on their own individual action in achieving social outcomes. However, the fact that the experiences of young people in the early twenty-first century are very different from their experiences a few decades earlier does not necessarily rule out the enduring and systematic impact of social structures. Younger people may well need very different and more individualized skill sets in negotiating contemporary processes of social reproduction. Furlong (2006) neatly captures this view: 'Cultural representations can change while economic conditions remain static. In a nutshell, youth is at the crossroads at which structured inequalities are reproduced' (p.xvi). Furlong and Cartmel (2007) also remind us that there is nothing new about uncertainty, disruption, the erosion of traditional institutions and more complex social relations and lifeworlds. Such processes have always been at the heart of social science and were the primary preoccupations of the founding fathers:

> While structures appear to have fragmented, changed their form and become increasingly obscure, we suggest that life chances and experiences can still be largely predicted using knowledge of individuals' locations within social structures: despite arguments to the contrary, class and gender divisions remain central to an understanding of life experiences.
>
> *(p.2)*

This takes us back to the more prosaic but important position of housing in structuring the life chances of young people. Given the focus of this book, this will be given more attention in a moment. However, a somewhat dated analysis of the housing decisions of young people by Ineichen (1981) nicely captures this relationship between individual choice and structural constraint in this context. Focusing on what was then a starker divide between home ownership and council housing in Britain, Ineichen examined the different housing 'careers' of a group of newly married couples in Bristol. The study showed that the rational response to the housing choices available to young people at that time exacerbated the social divisions which council housing was supposedly designed to ameliorate. Young people were usually making choices rationally, but not in conditions of their own choosing. Ineichen observed that the housing career approach could illustrate 'the ways motivation is restricted and shaped by the housing choices available; in other words, one of the processes by which structure is formed' (p.257).

Leaving home

So, across a wide range of societies, younger people are staying longer in the parental home. There is a growing sense of, and expectation of, independence among younger people, but the reality is often a dependent independence in relation to housing and income. But is this necessarily a problem? One of the initial motivations for putting this collection together was to explore the extent to which housing policy and housing market factors were important explanatory elements in these changing social patterns. Certainly, in the urban and housing studies literature, the housing affordability problem is commonly referred to as a key determining factor in the move to independent living among younger people.

The 2009 report on *Youth in Europe* (Eurostat, 2009) observes that 'Leaving the security of the parental nest to live independently is usually a challenging experience for young people' (p.29). In some cases, the challenge proves too difficult and there is an enforced return to the family home. Indeed, as Beer and Faulkner (Chapter 4) stress, national and cross-national statistics on the age of departure from the family home can be misleading because of these 'boomerang' (Abbey Mortgages, 2009) or 'yo-yo' (Biggart and Walther, 2006) effects. The 'final' age of departure from the family home may be much later than the statistics indicate. Equally, comparisons over time of the age of departure may be misleading if statistics have been collected on a different basis, if questions have been framed differently or if there are particular cohort or period effects (such as war). Younger households are, however, generally more vulnerable to income loss than more mature households because their average incomes are lower and they are unlikely to have substantial savings to enable them to cope with a sudden change in their economic fortunes. In 2007, the at-risk-of-poverty rate among European 18–24-year-olds in Norway and Denmark was around 30 per cent and was above average for that age group in almost all European countries. Younger households are often ineligible for various social transfers, are likely to be in more precarious jobs and may not have accumulated sufficient working years to qualify for safety-net benefits. Access to the safety net of social housing is especially relevant since young, single people are typically excluded. Of course, life on a shoestring can indicate very different trajectories for young households. The poverty of student life is usually short term and experienced in a very different context than that of, say, a young, unskilled migrant worker or a young lone parent. The importance of the timing of leaving home and the varying interpretations offered for an apparent delay in the age of departure in recent decades is captured in the title of a piece by Bell *et al.* (2006). In a policy brief derived from a longer study they pose the question, 'Failure to Launch or Launching Too Soon?' In their examination of patterns in Canada, the USA and four European countries, they find that in all six countries young adults of both sexes were staying longer in the parental home in the 1990s than in the 1980s. It is important to remember, however, that changing patterns of departure occur against highly varied social norms. Again, bearing in mind earlier strictures about 'boomerang' effects, in 2007 the average age of leaving home across the European Union varied for men from 23 to 30 and for women from 22 to 29 (Eurostat, 2009, pp.29–30). However, as the Bell *et al.* title indicates, a delay in leaving home may well be a sensible strategy and should not necessarily be interpreted in terms of 'failure' or constraint. The social class dimensions of departure are more nuanced and complex than they might seem. Those who leave home earlier may be less educated, less skilled men and women. Those who stay at home longer may be those staying longer in full-time education. The later departers may also be those with less need to leave in relation to space and comfort. Thus the apparently independent may be more vulnerable than the dependent. The significant and often enduring cultural differences in relation to leaving home indicate that it is unlikely that explanations for such patterns will be simple and mono-causal – or that a single factor, such as housing affordability, will fully account for any significant changes in patterns of departure. Guerrero's (2001) rigorous comparative study of the living arrangements of young people in France and Spain brings out the subtle and complex interaction among a range of factors. Guerrero asked why Spanish young people left home later than French youth. She pursued this question through a mix of detailed policy analysis and analysis of large official surveys of young people carried out in the early 1990s. She shows how labour markets and social policies structure incomes in different ways among young people in France and Spain. Social policies also provide very different levels of housing opportunity in the two countries. Taken together these factors combine to shape distinctively different youth strategies. In the French case, young people leave the nest early and one-generation, dependent households are frequent. In the Spanish case, young people leave much later and one-generation, dependent households are rare (Guerrero, 2001, p.290). But Guerrero also stresses that differences in social policies are embedded in, and reflect, different social and cultural norms, as does the broader literature on welfare regimes. There are, for example, different expectations and practices regarding the relationship between marriage and independence, the use of parental resources and the role of the family in France and Spain. There are also quite specific institutional differences which shape youth trajectories – notably, the less centralized higher education system in Spain. There is less need to leave home to attend an elite university in Spain – quite the opposite to France. This is important, Guerrero suggests, not only with regard to the living arrangements of a subgroup of mainly middle class youth but because of the 'diffusion' effects of student lifestyles: 'In most countries the expansion of consensual unions in the 1960s/1970s was largely due to their diffusion in the student subculture. Later, cohabitation diffused into other social groups' (p.292).

So why should we be bothered if young people are staying at home longer? After all, it could be argued that in a world of apparently greater risk and insecurity, trends that show the family staying together for longer may be good news for individual development and wider social cohesion. Perhaps the northern European norm of early nest-leaving is not necessarily one to be emulated or given policy support. Much depends, of course, on context, on past norms and on individual circumstances. Opportunities, choices and constraints are likely to be unevenly and unequally distributed among different groups of young people with regard to gender, ethnicity and social class. In some cases, however, sociologists have pointed to more fundamental threats to social structures being brought about by the behavioural changes of young people. The starkest example comes from Japan, where Yamada's book on 'parasite singles' (Yamada, 1999 and see Hirayama, this volume) occasioned a continuing debate in Japan about the underlying causes and consequences of the growing number of young people staying at home. Yamada suggested that this was a long term trend and involved a lifestyle of choice which was both parasitic and sybaritic. An elderly generation of Japanese had done very well from an expanding economy and positive asset growth in the pre-bubble economy. Now their children were reaping the benefits. The statistics are certainly striking. In 2006, they accounted for around 35 per cent of those aged 20 to 30 and their numbers were expected to grow further. Moreover, within the overall total of parasite singles there is apparently a subgroup of *hikikomori* – some one million young people who have mental health problems and rarely leave their rooms (see Horiguchi, 2011 for an extended discussion). More typically, however, they are outgoing, extrovert, have substantial disposable income and a lively social life.

The substantial demand for designer goods in Japan has been attributed to the parasite single phenomenon. And they have been blamed for Japan's economic and demographic problems (buying luxury rather than basic goods, and a very low fertility rate) (Tran, 2006; *Economist*, 2001). But as Tran (2006) points out, the Japanese tradition has been for parents to look after children until marriage and this should be borne in mind. Also, as expected, there is more than one factor at work, including changing attitudes among young women and a more hostile labour market, as well as affluent and accommodating parents (Genda, 2000). Nevertheless, the Japanese example shows that the changing strategies and behaviours of young people can have wider and potentially important social and economic consequences.

Housing and young people

Housing policies and the structure of housing markets are unarguably key factors in the shaping of youth trajectories. But this chapter has emphasized that housing is only one of a range of factors and there always is a risk of overstating the impact of the cost and availability of housing on patterns of new household formation. One complication is that the impact of housing supply is a bit like building a motorway – you get more traffic. Build lots of affordable housing designed and located for young singles and couples and it is highly likely that there will be a growth of such households. However, it has also been emphasized that housing policy choices reflect and are structured by culturally embedded social norms. Thus in societies where marriage and leaving home tend to be simultaneous life stages, and where consensual unions are socially discouraged, there is likely to be less political pressure or social support for housing subsidies for young people. Where there are supportive social and housing policies, young people can also take more of a risk. They can, in Guerrero's terms, leave home 'under precarious conditions' (2001, p.294). If things go wrong, there will be something of a safety net to fall back on and they will not be totally reliant on the family. Emmanuel, in this volume, argues that different patterns of leaving home in Europe long predate any affordability issues in the housing market. And Guerrero (2001) argues that changes in Spanish housing policy could well 'reduce the rate of young people moving out to marry and increase the number of consensual unions and nonfamily arrangements'. But, she continues, 'This does not exclude the possibility that in such a context, different social norms about consensual unions might persist between France and Spain, but they would be smaller than in the current configuration' (p.294). In other words, broadly similar housing systems and patterns of subsidy will still produce differences in the housing trajectories of young people for cultural as well as other reasons. What is undeniable is that young people today generally face very different housing market conditions than did the previous generation of young people. That is not to suggest that these changes have all been in a similar direction or with similar consequences. But it would be difficult to find many contemporary examples of housing policies which are more, rather than less, youth friendly than previously, or housing systems where access for first-time buyers is easier rather than more difficult. Lawson and Milligan's (2007) review of international trends in housing and policy responses found that one of the most prominent common challenges was rising housing costs and declining housing affordability. The recalibration and reallocation of risk by financial institutions have raised the bar for entry to home ownership even where house prices have declined. New environmental pressures have further restricted land supply in some areas, which some analysts and lobbyists blame for deteriorating affordability for young people, particularly in countries such as the UK and Australia (see, for example, Demographia, 2010). In China, where urbanization and home ownership levels have increased exponentially over the last decade, there are regular newspaper reports of young couples having to move further away from the booming east coast cities if they wish to own their own homes or have a reasonable amount of living space. A recent headline in the *People's Daily* (2010a) was 'Leave or stay, young Chinese struggle with high housing prices'. Xue, a young graduate, was quoted as saying, 'After days of consulting with relatives and friends, we decided to move to Taiyuan, where the average housing price is only one fourth of Beijing's 20,000 yuan per square meter.' Similarly, another report with the headline 'Housing and marriage' suggests that 'China may breed a new group of bachelors suffering from unaffordable housing prices' (*People's Daily*, 2010b).

Now, of course, we should beware of vested interests and journalistic hyperbole in some of these reports. We should also remember that getting your own home, rented or owned, has rarely been an easy transition, apart from for a privileged few. But governments, banks, real estate agents and others with a stake in property markets have over the years ratcheted up expectations among cohorts of young people – only for the system to then fail to deliver on these promises. Moreover, neoliberal doctrines which have been highly influential in housing debates have not only reasserted the primacy of the market in social and economic affairs but also the role of the family. In societies where social housing has been more widely available, cutbacks in investment and privatization policies and stricter eligibility rules have made access more difficult, particularly for younger single people. And the era of deregulated, highly competitive mortgage lending would appear to be at an end. Lower loan-to-value ratios require higher deposits (Heath, 2008). In housing, as in other spheres, parental resources – material and non-material – are going to be more important in the shaping of youth opportunity structures. Again to quote the *People's Daily* (2010a), 'Confronted with high house prices and yet an urgent need to buy an apartment in a few years after graduation, many young Chinese are turning to their parents for help.' Parents with larger houses and more space will be better placed to accommodate their offspring – to provide housing assistance in kind. Rich parents will be better able to provide help with deposits, rents or other costs associated with setting up home. There is of course nothing new in that, and in some societies, for example in East Asia or in the Southern Mediterranean region, the family has remained deeply embroiled in housing arrangements. There does seem, however, to be a more general transfer of risks and responsibilities in housing, and in other spheres, back to the family (Forrest and Hirayama, 2009; and see Franklin, 1995). In Modell *et al.*'s (1976) terms, with regard to achieving housing independence, the general consequence of a greater reliance on family resources amidst shifting attitudes and opportunities will be greater *spread*, less *age-congruity* and later *timing*. The transition to housing independence will be later, spread over a greater number of years and there will probably be less, rather than more, coincidence between different elements of the youth transition. Whether such a change is good or bad is quite a different matter and involves a whole range of culturally, socially and temporally specific judgements. But within youth cohorts there will be winners and losers – and the distance between them will grow. This is as true in contexts of austerity such as the UK or the USA as it is in contexts of growing affluence such as China. The ability to survive and negotiate difficult housing times or to take full advantage of expanding housing market opportunities will be shaped by differences in relation to both material and social resources.

Conclusion

The chapters which follow aim to capture the diversity of youth experiences across a range of cultural contexts and economic circumstances. In particular, they aim to draw out the importance of housing in the process of the transition to adulthood. This involves addressing different aspects of housing and paying close attention to the range of factors which can facilitate or constrain, encourage or deter, the move from the parental home. Some of the chapters offer a sceptical account of the impact of housing affordability on young peoples' housing choices. Others place housing costs at the core of their account of the difficulties faced by youth in their country. The tone and coverage of the different chapters reflect, inevitably, temporal and cultural specificities in relation to economic and social conditions and with regard to the socially constructed nature of youth. The aim has also been to encompass a wide range of economic circumstances and housing systems in order to draw out the commonalities and contrasts among different groups of young people. There are strong contrasts in relation to the pace and scale of social and economic change, captured to some degree by comparisons between Europe and East Asia. There are also some commonalities between countries such as Greece and Italy and Japan and China with regard to the role of more traditional family practices in relation to housing. Northern European societies such as Denmark have rather different histories as regards family structures, family practices and welfare provision. One of the most striking contrasts is between Japan and China, where young urbanites in the major cities have over the last two decades faced quite contrary trajectories of change. Both groups have experienced dramatic transformations, but in Japan many young adults have only known recession since the economic bubble burst at the end of the 1980s, the era of the 'lost decade' when the features of Japan's distinctive welfare capitalism – of job security, corporate paternalism and the male breadwinner model – began to be transformed by economic pressures. The same cohort in China, however, have experienced a sharp transition of a very different kind – the progressive impact of market reforms and the opening up of new employment opportunities, new lifestyles and a welfare system shifting from low quality but universal provision to one which is increasingly market- and cash-driven and more differentiated.

In closing, it should also be emphasized that, in the main, this book is focused on mainstream rather than marginalized youth. Although we touch upon issues of social exclusion in places, notably in Lieberg's discussion of the Swedish situation, this is not a book about young people on the economic and social margins. It is about, in the main, how the middle mass of young people in different ways and in different places are experiencing and negotiating a changed set of housing opportunities. These changes are captured most typically in the contrast between the relatively benign economic and policy regimes experienced by baby boomer generations and the more austere circumstances facing many younger people today. There are also important differences among younger cohorts regarding housing opportunities and trajectories, both within and between countries, most evident in relation to Japan and China.

Some of the authors approach the contemporary youth housing question with a strong emphasis on the shifting economic conditions of post-war capitalism, and in particular the impact of neoliberal policies and ideologies on youth opportunities and intergenerational dynamics. For others the departure point is the tension between continuity and discontinuity in family practices and family relations, between modernity and tradition. In other chapters, housing market dynamics are very much to the fore, particularly in relation to affordability. In most cases, the chapters range across all these issues to varying degrees. If there is a general conclusion it is that the interaction between youth and housing has to be understood in its particular cultural and historical context; that apparently similar trends in relation to the transition to adulthood may have different causes and consequences in different cultures; and that what is 'normal' in relation to the pattern of departure from the family home varies temporally and culturally.

The material and emotional aspects of housing touch upon youth in a number of important ways, including the need for financial assistance, patterns of asset-building, getting married or cohabiting and having children, and more subtle aspects of social identity and social competence. We must always be wary of exaggerating discontinuities and of overdramatizing the present. But it does seem that, across a wide range of societies, housing systems are in a particular state of flux. Young people are particularly exposed in a situation where previous certainties about home ownership or state housing provision have been seriously undermined but there is something of a policy and conceptual vacuum about where to go from here. However, it will also be younger people who will be at the sharp end of demanding and shaping these different housing futures.

References

Abbey Mortgages (2009) *Britain's Baby Boomerangers,* Press Release, 9 February.

BBC World News (2003) 'The kippers who won't leave home', 17 November.

Beck, U. (1992) *Risk Society: Towards a New Modernity,* London: Sage.

Bell, L., Burtless, G., Gornick, G. and Smeeding, T. (2006) *A Cross-National Survey of Trends in the Transition to Economic Independence,* Network on Transitions to Adulthood Research Network Working Paper.

Biggart, A. and Walther, A. (2006) 'Coping with Yo-Yo-Transitions. Young adults' struggle for support between family and state in comparative perspective' in Leccardi, C. and Ruspini, E. (eds) *A New Youth? Young People, Generations and Family Life,* Aldershot: Ashgate, 41–62.

Billari, F. (2004) 'Becoming an adult in Europe: A macro(/micro)-demographic perspective', *Demographic Research,* Special Collection 3, article 2, 15–44.

Demographia (2010), *6th Annual Demographia International Housing Affordability Survey: 2010,* Christchurch, New Zealand: Performance Urban Planning.

Doogan, K. (2009) *New Capitalism? The Transformation of Work,* Cambridge: Polity Press.

Economist (2010) 'Special report: Japan – into the unknown', 20 November.

Eurostat (2009) *Youth in Europe,* Brussels: European Commission.

Forrest, R. and Hirayama, Y. (2009) 'The uneven impact of Neo-liberalism on housing opportunities', *International Journal of Urban and Regional Research,* 33(4), 998–1013.

Forrest, R. Kennett, P. and Leather, P. (1999) *Home Ownership in Crisis? The British Experience of Negative Equity,* Aldershot: Ashgate.

Franklin, A. (1995) 'Family networks, reciprocity and family wealth' in Forrest, R. and Murie, A. (eds) *Housing and Family Wealth,* London: Routledge.

Furlong, A. (2006) 'Foreword' in Leccardi, C. and Ruspini, E. (eds) *A New Youth? Young People, Generations and Family Life,* Aldershot: Ashgate, xv–xviii.

Furlong, A. and Cartmel, F. (2007) *Young People and Social Change,* Maidenhead: Open University Press.

Genda, Y. (2000) 'Youth unemployment and parasite singles', *Japan Labour Bulletin*, Special Topic, 39, 3.

Giddens, A. (1991) *Modernity and Self-Identity*, Cambridge: Polity Press.

Guerrero, T. J. (2001) *Youth in Transition: Housing, Employment, Social Policies and Families in France and Spain*, Aldershot: Ashgate.

Heath, S. (2008) *Housing Choices and Issues for Young People in the UK*, York: Joseph Rowntree Foundation.

Hillman, K. and Marks, M. (2002), *Becoming an Adult: Leaving Home, Relationships and Home Ownership among Australian Youth*, LSAY, Longitudinal surveys of Australian youth research report 28.

Horiguchi, S. (2011) 'Coping with hikikomori: socially withdrawn youth and the Japanese family' in Alexy, A. and Ronald, R. (eds) *Home and Family in Japan: Continuity and Transformation*, London: Routledge.

Ineichen, B. (1981) 'The housing decisions of young people', *British Journal of Sociology*, 32(2), 252–258.

Jones, G. (1995) *Leaving Home*, London: Open University Press.

Lawson, J. and Milligan, V. (2007) *International Trends in Housing and Housing Policy Responses*, Sydney: AHURI.

Leccardi, C. and Ruspini, E., eds (2006) *A New Youth? Young People, Generations and Family Life*, Aldershot: Ashgate.

Modell, J., Furstenberg, F., Jr. and Hershberg, T. (1976) 'Social change and transitions to adulthood in historical perspective', *Journal of Family History*, 12, 7–32.

People's Daily online (2010a) 'Leave or stay, young Chinese struggle with high housing prices'. Online. Available at: <http://english.peopledaily.com.cn/90001/90776/90882/6858033.html> (accessed 10 March 2011).

People's Daily online (2010b) 'Housing and marriage'. Online. Available at: <http://english.peopledaily.com.cn/90001/90778/90860/7240804.html> (accessed 10 March 2011).

Rindfuss, R. R. (1991) 'The young adult years: diversity, structural change and fertility', *Demography*, 28(4), 493–512

Roberts, K. (2006) 'Young people and family life in East Europe' in Leccardi, C. and Ruspini, E. (eds) *A New Youth? Young People, Generations and Family Life*, Aldershot: Ashgate, 203–223.

Smith, S. and Munro, M. (2008) 'The microstructures of housing markets', *Housing Studies*, 23(2), 159–162.

Thornton, A. and Fricke, T. (1987) 'Social change and the family: comparative perspectives from the West, China, and South Asia', *Sociological Forum*, 2(4), 746–778.

Thornton, A. and Lin, H. (1994) *Social Change and the Family in Taiwan*, Chicago: University of Chicago Press.

Tran, M. (2006) 'Unable or unwilling to leave the nest? An analysis and evaluation of Japanese parasite single theories', *electronic journal of contemporary Japanese studies*, Discussion Paper 5. Online. Available at: <http://www.japanesestudies.org.uk> (accessed 1 October 2011).

Yamada, M. (1999) *Parasaito Shinguru no Jidai [The Time of Parasite of Singles]*, Tokyo: Chikuma Shobo.

PART I

The family, demography and the transition to adulthood

2

BALANCING AUTONOMY, STATUS AND FAMILY IN THE TRANSITION TO ADULTHOOD

Class and housing aspects of the Southern European model in Athens, 1987–2004

Dimitris Emmanuel

Introduction: the Southern European model and the international context

Southern Europe is known for its mild climate and its Mediterranean cuisine. It is also known for "mama's boys" – men that live with their parents up to their early thirties. Indeed, the share of young adults, especially men, living with their parents in Greece, Italy, Portugal and Spain – the four "Southern European" (SEU) countries of what used to be the EU15 – has been, during the last few decades, far greater than that of Northern Europe and North America.[1]

What is less known is that, despite the social and sexual revolution that has shaken traditional family and household structures since the 1970s throughout the advanced west, this gap has been *widening*: the share of those living with parents has increased substantially in the four SEU countries since the 1980s. In 1987, it ranged from 63 per cent (Greece) to 84 per cent (Spain) for the 20–24 age group and 39 per cent to 49 per cent for the 25–29 age group; by 1995, the respective shares have increased dramatically, to 72–89 per cent (for ages 20–24) and 49–59 per cent (for ages 25–29). During the same period, countries in the rest of the EU15 showed modest increases, stability or even decrease (Tsanira, 2009; see also Moreno, 2006). The available data for the broader age group of 18–34 for 2008 show that these processes of increasing coresidence in ways that widen the gap between the South and the North have continued, albeit at a slower pace than previously (Eurostat, 2010a, 2010b). Within this broader category of "youth" (ages 18–34), the proportion living with their parents in 2008 was more than 50 per cent in the four SEU countries, whereas in the Nordic countries the share was below 20 per cent, in the Netherlands and France around 30 per cent and in Germany, Belgium and the UK around 40 per cent. There are equally impressive differences in the case of those living *away* from the parental home: while the share of the young aged 18–28 who live alone is well below 5 per cent in SEU (with the exception of Greece, with about 8.5 per cent, probably due to immigrants), in the majority of cases in Northern Europe it is above 10 per cent and in the Nordic countries ranges from 20 per cent to more than 30 per cent (Eurostat, 2010b: 90). Similar wide differences are observed in the share of the young living in consensual partnerships without marriage (Tsanira, 2009; Eurostat, 2010b: 91).

The aim of this chapter is to shed light on the changing housing arrangements of young people in urban Greece during their transition to adulthood and to examine the role of class and housing using material for the Athens Region. As will become evident, there is a strong case that the patterning and change of these arrangements cannot be understood within a purely *local* approach. Both in the historical long term as well as during more recent decades, demographic patterns and household structures have been formed by broad processes that must be examined from an international and comparative vantage point in order to be understood. This applies *a fortiori* in this period of globalizing influences. Thus, understanding the Greek case at the level of social and demographic patterns and trends and then going into the matter of their interaction with the housing system involves its placement within a broader picture of contrasting or similar international patterns. The major contrasts in the living arrangements of the young between the European North and South and the respective differing (or similar) processes of change that we have been reviewing are arguably interconnected in meaningful ways with what may be considered distinct *systematic patterns* or *models* of the transition to adulthood that apply in the given time period. There may be two or, preferably, more models – in order, for example, to take into account important variations within Central and Northern Europe. In the case of the Southern countries we will follow standard European practice and lump them together, mainly for simplicity's sake, into one model.[2] Thus, in what follows, we will use the concept of a Southern European model as a broad organizing category within which we may situate the Greek case. This model contrasts with Northern European and Northern American countries in three main respects: the high rate of coresidence with parents, the dramatic increase in coresidence since the 1980s and, lastly, the limited extent of cohabitation outside marriage or, conversely, the extent to which exit from coresidence, and more generally independent adulthood, depends on forming a socially acceptable household based on marriage.

In what follows, we will first suggest an explanatory framework for these major contrasts. This will also help put the role of housing and the housing system within a wider perspective, distinct from the narrow focus of local and medium-term microeconomic and housing market analysis. Second, we will examine in more detail the characteristics and situation of both coresidents and the independent young and the trends in coresidence during the period extending from 1987 to 2004 in the light of our explanatory framework. This analysis will also examine the role of differences in the coresidence/independence pattern across classes – an aspect that is seldom examined in the relevant literature. Lastly, we will examine the extent to which conformity to the dominant model produces, especially from the point of housing, dysfunctions suffered either by the young or by parenting adults or by both among the various groups of households.

Wading through the explanatory muddle: Southern familism, welfare regimes and demographic transition

There are roughly five ways to approach the problem of understanding international differences and national patterns and trends in the household arrangements of the transition to adulthood. The three more familiar ones are: Southern "familism" versus the different ways of the North (or vice versa); the role of the welfare state or, in its more modern version, differences in welfare regimes; lastly, the role of various socio-economic conditions and trends in education, incomes, employment and housing. The other two approaches, although supported by a truly voluminous scientific literature, are more esoteric and command less public attention: microeconomic models of the family and the household, and grand models of demographic transitions. Let us briefly make some comments on these approaches. Our intention is not to make a systematic review and evaluation but simply to clear the ground of some misconceptions and point out the elements that will inform our particular approach.

The lack of a "proper" strong welfare state evident in Greece and to varying extents also in the other Southern European countries has been a very popular explanation for various matters, including the ones examined here. Conversely, the existence of one and the impact of variations in welfare policies are often used as an explanation of Northern European ways. This latter case may be perfectly reasonable for analysis *within* a particular national context or group of nations with comparable social and historical contexts. In the former case, however, where the *absence* of an essentially extraneous factor is used for explanation, a host of problems arise. The argument goes as follows: the absence of a strong welfare state or, more specifically, one that is not mainly focused on pensions, the elderly and the middle aged (as is the rule in SEU countries) accounts for both the importance and strong role of the family ("familism") and the high degree of coresidence among the young. This, in its more simplistic forms, often constitutes either a truism or fallacious reasoning from counterfactuals.[3] Otherwise, these arguments hide a strong *functionalist* theoretical assumption that usually cannot stand logical scrutiny. The underlying assumption is that the functions performed by a strong welfare state are *necessary* in modern societies. Therefore, their absence will trigger a response that creates a *substitute* – familism and family support through coresidence. However, in order to convincingly make a functionalist argument for the existence of some process one must show both the necessity of the function, the relative, at least, uniqueness of this particular solution to the functional necessity, and the mechanism that makes the solution possible and reproduces it. This is a very tall order for any explanatory argument to accomplish, but especially so in this case in view of the historical and worldwide rarity of strong welfare states. In this case there is also a chicken and egg problem. Is it that the society produces the welfare state it is fit for or vice versa? Is, for example, the lack of a strong welfare state due to the existence of familism or is familism due to the lack of a strong welfare state? Do the young in Nordic countries leave the parental home early because they receive welfare benefits or does the state offer benefits because the young leave early and face high risks of poverty? It is indicative of the facile appeal of functionalist approaches that often both sides of these questions are answered in the affirmative.

The appeal of Esping-Andersen's Welfare Regimes typology as an organizing and explanatory framework of the issues we examine[4] is certainly based in large part on this substratum of beliefs about the crucial functional role of the welfare state. His typology, especially after its expansion in order to include additional social elements and a better account of Southern Europe (1999), is also more ambitious: it may be understood as an account of the whole *social formation* and thus it has great appeal to those fond of holistic explanations. More crucially for our subject, it roughly correlates with the differentiation of Europe in the household arrangements of the young along the North–Centre–South axis. Esping-Andersen's types may be understood as useful *descriptions* of historically formed divergent structures with special reference to the social role of the state. When, however, this popular typology is applied as a major explanatory factor for *social* structures, it suffers from similar problems to the functionalist accounts outlined above. Aside from the logical and epistemological problems there are obvious substantive problems. Consider the case of "familism" and its relation to the support of the young: from the work of such major historical demographers as Laslett (1983) and Hajnal (1983) we know that since the late Middle Ages there have been fundamental differences across the major regions of Europe in this regard. Later work has shown that these broad schemas may have been oversimplifying, given the greater complexity observed and the existence of significant regional and historical variations. Nevertheless, the existence of persisting major differences in family and household arrangements between North and South throughout the nineteenth century and up to the first decades of the twentieth is not in question (Kertzer, 2002). The original social and economic circumstances and rationale that formed these patterns may have become irrelevant in the modern urbanized world, but as Reher (1998) has argued in his influential work, the diverging forms of families with "strong" and "weak" ties have persisted as functioning systems governed by particular sets of cultural norms.[5] The point is that these socially pervasive patterns existed well before the emergence of the welfare state and that they were embedded in society in ways that made for their stubborn persistence. Does it make any sense, then, to view familism as the product of particular forms of the welfare state? Was the absence of welfare programmes the factor behind the behaviour of families in nineteenth century Greece? By the same token, were young Swedes, leaving home early during that time, given support through state subsidies? Thus, the importance of "familism" in the South takes historical and explanatory precedence over any Welfare Regime influences. It is true, of course, that the concept of familism has been used to excess and more often than not in an undiscriminating manner – especially in Southern European housing studies – with the result of an "over-social" understanding of many patterns and processes and a disregard for salient economic factors and economic rationality.[6] Nevertheless, and keeping in mind these reservations, we cannot but keep the strong role of the family and family ties at the center of our analysis in what follows.

Having said this, we must immediately add that both in the European South and the rest of Europe as well as most of the "advanced"West the institution of the family and family relations have been undergoing major changes affecting both the behavior and values of the parental unit and those of their young offspring. Thus, familism as an important set of influences cannot be viewed statically or in isolation but must be seen in combination with the forces exerted by these changes. This brings us to the matter of the role of demographic transitions. During the first half of the twentieth century and up to the 1960s and 1970s, there has been a major transition towards demographic stability based on the gradual reduction of fertility that paralleled the reduction of morbidity. With advancing economic development and urbanization, family formation moved towards the middle-class ideal of a child-centred household based on marriage at an early age and devoted to the proper raising and social advancement of a limited number of offspring. However, since the late 1960s, the 1970s or the 1980s, depending on the country, demographic trends have shown a shift towards a new pattern with the following characteristics (van de Kaa, 2002):

- substantial decline in period fertility, partly resulting from postponement of births
- substantial decline in the marriage rate and an increase in first marriage age
- strong increase in divorces (where allowed) and in the dissolution of unions
- strong increase in cohabitation among young people
- strong increase in the proportion of extra-marital births
- catalytic shift in contraceptive behaviour.

Following the influential work of demographers Dirk van de Kaa and Ron Lesthaeghe, an increasing number of demographers and sociologists have been convinced that we are witnessing a "Second Demographic Transition" sweeping across Europe and North America, albeit at varying rates and starting times. According to Lesthaeghe (2010) these changes are evidenced to varying extents in most of the relatively developed countries of the world. Now, the interesting part of the theory of the "Second Transition" is that, as its proponents convincingly argue, it is the result of a major shift in values, lifestyles and social norms. The conceptualization of this shift varies: from van de Kaa's move towards "individualism" to Lesthaeghe's suggestion that we are dealing with a movement towards Inglehart's "post-materialist" values and Maslow's higher needs. The essential point of these arguments is that we have a movement away from the conservative, middle-class concept of the family devoted to stability, material security and the successful raising of children, associated with the first transition, towards more individualistic values of personal self-fulfilment, in which marriage (or cohabitation with a partner) and procreation are matters of individual lifestyle choice that may (or may not) take place at any point during the first half of the life-cycle – usually later rather than earlier.

This is not the place for a review of the demographic and sociological evidence, but we may accept that certainly *something* with the scope and character of the Second Transition has taken place in both Northern and Southern Europe during the last thirty years. The crucial and undeniable common evidence is the major change in the time of marriage and the fertility rate – which is partly the result of late marriage. Coming back to van de Kaa's list, it is obvious that some aspects of the Second Demographic Transition, such as divorce rates, cohabitation instead of marriage and extra-marital births, do show an increase in the South, but at much slower rates than in Northern Europe and North America. These differences, however, may be understood as stemming from the interplay of a common process of change with widely differing social contexts and cultural backgrounds. What are the origins and driving forces of this common change, akin to a social revolution? From the viewpoint of Southern and Eastern Europe and certainly from the viewpoint of Greece, it suffices to say that it started in the more economically developed parts of the "advanced" West and that its influence is due to globalization processes. Globalization is an overused concept but in this case offers a realistic framework. Whatever the causes of the social and cultural underpinnings of the Second Transition – be they the social and sexual revolution of the 1960s and 1970s riding on post-war affluence or whatever else – the fact is that the globalizing influence of mass media and mass culture as well as internationalized education have exerted a powerful influence along these lines on the young – and their parents – in all European countries.

Thus, alongside the concept of Southern familism (SF), we will retain the largely external influence of the Second Demographic Transition (SDT) as a major component of the framework required for understanding the household arrangements of the young and their change during the last decades. While, however, the importance of the SDT model, with its emphasis on changing values and norms, has been amply recognized in the case of Northern and Central European countries (see Lesthaeghe, 2010 and De Jong Gierveld *et al.*, 1991, among others), its direct application in the case of SE countries appears problematic: how can we reconcile the *increase* in the rate of coresidence with parents with a shift towards values of individualistic independence among the young? Dalla Zuanna (2001) has argued that in Italy, at least, in contrast to what the SDT model predicts, conservatism and the importance of familism have increased. It is a renewed familism that has led to the longer stay in the parental home, the postponement of marriage and the dramatic drop in fertility rates to well below NC European rates. Interestingly, he also points out that *within* Italy, it is the more modern and secularized among the young that postpone marriage the most and have the lowest fertility. Leastheghe (2010), faced with the conundrum of Southern countries, resorts, against his own theory one would say, to an eclectic combination of factors: strong familism, the welfare regime (i.e. lack of public support) and conditions in the labour and housing markets. These factors do indeed make the behaviour of the young understandable within the given context. But why the increase in coresidence and the apparent retraction of the value of independence? Have the young in the South, despite the presumed strong globalizing influences, been unaffected by the values fueling the Second Transition, save for the practical benefits of postponing marriage?

A possible answer to this question may be found in a certain bias of the value model incorporated in the SDT, due to the influence of the theory of "postmaterialism" (Inglehart, 1997). A number of national and comparative studies of changes in values have argued that the theory of postmaterialism, with its emphasis on inward-oriented "ascetic" (non-materialist) individualism, attracted to change, self-realization and community concerns (e.g. the environment) has neglected the significance and widespread incidence of an equally postmodern set of values that, while consistent with orientation to change and rejection of tradition and authority, leans more towards outward-oriented materialist values related to egoism, concern for status, consumption and hedonism (Hellevic, 1993). Thus, the global influence of the SDT may exert pressures of a dual or even conflicting character, which may have significantly different effects in different social and cultural contexts. In the case of SEU countries, the SDT has apparently been associated with the growth of a type of individualism that is more concerned with consumption-based status and middle-class appearances rather than autonomy and rejection of traditional family norms. This point has often been made in relation to the so-called carefree living of the young while staying within the parental nest. More importantly, however, it applies equally to forming a household with a partner at a later time based on a marriage that has the prerequisites for an acceptable level of consumption status.[7] Such attitudes, of course, are fully sanctioned and encouraged by the parental unit. To the extent that these characteristics among the young have been strengthened in Southern countries, with the unfolding of the Second Transition in combination with the persistence of strong familism, both the comparatively high level of coresidence and its exceptional increase during the last two decades can be accounted for.

Microeconomics and games: balancing autonomy, status and family

While the theories examined so far have a broad scope suitable for understanding comparative and historical patterns and processes of social change, most accounts of the household arrangements of the young – especially accounts from official statistical agencies (Eurostat, 2010b; Berrington et al., 2009) – focus on the role of the spread of education, conditions and trends in labour and housing markets and incomes. This, at first glance, makes a lot of sense. In fact, however, cross-national analysis of the role of these factors produces very mixed and ambivalent results (Bell et al., 2007; Newman and Aptekar, 2007). From the vantage point of our previous analysis this should come as no surprise: if global shifts in values and norms and major divisions in cultural patterns are the main factors involved, medium-term fluctuations in markets will most probably have minor and contradictory impacts. Moreover, there is a built-in ambiguity in the significance of these conjectural factors. Higher incomes may facilitate coresidence with parents but may also make possible the financing of living alone or with a partner. Extensive unemployment or temporary employment among the young may increase the appeal of the security of the parental nest but may also be the corollary of limited participation in the labour market due to extensive family support. The fast increase in higher education enrolment during the 1990s in many countries – including Greece – may explain a part of the increase in coresidence, but this applies to the 20–24 age group, whereas the most dramatic changes in coresidence rates took place among the 25–34 cohort. Housing conditions either in the parental home or among the independent young and the general availability of housing at accessible cost are equally indeterminate factors. The availability of housing space is strongly associated with the level of income and wealth and thus its influence is confounded. In addition, the availability of housing space depends on the size of the household, which in turn depends on the extent of coresidence. In the case of independent young households facing difficult housing conditions, we may have a strong self-selection factor in contexts where coresidence is the norm. As a result, such housing conditions are not representative of actual housing opportunities for the young. Lastly, and more crucially, housing and living conditions have improved substantially in the SEU countries since the 1980s. This cannot be reconciled with an argument that difficult labour and housing market conditions are the determinants of the increase in coresidence.

In a nutshell, we should expect economic trends and, more generally, economic factors to have a relatively secondary impact, and their influence to interweave with the complex influence of values and cultural factors. There are a host of microeconomic modelling studies on this subject, attempting something along these lines: to combine standard or game-theoretic utility maximization theory with non-economic factors such as the altruism of parents and the utility offered by the family (or the disutility of coresidence for the parents) or, conversely, the utility of independence for the young.[8] More often than not these approaches have mixed results regarding the role of income (especially that of parents) and the role of costs – including housing – that largely vary depending on the country. There are also contradictory views and results regarding the parental and filial motives involved – especially the extent and nature of parental altruism.[9] Nevertheless, these are theoretically and analytically rigorous efforts to tackle the issues examined here at the micro-level of individual action. Their problem is their excessive reliance on the established neo-classical formalism of utility maximization and, mostly as a consequence, the narrow empirical range of analysis: too much has to be deduced from responses to changes of a single variable – income.

If, in a more sociological vein, we drop this restrictive neo-classical baggage, a view of particular household arrangements of the young as the outcome of quasi-utilitarian games played out by parents and their offspring at certain phases of the life cycle may indeed have significant explanatory and heuristic value. We have already indicated that these outcomes may be viewed as particular patterns of balance between the values and pressures of family ties and family control, on the one hand, and the drive for individualism and autonomy on the part of the young on the other. We also noted that, especially for Southern countries, there seems to be a strong concern for consumption-based status on the part of the young, combined with an equally status-oriented concern for social mobility and a socially accepted, well-provided marriage on the part of the parents. The parents will offer financial support and practical help in everyday life to achieve an outcome according to their wishes – an orderly and socially acceptable progress towards education, a good job and a good marriage. In SEU countries this is, supposedly, safeguarded by prolonged coresidence, in which the young gain an easier life and better consumption standards at the cost of losing most of their present and future autonomy.[10] On the other hand, parents may also value the young's need for autonomy and therefore support a move to a quasi-independent household. Or, on the other extreme, they may value autonomy so much that they demand – or take for granted – that their offspring will leave the nest and make do by themselves or, if they stay, contribute their share of expenses and household work. In all this, costs are also involved: the costs of support and the less tangible costs of coresidence in the same home for the parents, as well as the costs of independent living for the young. Consider the simple two-actor bargaining game presented in Figure 2.1. Parents have two options: to offer or not to offer financial and practical support. The young similarly have two options: stay in the parental home or live independently.

Each outcome is associated with certain payoffs. For the parents there are certain costs, on the one hand, and the benefits of preserving family ties and family control and keeping or improving social status, on the other. For the young there are also the costs and benefits of autonomy and the benefits of consumption status. If this is a non-coordination game, the young will choose option 3 and Southern parents will most probably choose option 1. These are both Nash equilibria and therefore there is no cooperative solution. However, this most probably is a coordination game, where both parties gain by making mutually consistent decisions due to the existence of either externalities (economies of scale, benefits for the family as a

		Parental Support	
		+	−
Young coresidence	+	1. Financed coresidence	2. Non-financed coresidence (young contribute their share)
	−	3. Financed independence	4. Non-financed independence

FIGURE 2.1 Outcomes of a two-actor game.

whole) or pressure exerted by one player on the other (social pressure, financial incentives). In the Southern context, if indeed status and consumption considerations are as important for both parties as we assume, the value of autonomy is weak vis-à-vis the value of the family, the costs of coresidence are not considered high, and option 1 offers the maximum sum of welfare and is Pareto efficient (with compensation). This utilitarian criterion is not considered sufficient for reaching equilibrium in egoistic rational games, but may be so when social pressures apply. Needless to say, this sketch of a game-theoretic framework does not aspire to a theory – given the fact that, lacking hard data, we can always adjust the balance of values, costs and benefits to fit the case. It can offer, however, useful suggestions towards interpreting the material we will be reviewing.

The Second Transition and the rise of coresidence, Athens 1987–2004

Examining the Greek case in the light of our previous discussion presents certain methodological problems. The in-depth analysis of the household arrangements of the young in the transition to adulthood is best tackled with longitudinal panel data, so that we have information on the household before the decision of the young to leave (or stay), and also know the character of the household of origin for the young in independent households and follow their subsequent trajectories. Such panel data are scarce in Europe and certainly so in Greece. Thus it is understandable that most econometric studies of the subject have used the material of the European Community Household Panel (ECHP). The ECHP, however, covers the late 1990s and the early 2000s and does not cover the decade or so of major changes before that time. Moreover, similar to the European Survey of Income and Living Conditions (EU-SILC) that followed, it has certain serious limitations from a socioeconomic perspective. It offers detailed data on current income and its sources (including subsidies) but no real data on *consumption*. Now, current income is important, but it is also a notoriously untrustworthy variable in many contexts and, furthermore, cannot measure the more permanent and "structural" differences in the resources available to households – hence the need for more complex concepts such as "permanent income" and "lifetime resources." The level of consumption, on the other hand, given its relative stability and the fact that it is determined by both past experience and considerations about the future, offers a good surrogate for available resources. Data on consumption, moreover, offer better material for the analysis of housing and living conditions. Given these considerations, we decided to draw material from a database derived from the Greek Household Expenditures Surveys (HES) covering 1987, 1993, 1998 and 2004.[11] Using the Expenditure Surveys means that we cannot directly examine the *decision* to leave home nor can we have data on the origin of the young living in independent households. Thus, we can only examine *snapshots* of the extent and character of coresidence and compare households with and without young living with their parents. This, unfortunately, is complicated by the fact that some parents may have a certain number of children while others have none or have fewer. These complications will have to be kept in mind or, if possible, handled with adequate adjustment of the data. Nevertheless, we believe that the material is robust enough for understanding the broad pattern and its differentiation across class lines, and inequalities in housing situation.

Table 2.1 shows for the Athens Region (the department of Attika) the share of the young aged 19–33, as a whole and in three successive five-year cohorts, that live in the parental home.[12] As expected, there is a continuous, sharp increase between 1987 and 2004, most especially in the 24–28 and 29–33 cohorts.[13] Table 2.1 also shows both the share of the unmarried among the young and the share of coresidents among the unmarried for 1987–2004.

While both the high coresidence rates typical of Southern Europe and their sharp increase since the 1980s are evident, we have no clear picture of the nature of this change. It has been pointed out (White, 1994) that the relevant denominator for measuring the share of coresidence is not the young population as a whole but the *unmarried* part. Thus we may distinguish between the effects of postponing marriage and the propensity to live with parents when unmarried. This is doubly relevant for the Greek context, where leaving the nest is strongly associated with marriage. Two things become immediately apparent from Table 2.1: first, the share of the unmarried young increased dramatically from about 49 per cent among the 19–33 age group in 1987 to about 73 per cent in 2004, with most of the change taking place among the older cohorts, 24–33; second, the share of coresidence among the unmarried is very high but shows a very modest increase of 1.5 per cent, after a slight decrease of 3 per cent during the 1990s. Thus, the main factor behind the increase in coresidence has been the dramatic increase in the extent of postponing marriage. For some, for example Dalla Zuanna, (2001), referring to the case of Italy, strong familism and coresidence themselves fuel marriage postponing and help us understand the ultra-low fertility rates of Italy (and the equally low ones of Greece, we may add). This may be true to some extent, but the fact is that the dramatic drop in fertility in Greece took place during the 1980s,[14] *before* the period we examine and thus before the dramatic fall in marriage rates among the young due to postponement. We do not have similar evidence for the 1980s on the behavior of the young, but, at best, we may assume that there was a drop in marriage rates – as was the case for the general population – in tandem with the fall in fertility. In any case, it appears more reasonable to view both changes as related to the broader one of the Second Demographic Transition.

Class differences and diverging class paths

While the role of income differences has often been examined in studies of coresidence, the extent of differences across major class divisions has not. Class analysis offers two advantages: first, it offers a broad picture of the role of economic inequalities that goes beyond transient income and such complications as the effect of

TABLE 2.1 Coresidence among the young and the unmarried young in Athens, 1987–2004.

Age range	Living with parents (%)			Unmarried (%)			Unmarried living with parents (%)		
	87/88	98/99	04/05	87/88	98/99	04/05	87/88	98/99	04/05
19–23	71.9	79.0	82.9	83.2	94.4	94.8	83.0	82.6	85.8
24–28	43.2	56.9	69.3	48.6	74.8	80.9	79.4	74.4	84.1
29–33	16.2	27.4	33.3	19.1	37.0	46.2	71.5	70.5	70.3
All 19–33	42.5	53.4	60.6	48.8	67.7	72.7	80.2	77.1	81.7

demographic variables and the life cycle; second, it leaves room for the possible effect of class-specific values, practices and cultural norms. The concept of social class, of course, is controversial and affords many approaches suited to different objects of analysis. For the present context, as well as for the analysis of urban life patterns and living conditions more generally, a Weberian approach based on the structural inequalities in "life chances" that shape the living conditions of particular socio-economic categories seems the most appropriate.

We have developed a simple model adjusted to the data limitations of Household Expenditure Surveys, which ranks socio-economic *categories* of households (instead of individual households, as in stratification models) according to their average consumption expenditure per adult equivalent.[15] The socio-economic categories are distinguished by such determinants as economic activity, occupation, position in employment, and education. These, given the sample limitations of expenditure surveys, are rather broad. The ranking order of socio-economic categories is divided into four classes in a way consistent with socially meaningful divisions.[16]

This model has been adopted for Athens on the basis of the 1998/99 HES, and has also been applied to the data for 1987 and 2004 for reasons of consistency, though there are certain secondary deviations due to the upwards or downwards movement in particular categories (for example farmers moving up to the working class). In the case of 1998 and 2004 there is the additional complication of foreign economic migrants that steadily moved into Athens from the early 1990s. Thus, migrant households will, when appropriate, be removed from the data in order for more valid comparisons with 1987. This is possible for the 2004 data (when migrants in Athens amounted to about 8 per cent of households, concentrated in classes 3 and 4) but not for 1998 when they were quite probably at about half the 2004 number. Table 2.2 shows the class differences in the extent of coresidence and in the pattern of changes during the period 1987 to 2004.

Since these snapshot data do not offer information about the class of non-coresiding young, we measure the extent of coresidence per class simply by presenting in Table 2.2 the share of *households* that include *at least one* young person living with parents. This is a very rough measure since it is also affected by the number of offspring a family has, which depends, for example, on its stage in the life cycle. In order to limit the effect of such demographic influences, we restricted the households examined for each young cohort to a certain age band for the head of household: 40–60 for the young cohort aged 19–23, 45–65 for the young aged 24–28 and 50–70 for the young aged 29–33. Thus the resulting differences will be informative enough.

The main points to be made about the shares shown in Table 2.2 are the following:

•   The share of Upper Middle Class households with coresiding offspring is consistently the lowest one throughout the period and in all age groups. This is most probably due, first, to a higher rate of supporting the young to live independently, and second, a higher rate of supporting students abroad and in

TABLE 2.2 Class differences in coresidence, Athens.

Class	Percentage of households with at least one dependent young person		
	HES87	HES98	HES04*
Age of head 40–60, young 19–23			
1. Upper Middle Class	17.2	21.0	17.9
2. Lower Middle Class	32.1	25.0	25.1
3. Working Class	25.8	31.2	31.1
4. Lower Class	25.1	29.3	16.3
Age of head 45–65, young 24–28			
1. Upper Middle Class	9.4	19.2	19.4
2. Lower Middle Class	20.3	22.8	27.2
3. Working Class	14.0	26.6	31.6
4. Lower Class	18.2	30.5	22.0
Age of head 50–70, young 29–33			
1. Upper Middle Class	3.6	8.9	8.2
2. Lower Middle Class	8.4	12.2	14.2
3. Working Class	7.2	14.1	13.1
4. Lower Class	8.2	14.9	18.7

* Figures for 2004 do not include foreign economic migrants

> other Greek cities. Thus it is the Lower Middle Class and the Working Class that have to support coresiding young to a larger extent. Even the Lower Class, which has a larger share of pensioners, shows relatively high extents of coresidence.
>
> • While the Lower Middle Class showed the highest proportion of households with coresidence in 1987, by 2004 the highest shares are found among the Working Class.
>
> • The greatest increase in coresidence has taken place in the 24–33 age group. This change, moreover, cuts across classes: both the Upper Middle Class and the Working Class more than doubled the share of households with coresiding young in this age group.

The social traits of coresidents and the independent young

The extent and nature of the social changes that took place since the 1980s can be made clearer with a comparison of the traits of both the "dependent" young living with parents and the "independent" young in 1987 and 2004 (Table 2.3). This comparison can also help clarify the role of such factors as the expansion of education and participation in the labour market, which for many have been important determinants of the increase in coresidence.

TABLE 2.3 Young people aged 19–33 in Athens in 1987 and 2004: basic characteristics.

	"Dependent" young (%)			"Independent" young (%)		
	19–23 years	24–28 years	29–33 years	19–23 years	24–28 years	29–33 years
HES 2004						
Employed	28.9	71.9	83.6	30.7	67.9	81.1
Unemployed	8.8	14.5	9.0	2.7	8.5	4.8
Students	58.0	14.5	2.3	54.7	5.5	0.3
Married	1.7	1.3	0.6	18.6	52.7	75.2
Rented homes with young people	27.6	23.1	10.6	81.3	65.8	49.2
HES 1987						
Employed	38.8	68.7	71.5	28.0	55.5	68.8
Unemployed	15.6	16.6	14.2	5.5	4.2	2.8
Students	33.6	6.3	0.4	30.1	2.2	0.3
Married	4.3	11.7	23.6	55.7	84.1	92.3
Rented homes with young people	22.5	14.6	21.0	61.4	50.9	45.0

We can make the following remarks:

- Marriage rates among the young living with parents in 1987 were low but significant, showing the partial persistence of the traditional pattern prevalent in conditions of lower economic development. By 2004, these rates have become insignificant.
- The extent of marriage among the independent young was, in contrast, very high showing the strong interconnection between leaving the nest and getting married. This connection is still apparent in 2004 but the share of married young heads of households has fallen drastically in the 19–23 and 24–28 cohorts.
- The extent of employment and the rates of unemployment do not conform to the preconception that it is difficult labour market conditions that drive the young into the protection of the parental home. Employment rates have generally increased – save for the 19–23 age group, in which we have the major expansion in higher education. The unemployment rate has shown an increase only in the case of the independent young aged 24–33, and by relatively modest percentage points. Moreover, this has to be qualified by the parallel increase in labour market participation and the fact that the independent young have gradually become a minority whose relative level of resources measured by consumption per capita has worsened considerably compared to their 1987 position.[17]

- The effect of the rapid expansion of higher education, especially among young women, is evident in the 19–23 cohort of both categories. The share of students among the 24–33 group, on the other hand, is very low or insignificant. Therefore, the argument that it is education that has driven changes in these cohorts finds little support.

- Although the proportion of rental housing has fallen in Athens as a whole between 1987 and 2004, especially if we exclude foreign migrants (from about 30 per cent to 22 per cent), there is an increase in the share of rented homes with young people living in them – mainly among the independent young. This is, however, due to the influx of young foreign migrants: the extent of renting among independent young Greeks (about 51 per cent) has not changed much compared to 1987.[18]

The most impressive fact in Table 2.3 is the extent of employment among both the dependent and the independent young and its increase since 1987. This puts the prevailing image of the "carefree" young enjoying a good life with the help of family support and income from occasional part-time employment in a new light, to say the least. In fact, the 2007 EU-SILC data for the Athens Region show that part-time employment among the young does not exceed 5 per cent and that full-time employment does not differ much from the general average in hours per week. Moreover, their earnings do not differ much from the average, given the role of age and experience in Greek salary structures. While the monthly average for all salary and wage earners was ⬜1053, the employed among the 19–23 cohort earned on average ⬜700 per month (justifying the famous "⬜700 generation" tag), the 24–28 cohort ⬜831, and the 29–33 cohort ⬜937. On the basis of the 2004 evidence, their earnings seem to have made a significant contribution towards the consumption level of the household – especially among the Working Class and the Lower Class, conforming to some extent with the pattern prevalent in the past. In order to substantiate this, we examined the relative housing and consumption conditions of households with working dependent young (aged 19–33) compared to the average of all households with young aged 19–33 in the same social class in 2004, with foreign economic migrants separated in a distinct "Class" 5.[19]

The evidence on relative conditions shows that the presence of dependent young has a significant negative impact on both housing and consumption per capita levels relative to each class average – especially so in the case of the Lower Middle Class. This is, of course, mainly due to the addition of household members and the consequent fall in per capita indicators. This negative impact, however, is not present in the subgroup with working young: the index for housing of households with working young is similar to the class average across all classes, while the index for consumption shows increasing proportional benefits as we move down the class scale – from +3 per cent (Class 1) to +7.6 per cent (Class 4). These facts on the contribution of the working young to the family do not, of course, "refute" the thesis that consumption-status-oriented individualism has been on the increase among the young and that coresidence is in large part the result. The majority of the young earning a stable income *could* actually move out of the nest, especially after forming a two-income partnership. However, this would add greatly to their responsibilities and reduce their consumption substantially. The facts on employment and earnings show that what is being avoided is not hardship and responsibility in general but those associated with *marriage* (and the prospect of child rearing), versus the comfort and semi-autonomy offered by the family. As we noted in a previous section, it is the postponement of marriage that shapes up as the crucial factor in the changes we have been examining. On the other hand, "marriage postponement," a term used by demographers, is in many ways misleading in this context, as it presupposes a conscious choice among alternatives. Apparently, marriage for most of the under-30s has essentially become a non-option – something which is not on their current agenda and which may happen in the distant future when sufficient conditions are secured or, as the Second Transition theorists argue, as an act of self-fulfillment.[20]

Class, housing and coresidence: incidence of economic hardship and housing deprivation

The functioning of the Southern model of coresidence depends, obviously, on adequate economic resources and housing space on the part of parents. How is this reconciled with the prevalence of coresidence across all classes and, more importantly, its greater concentration among the economically weaker ones? It is evident that, to a large extent, it is not. As Table 2.4 shows, coresidence must often coexist with extensive economic hardship and housing deprivation.

The first column of Table 2.4 shows the "urban" poverty rate among households with young aged 19–33 and a head of household more than 33 years old, for each class in Athens in 2004 ("Class" 5 is composed of foreign migrants), according to an *ad hoc* poverty line suitable for measuring relative deprivation in terms of living conditions in a particular urban context. The "urban" poverty line corresponds to

TABLE 2.4 Urban poverty and housing hardship in households with coresiding adult young and a head of household older than 33 years, Athens 2004.

Class (2004)	Households with adult young and head older than 33 years (%)		
	Urban poor	Below minimum housing need	Below minimum housing need + 15 sq. m.
1. Upper Middle Class	5.0	19.3	43.1
2. Lower Middle Class	21.5	30.7	55.7
3. Working Class	29.7	47.5	70.6
4. Lower Class	38.3	48.1	70.7
5. Foreign Migrants	77.5	83.1	92.1
All groups	28.7	41.7	64.1
Classes 1–4	21.7	34.2	55.7

half of the average consumption per adult equivalent for all households in the Athens Region. It is obvious that a sizeable part of the Working and Lower Classes – and even the Lower Middle Class – that have adult young in the home face acute economic hardship. The extent of *housing* hardship (columns two and three) is even greater. On the basis of a conservative minimum standard need for housing space according to the size and composition of the household, designed for social policies of the 1980s,[21] almost half of the households with young in Classes 3 and 4 live in less than the minimum required space. The problem also affects nearly one-third of the households in the Lower Middle Class.

Now, these measures of housing deprivation are based on a minimum standard that belongs to a different age. Today, with the move to a service economy and the so-called "information society," the need for the proverbial "room of one's own" is paramount for both the young *and* their parents. In the last column of Table 2.4 we increased the minimum standard for housing space by 15 square meters so we can roughly take these new needs into account. With these new standards of need the extent of housing deprivation for those with coresiding adult young across all classes is literally unacceptable. By these figures, apparently only the lucky housing rich in the upper housing subclasses can live in space adequate to the requirements of coresidence: both parents and young among the rest – especially in the less advantaged classes – must suffer relative overcrowding. These facts show clearly that the Southern model of housing for the young may have become dominant but it certainly suffers from unacknowledged major dysfunctions in the Greek case.

Conclusion

The review of the evidence for Athens for the period 1987–2004 has shown that both the high levels of coresidence and their impressive increase in this period conform to the Southern European model of household arrangements for the young during the passage to adulthood. The international and historical evidence suggests that this "model," as it has evolved since the 1980s, is the product of the twin pressures of strong "familism" and the shift in values, norms and lifestyles brought by the Second Demographic Transition that swept European countries. This shift in values and lifestyles apparently took a more materialistic and status-oriented form in the European South. The evidence from Athens shows that this has not particularly changed the pattern of choices among the *unmarried* young, but has changed the set of attitudes towards marriage, resulting in a dramatic fall in marriage rates among the young aged 19–33. The increase in coresidence, given the role of strong familism and the prevailing balance between the values, costs and benefits associated with autonomy versus family support, was the direct product of this fall in the marriage rates – though increased coresidence may in turn have added some impetus to this negative trend.

These changes had swept across all social classes in Athens in ways consistent with the hypothesis of the universal and globalizing influence of the Second

Transition. Trends in housing and economic conditions appear to have had little effect on the progress of these changes. Moreover, the model of extensive coresidence and its increase during the 1990s applied across all social classes, despite the differences in the size of dwellings and the level of financial resources. Only in the case of the Upper Middle Class does a higher level of income and wealth, in comparison to other classes, seem to exert a negative influence on the probability of coresidence, due to the greater ease with which the young can be financially supported in setting up independent households, and to different attitudes towards autonomy. *Within* each class, the size of the parental dwelling may well exert a positive influence on the probability of coresidence. But taking the broader perspective the model of coresidence is dominant even among the less fortunate in terms of housing space and financial resources. Given Greek housing conditions, the underside of this "triumph" of Greek families in keeping their young in the home is the extensive incidence of major dysfunctions of the prevailing familistic "model" in terms of economic hardship and housing deprivation.

Dalla Zuanna (2001), in his famous paper on Italian "ultra-low" fertility and the negative role of strong familism, argued that the victory of the strong family in supporting the young through coresidence while they delay marriage for increasingly longer periods is a Pyrrhic one: the drastic reduction of fertility rates due to marriage postponement will lead to the rapid decline and ageing of native populations. The prolonged stay with the parents will reproduce the inability of young males to face the responsibilities of marriage with modern working women in ways that do not conform to the traditional division of labour between genders followed by their mothers, and will therefore further undermine marriage and fertility. We may add that this "victory" is a Pyrrhic one in a more immediate sense also: it causes serious household dysfunctions especially among Lower Middle Class and Working Class households. These dysfunctions, experienced by the young in combination with the cultural pressures of status-oriented consumerist individualism, will also erode the value of forming a family and raising children.

Notes

1 The "New Member" countries that make up the new EU25 – mostly countries in Eastern Europe – show similar or higher shares. However, compared to SEU, Eastern European countries form a distinct category of their own, with significantly different levels of economic development and urbanization as well as different socio-cultural traditions. As a result, the structure of coresidence with parents has characteristics that do not allow direct comparisons with the SEU cases – the large numbers of married couples living in parental households, a very rare arrangement in SEU countries, is a case in point. Thus, in what follows we will stay within the limits of EU15.

2 Mandic (2008), after a cluster analysis of the relevant characteristics, distinguishes three models for Europe: a Central-Northern, a South-Western (our SEU) and a North-Eastern – mainly the New Member countries of Eastern Europe.

3 To give a crude example of such an argument: (a) if country X was like Sweden, institution Y would be different; (b) country X is not like Sweden; therefore (c) institution Y in country X is what it is! Although counterfactuals may help in the formulation of

hypotheses (e.g. through thought experiments) they do not prove anything by themselves. This is doubly true, of course, for irrelevant counterfactuals.

4 See, among others, Allen *et al.*, 2004, especially Chapter 4; Mandic, 2008; Karamessini, 2007; Minguez, 2003.

5 For the significance of Reher's thesis for SEU, see Micheli (2000) and Karamessini (2007). For early leaving of the parental nest and the related housing choices in relation to the Nordic countries, see Lauster (2003).

6 For a critique of the rigid application of the familistic model of housing wealth accumulation geared to intergenerational transfers, see Emmanuel (1994).

7 For similar points regarding the views of the young in the case of Greece, see Tsanira, 2009. In a multidimensional statistical analysis of the attitudes towards various values recorded by the European Social Survey in Greece, it was found that in the two-dimensional space defined by the axes conservatism–change and atomistic–collective, the group aged 15–34 was located in the quadrant where the sets of attitudes signifying appearances, status, recreation and adventure were also located (Voulgaris, 2007).

8 See the concise review in le Blanc and Wolff, 2003. On the role of altruism see, among others, Laferrère, 2006; Manacorda and Moretti, 2002.

9 This often depends on the national context. While in France altruists are those financially supporting coresidence, in Italy, given the strong wish to keep the family together, altruists are those supporting the independence of the young!

10 Manacorda and Moretti (2002) consider this a "bribing" relationship. This assumes a certain cynicism on the part of the young, a readiness for leaving the family if the "bribe" is not adequate and the absence of simple conformist motives.

11 These are also referred to as the 1987/88, 1993/94, 1998/99 and 2004/2005 surveys, since part of the sample is usually gathered during the first two months of the following year.

12 Defined as "offspring of the household head or his/her spouse." We've chosen three five-year cohorts that do not coincide with the standard demographic 20–24, 25–29 and 30–34 divisions in order to avoid distorting the pattern of coresidence both at the beginning (relative to the age of entering higher education) and the end (coresidence falls sharply in the early thirties).

13 Interestingly, the shares throughout this period do not differ much between the Athens Region and Greece as a whole.

14 During the 1980s live births fell by 35 per cent, from more than 15 per 1000 inhabitants to about 10 (data from EL.STAT, www.statistics.gr, statistical themes – population, vital statistics, time series: Births, Years 1932–2010).

15 A method familiar from poverty studies, though these commonly use income instead of consumption. For the problems of using current income, see our previous remarks. Our model was first introduced in Emmanuel *et al.*, 1996.

16 The model adopted for Athens on the basis of the 1998/99 HES is as follows: 1. *Upper Middle Class* (Managers, Professions, Rentiers, Upper Clerical); 2. *Lower Middle Class* (Lower Technical Professions, Petty Entrepreneurial, Lower Clerical, Upper Pensioners, Student Householders, Upper Houseworkers); 3. *Working Class* (Craftsmen and Operators, Tradesmen, Sales and Service Workers); 4. *Lower Class* (Unskilled Labourers, Farmers, Lower Pensioners, Lower Houseworkers, Unclassified Unemployed).

17 Based on estimates of consumption per adult equivalent for 1987 and 2004, after excluding foreign migrants from the 2004 data.

18 Thus, if we add the percentage of dwellings supplied by family and relatives free of charge (about 10 per cent), 40 per cent of the independent young live in owner occupation – somewhat less than the 43 per cent in 1987 despite the major expansion in housing credit after the late 1990s due to Greece's entrance into the EMU (Economic and Monetary Union). In fact, 22 per cent of the 24–28 cohort and 32 per cent of the 29–33 cohort among the independent young in owner occupation had received housing loans. This stability in the ownership rate must be due to the fall in the marriage rate and the consequent reduction in the flow of parental property and savings transfers. It should

be noted that this factor accounted, more or less, for more than half of moves into owner occupation in Athens in the late 1980s (Emmanuel, 1994).

19 We estimated a housing size/need index based on dwelling area, in square meters, divided by the need for space for the corresponding household structure and size (see also the discussion of Table 2.4), and an expenditure per capita index based on total consumption per adult equivalent.

20 It is indicative that, when a European Barometer asked, in 2007, for the main reasons why young adults stay in the parental household, in all countries only an insignificant number picked the option "Get married later than used to" (European Commission, 2007, p.72).

21 The standard assumes the need for a sitting room, a room for each couple, a room for each adult member and one room for every two non-adult members with the exception of 15–18-year-olds of different sex. Each room plus circulation requires 20 square meters and a further 10 square meters are needed for common spaces. See Emmanuel *et al.*, 1996, pp.100–101.

References

Allen, J., Barlow, J., Leal, J., Maloutas, T. and Padovani, L. (2004) *Housing and Welfare in Southern Europe*, London: Blackwell.

Bell, L., Burtless, G., Gornick, J. and Smeeding T. M. (2007) "Failure to launch: cross-national trends in the transition to economic independence," pp.27–55 in Danziger, S. and Rouse, C. (eds) *The Price of Independence: The Economics of Early Adulthood*, New York: Russell Sage Foundation.

Berrington, A., Stone, J. and Falkingham, J. (2009) "The Changing Living Arrangements of Young Adults in the UK," *Population Trends*, 138: 27–37.

Dalla Zuanna, G. (2001) "The banquet of Aeolus: a familistic interpretation of Italy's lowest low fertility," *Demographic Research*, 4(5): 133–161.

De Jong Gierveld, J., Liefbroer, A. C., Beekink, E. (1991) "The effect of parental resources on patterns of leaving home among young adults in the Netherlands," *European Sociological Review*, 7(1): 55–71.

Emmanuel, D. (1994) "On the Structure of housing accumulation and the role of family wealth transfers in the Greek housing system", pp.168–201 in R. Forrest and A. Murie (eds) *Housing and Family Wealth*, London: Routledge.

Emmanuel, D., Velidis, S. and Stroussopoulou, E. (1996) *Low Income Housing in Greece*, Athens: DEPOS (in Greek).

Esping-Andersen, G. (1999) *Social Foundations of Postindustrial Economies*, Oxford: Oxford University Press.

European Commission (2007) *Young Europeans: A Survey Among Young People Aged Between 15–30 in the European Union – Analytical Report*, Flash Eurobarometer report, European Commission.

Eurostat (2009) *Youth in Europe: A Statistical Portrait*, Luxemburg: Eurostat.

Eurostat (2010a) "51 million young EU adults lived with their parent(s) in 2008," *Eurostat: Statistics in Focus*, 2010(50). http://epp.eurostat.ec.europa.eu/cache/ITY_OFFPUB/KS-SF-10-050/EN/KS-SF-10-050-EN.PDF (accessed May 10, 2012).

Eurostat (2010b) *Income and Living Conditions in Europe*, Luxemburg: Eurostat.

Hajnal, J. (1983) "Two kinds of pre-industrial household formation system" in Wall, R., Robin, J. and Laslett. P. (eds) *Family Forms in Historic Europe*, Cambridge: Cambridge University Press.

Hellevik, O. (1993) "Postmaterialism as a dimension of cultural change," *International Journal of Public Opinion Research*, 5(3): 211–233.

Inglehart, R. (1997) *Modernization and Postmodernization: Cultural, Economic, and Political Change in 43 Societies*, Princeton, NJ: Princeton University Press.

Karamessini, M. (2007) "The Southern European social model: changes and continuities in recent decades," *Discussion Paper Series*, No. 174, Geneva: International Institute for Labour Studies. http://www.ilo.org/public/english/bureau/inst/publications/discussion/dp17407.pdf (accessed May 15, 2012).

Kertzer, D. I. (2002) "Living with kin," pp.40–72 in Kertzer, D. I. and Barbagli, M. (eds) *Family Life in the Long Nineteenth Century, 1789–1913,* New Haven and London: Yale University Press.

Laferrère A. (2006) "Leaving the nest: parental income, housing and altruism." http://www.eea-esem.com/files/papers/EEA-ESEM/2006/1295/Nestleaving-2006V2.pdf (accessed May 15, 2012).

Laslett, P. (1983) "Family and households as work group and kin group: areas of traditional Europe compared" in Wall, R., Robin, J. and Laslett, P. (eds) *Family Forms in Historic Europe,* Cambridge: Cambridge University Press.

Lauster, N. (2003) "A room of one's own or room enough for two? Housing and leaving home for family and non-family destinations in Sweden, 1968–1992," paper presented at the annual meeting of the American Sociological Association, Atlanta. http://www.allacademic.com/meta/p106654_index.html (accessed May 10, 2012)

le Blanc, F. D. and Wolff, F.-C. (2003) "Transfers and coresidence under altruism." http://www.sc-eco.univ-nantes.fr/~cebs/Pages/wolff/lw0403.pdf (accessed May 10, 2012).

Lesthaeghe, R. (2010) "The unfolding story of the Second Demographic Transition," *Population and Development Review*, 36 (2): 211–251.

Manacorda, M. and Moretti, E. (2002) *Intergenerational Transfers and Household Structure: Why Do Most Italian Youths Live With Their Parents?* Discussion Paper No. 536, London: Centre for Economic Performance, London School of Economics and Political Science. http://cep.lse.ac.uk/pubs/download/DP0536.pdf (accessed May 10, 2012).

Mandic, S. (2008) "Home-leaving and its structural determinants in Western and Eastern Europe: an exploratory study," *Housing Studies*, 23(4): 615–637.

Micheli, G. (2000) "Kinship, family and social network: the anthropological embedment of fertility change in Southern Europe," *Demographic Research*, 3(13). www.demographic-research.org/Volumes/Vol3/13 (accessed May 10, 2012).

Minguez, A. M. (2003) "The late emancipation of Spanish youth: keys for understanding," *Electronic Journal of Sociology*, 7.1. http://www.sociology.org/content/vol7.1/minguez.html (accessed May 15, 2012).

Moreno, L. (2006) "The model of social protection in Southern Europe: enduring characteristics?" *Revue Française des Affaires Sociales*, 2006(1): 73–95.

Newman, K. and Aptekar, S. (2007) "Sticking around: delayed departure from the parental nest in Western Europe," pp.207–230 in Danziger, S. and Rouse, C. (eds) *The Price of Independence: The Economics of Early Adulthood*, New York: Russell Sage Foundation.

Reher, D. S. (1998) "Family ties in Western Europe: persistent contrasts," *Population and Development Review*, 24(2): 203–234

Tsanira, E. (2009) "The transition to adulthood in Athens: behaviour patterns, attitudes, views," pp. 321–350 in Maloutas, T., Emmanuel, D., Zacopoulou, E., Caftanzoglou, R. and Hadjiyanni, M. (eds) *Social and Spatial Transformation in 21ˢᵗ Century Athens*, Athens: National Centre for Social Research (in Greek).

van de Kaa, D. J. (2002) "The idea of a second demographic transition in industrialized countries," paper presented at the Sixth Welfare Policy Seminar of the National Institute of Population and Social Security, Tokyo, Japan, January 29, 2002. www.ipss.go.jp/webj-ad/webJournal.files/population/2003_4/Kaa.pdf (accessed May 10, 2012).

Voulgaris, Y. (2007) "Greece seen at the mirror of Europe: national political cultural trends and globalization" pp.40–63 in Kafetzis, P., Maloutas T. and Tsiganou, I. (eds) *Society – Citizens and Politics: The European Social Survey – ESS*, Athens: NCSR (in Greek).

White, L. (1994) "Coresidence and leaving home: young adults and their parents," *Annual Review of Sociology*, 20: 81–102.

3

THE FIRST STEPS INTO THE ITALIAN HOUSING SYSTEM

Inequality between generational gaps and family intergenerational transfers

Teresio Poggio

Introduction

The problem of the delayed transition to adulthood has arisen in almost all the developed countries but it is of particular importance in Italy. Young people stay longer in the parental home and delay new family formation, compared to what used to happen in previous generations and to what happens in many other European countries nowadays. According to estimates for 2009, 59 per cent of never-married individuals in the age group 18–34 lived with their parents. Even when considering only those who have reached economic independence, the corresponding figure remains a remarkable 42 per cent (ISTAT 2010).

Cross-national differences are rooted in European history and cultures: it is a rather common practice for young adults in Southern Europe to leave the parental home at a later time than their contemporaries in Northern Europe. However, both the widening of this gap between these two groups of countries (Emmanuel, in this volume) and the observed differences across Italian cohorts are a reason for concern.

Cultural, economic and social changes have driven the observed delay. Factors linked to these changes may be grouped into two broad families: the increased capabilities of individuals and external structural economic constraints. On the one hand, it has been argued that delayed nest-leaving and family formation may depend on the increased expectations of younger generations and on changes in social norms regulating the transition to adulthood. Remaining in the parental home allows the maintenance of higher levels of consumption and the postponement of choices that used to be more impelling and stringent for previous generations, like securing a job and getting married, for example. On the other hand, delaying the transition to adulthood is also due to external economic constraints and uncertainty – not experienced by previous generations – related to changes that have taken place in the labour market and in the housing and welfare systems. It is reasonable to assume that both families of factors are implicated but assessing the relative importance of each of them is still open to research.

The aim of this chapter is more modest and also twofold. First, I would like to contribute to the discussion on the delayed transition to adulthood for Italy by focusing on the second family of factors. Consistent with the scope of the book, the discussion is specifically focused on constraints emerging from the housing system. Second, I would also like to use the Italian case for a broader discussion on the role of intergenerational transmission – in terms of housing-related transfers – in shaping the housing careers of young households. Italy may well represent a case study on this topic. The main interest is in shedding some light on the complex interplay between intergenerational inequality, other traditional cleavages – social class, gender and ethnicity – and social inheritance, which is inherent to family intergenerational transfers. The discussion is primarily developed through reliance on existing literature. Some results from original research on housing-related intergenerational transfers are also discussed.

Background

Intergenerational gaps and generational inequality

In the analysis of the delay in the transition to adulthood, two different research perspectives correspond to the two families of factors mentioned in the introduction. The main focus of the first perspective is on long-term improvement of living conditions, changes in values, social norms and on the increased autonomy and capabilities of individuals, overall (see Emmanuel, in this volume, for a detailed discussion). The long-term trend toward improvements in income and living conditions allows the younger generations a greater degree of freedom from material constraints. Young people have greater opportunity to postpone their choices concerning the various steps of the transition to adulthood (Buzzi 2007). They also have higher expectations than in the past. Adult offspring can enjoy a higher level of consumption and have more opportunities for leisure while they remain in the parental home.

It should be noticed that parent–child relations have also changed and the parental nest has become more comfortable for young adults. Social norms have become less stringent with regard to the contribution from younger members to the household income, or to housework. Young people can also demonstrate more freedom in their behaviour and even find the space for intimacy, with their non-cohabiting partner, in the parental home (Sartori 2007).

The main focus of the second perspective, and of this discussion, is on socioeconomic determinants and on intergenerational inequality arising from structural constraints and from the effects of globalization on the national welfare systems (Mills and Blossfeld 2005). During the last decades of the twentieth century, advanced economies have progressively become more integrated and interdependent. The information and communication technology revolution has provided the grounds for highly coordinated and synchronous world markets. The absence of effective governance of the international economy, the relative autonomy of many multinational corporations and the increased interdependence between different regions of the globe have also led to increased uncertainty in markets. As an overall result, each national economy has faced both openness to intense global competition and high levels of uncertainty. Governments have usually responded with policies oriented to neoliberalism, deregulation of the labour markets and reduction of welfare spending in order to cope with the new competitive context. Young people are expected to experience harder conditions – in comparison to older generations – as they have entered a more uncertain and less protected labour market, they have lower relative earnings and they also have to cope with a reduction in the level of social protection from the welfare state (Mills and Blossfeld 2005). The impact of these external constraints is differentiated, notably by educational level (Mills and Blossfeld 2005, Bernardi and Nazio 2005).

Previous research on young people and the labour market has highlighted the difficulties experienced by younger generations today. Bernardi and Nazio (2005) provided evidence on the first steps into the labour market: when compared to previous ones, younger generations are more likely to be unemployed and less likely to have a permanent position in a first job. When they are working, they have less opportunity to ensure stable contractual terms of employment and they are also more at risk of becoming unemployed. These difficulties, more common among those with lower levels of education, were found to influence delay in family formation.

In their work on 'atypical' – i.e. less protected – employment, Barbieri and Scherer (2009) found that these forms of employment are more common among younger cohorts, when compared to those who entered the labour market during the 1970s. They also found that non-standard employment especially affects those who are better educated.[1] One can note that atypical employment may still represent a better option than working without any contracts and guarantees, a condition that was rather common for those entering the labour market in the 1950s and 1960s (Schizzerotto 2002) and that is not uncommon today, especially for those with a low educational level. However, what is specific to younger cohorts is not only the risk of experiencing unprotected forms of employment when entering the labour market but also the risk of remaining entrapped in this precariousness and insecurity (Barbieri and Scherer 2009, Bernardi and Nazio 2005). In general, young people are likely to have uncertain and reduced economic capabilities.

Globalization has affected individual life chances as well, through its impact on the housing system. Housing is emerging as a relevant – and relatively independent – domain in which inequality becomes structured, especially if one considers the increased dependence of life chances on housing wealth and its transmission (see the following and Forrest 2008). Housing prices have risen in many European countries and investments in social housing were reduced even before the retrenchment of the welfare state in other domains. The liberalization and globalization of the mortgage markets have led to better availability of credit but also to increased exposure of households to the dynamics of international financial markets (Ball 1990). In the Italian context, new entrants into the housing market – young people and immigrants – experience increased difficulties: they face higher rents and housing prices; they are more dependent on the mortgage markets; and housing policies discriminate against them (Baldini and Poggio 2012).

Intergenerational family transfers

The gaps between young and elderly generations are often represented in terms of a 'conflict' between young people and relatively 'privileged' elderly cohorts. This caricature is too simplistic, because it does not consider private intra-family transfers, which also play a role in redistribution between generations and in the structuring of social inequalities.

Following Attias-Donfut and Arber (2000), it is possible to assume three different perspectives on intergenerational relationships by considering three different specific meanings of generation. First, a *family generation* denotes the relative position within family lineage: being a child, a parent, or a grandparent, for instance. Second, a *social generation* denotes a cohort sharing some common experiences and visions of the world, because of similar significant historical experiences. Finally, the concept of *welfare generations* is used to distinguish individuals in different age groups – at a given point in time – according to their contribution to the funding of the welfare state and according to the benefits they receive from it.

Scientific and public debates are mostly focused on the social and on the welfare generations' cleavages. This approach accounts for the main changes in the economic, social and political contexts which have taken place since the end of World War II and contributed to shaping in different ways individuals' life chances (*social generations*), including their housing careers. It also accounts for the distribution of current social expenditures across age groups with regard to the various social risks (*welfare generations*). Both social and welfare generations refer to processes taking place in the public sphere.

Narrowing the focus to the relationships between different *family generations* allows for a better understanding of generational cleavage and of its interplay with other factors in the structuring of social inequality. Different positions within the family lineage imply different roles, capabilities and power. Private, intergenerational material transfers that take place between such positions are of particular interest. This is especially true in those countries like Italy, in which the family traditionally plays an important role in the distribution and redistribution of resources. Redistribution from the elder to the younger generation – via family transfers – partially compensates for possible generational inequalities arising in the public sphere (Attias-Donfut and Wolff 2000, Castles and Ferrera 1996). However, it should be noted that this private compensation is only partial: it clearly depends on resources available to the elderly generation, which are differentiated across social strata.

From a methodological point of view, the analysis of intergenerational family transfers contributes to collocating individuals in the context of their primary social relations. It assumes family practices – sometimes strategies – as a relevant level of analysis when addressing social inequality and its transmission. This also serves to collocate the debate on generational inequality within a more compre-hensive perspective, which also takes into account intra-cohort inequality – based on class, gender and ethnicity – and social inheritance.

Housing in a familialistic welfare system

Family is a primary actor in the Italian welfare system. This is partly the result of specific cultural traits and social values. The structural role of the family as an economic agent should not be underestimated, however. Industrialization – and the shift toward a service economy afterwards – has coexisted with an ongoing role for the household and the family as important economic units. Even today they are directly involved in production: self-employed workers make up about one quarter of the labour force. Many of their activities are linked to family businesses or imply some support by family members. Registered unpaid family workers indeed represented 1.8 per cent of the labour force in 2006 (Poggio 2012).

Family plays an even greater role in the redistribution of income and in welfare provision (Ferrera 1996, Naldini 2003). The Italian welfare state was not fully developed before the 1970s. Even after its full expansion, its provision of services and transfers has been relatively poor by European standards. Several policy areas have been rather neglected, notably housing and care. The same is true for several social groups, including young people. In such a context, it is not surprising that families have had to provide some social protection to their members directly, in partial continuity with pre-industrial practices. This role of the family is also highly institutionalized. Beyond social norms, the inheritance law and the Civil Code establish several reciprocal obligations between family generations, including duties of maintenance and care. In many welfare domains the state provides support only in the second instance, if family fails, according to a 'subsidiarity' principle. Because of the important role family plays in social protection and because of the normative expectations about this role, Italy has been referred to as a 'familialistic' welfare system (Esping-Andersen 1990).

Housing is an important pillar of this familialistic welfare system (Poggio 2012). Co-residence between adult generations is a traditional way to pool family resources: income and care, as well as housing. In the past it was quite common for young couples to share a dwelling with their parents. Today this is more common for single individuals, before nest-leaving. Proximity between generations remains in any event an important principle informing localization choices, as it facilitates mutual support and care provision within the family network (Poggio 2008).

Precautionary savings have represented an important way to deal with social risks. Family strategies of asset accumulation have, in fact, provided some informal pension and insurance arrangements to members in unpaid family work, or who were not participating in formal social security schemes (Castles and Ferrera 1996, Poggio 2012). Home ownership has traditionally been considered a safe and good investment, with good reason. Self-building has also been a relatively successful asset-building strategy for working class households (Tosi 1995, Poggio 2012).

At present, about 70 per cent of Italian households own their home. Many homeowners accessed this property thanks to intergenerational transfers: the dwelling was given to them, inherited or purchased – or built – with financial support from their parents. Another 10 per cent of Italian households – especially the younger and the more elderly ones – live in housing provided for free, in almost all cases within the family network. This intermediate tenure typically represents a step in the process of the intergenerational transmission of home ownership.

In-kind family support – family dwellings, plots of land which can be built on, unpaid labour and other factors in self-building – was particularly important until the 1980s. The lack of effective regulation of land use and building standards – and tolerance of illegal building – have provided households with good opportunities for partial and total self-building (Allen *et al.* 2004, Tosi 1995). This has represented a cheap route to home ownership, even if it is at the cost of an irrational use of land and poor standards.

The transmission of home ownership and the structuring of social inequality

The reproduction of social inequality is inherent to the discussed forms of intergenerational transmission of home ownership. Access to this tenure, in fact, largely depends on family wealth and on the degree of control parents have over other material and social resources. Previous research shows that support for home ownership varies by class of origin – and also by gender – and tends to cumulate with family investments in their offspring's formal education (Bernardi and Poggio 2004, Guiso and Jappelli 1996, Poggio 2008). As a partial exception, the availability of the previously mentioned informal – sometimes illegal – and cheaper routes to home ownership in the past allowed some redistribution to take place in the housing system.

Research in the field provides evidence for increasing inequality emerging from the housing system itself. First, home ownership is widespread and is now considered the standard tenure in Italian society. This establishes challenging minimum requirements for housing independence (Facchini and Villa 2005, Kemeny 1981, Spilerman *et al.* 1993): new entrants into the housing market are not only asked to spend a significant share of their income on housing, in a homeowners' society they are also required to have some form of control – their own savings or family wealth, or the capacity to borrow – over large amounts of money, corresponding to current housing prices. Further, home ownership in the early stages of the life course may be a burden for young households, as there is a structural trade-off between early home purchase and the cost of raising children (see also Castles and Ferrera 1996). At an aggregate level, low fertility and postponement of first parenthood is associated with high home ownership rates and limited mortgage provision (Mulder and Billari 2010).

Second, family help – structurally sustained by the inheritance and gift tax system – has become more important than in the past when entering home ownership (Bernardi and Poggio 2004, Poggio 2008). This is also due to a tendency, since the 1980s, towards an entry into this tenure to be anticipated within the family life course.

Third, financial transfers – as against in-kind forms of support – have become a more important way to support younger family members within a housing system that has become more market driven. The possibility for some redistribution to continue through cheap and informal routes to home ownership has definitely been undermined (Bernardi and Poggio 2004, Poggio 2008).

Against such a background, and in the context of the previously discussed uncertainty over incomes from the labour market, housing autonomy and housing conditions tend to depend, more than in the past, on family wealth.

Main changes that have occurred in the socioeconomic context and in the housing system

The main traits of the Italian welfare and housing systems have already been outlined. In order to account for opportunities and constraints experienced by different generations in their transition to adulthood, it is possible schematically to distinguish three main periods.

From the 1950s to the early 1970s

The first few decades after the war were characterized by rapid economic growth and by the expansion of urban areas. Massive internal migrations took place in this period, from Southern Italy and from the countryside to major cities in the North of the country. Rapid industrial development, migrations and the need to repair war damage drove a housing demand oriented to new construction. Building activities took place in a context of weak or no planning constraints. Both speculative builders and self-developing homeowners could take advantage of this circumstance.

Private companies invested heavily in the rental market. A large-scale social housing plan was also implemented in the same period. New dwellings in the rented sector – with water, electricity and heating facilities – were rather attractive and sustained geographical mobility. Renting was a relatively common experience, especially for young households. According to Census data, the rental sector accounted for 44 per cent of Italian households in 1971.

Rising and relatively stable incomes and the progressive emergence of dual-earner couples sustained the demand for home ownership. The availability of informal and cheap routes to home ownership, and the privatization of social housing, also made it possible to satisfy this demand for low-income households, at least to a certain extent.

From the 1970s to the early 1990s

The late 1960s and early 1970s represented a period of important welfare and housing reforms (Bernardi and Nazio 2005). On the other hand, a high unemployment rate was experienced between the 1970s and the 1990s, especially among young people. A complete restructuring of industrial production took place after the international crisis of the 1970s. Smaller industries and the service economy progressively acquired greater importance. Labour demand, and hence housing demand, increasingly moved from major cities to mid-size towns and – to some extent – back to the countryside. The period of mass migrations also came to an end.

During the 1970s land use and building standards regulations were introduced and progressively implemented. Housing development was nevertheless not subject to strict regulations, except in major urban areas. Illegal building was in any case tolerated. The full implementation of the new regulations took place only during the 1980s. Housing policy reforms were introduced after a period of social conflict in urban areas. A 'ten year plan' was implemented in order to relaunch social housing provision, but the new production in this segment never reached the level of previous decades. A 'fair rent' regime was introduced in the rental market, as a way to balance reasonable returns for landlords and a minimum level of social protection for tenants. In fact, it failed in both its objectives. In the 1980s the rental sector collapsed and households were pushed into home ownership as a way of obtaining a decent, secure and affordable dwelling. The home ownership rate increased by 20 percentage points in the period 1970–90. The 1991 Census registered a 68 per cent home ownership rate, which still roughly equates to the current figure.

From the mid-1990s to the present

The restructuring of the Italian economy during the 1980s had important consequences for both the spatial structuring of housing demand – de-urbanization – and the working conditions of young people. Employment progressively became less regulated and less protected (Bernardi and Nazio 2005). During the past two decades, Italy has also experienced large-scale immigration from other countries. A restart of internal migration has also been reported in the new millennium (De Santis 2008). Both international and internal migrations sustain housing demand in the country, swelling the ranks of new entrants to the housing market.

The 'fair rent' regime was progressively dismantled between 1992 and 1998. Investments in social housing had been continuously decreasing and this sector today accounts for about 4 per cent of the residential housing stock. Provision for young people is limited in this sector, because of both the aforementioned dynamics of social investments in the field and the typical housing allocation rules. A housing allowance scheme was introduced in 1998 but is not very effective (Baldini and Poggio 2012).

Housing affordability problems have dramatically increased in the new millennium, as a result both of the dynamics of free market rents and of the change in social composition of those renting (D'Alessio and Gambacorta 2007): being a tenant is today more associated with low income than in the past. The average impact of rent on employees' individual earnings rose from 15–20 per cent during the 1980s and 90s to about 30 per cent in the mid-2000s (Poggio 2009). The social production of home ownership has become more market driven. The liberalization of the private rented market and the expansion of the mortgage market boosted housing demand. Housing prices skyrocketed, substantially nullifying the effect of better mortgage conditions. It has been estimated that employees needed about 14 years' worth of their salary, on average, in order to buy a home in the mid-2000s, while no more than eight years' worth were needed during the 1980s and 90s (Poggio 2012).

Summary

The changes outlined above have important implications for the opportunities that different generations have been presented with when entering the labour and housing markets. To summarize, those who entered into adulthood during the 1950s and 1960s probably experienced the most severe hardship and most dramatic changes during the first part of their life. However, fast economic growth allowed them to rapidly improve their living and housing conditions. Young people could benefit from large investments in new housing, both in the private market and in the social sector. They could also find opportunities for self-development and self-building, representing continuity with informal family practices in rural communities.

People moving to their adulthood during the 1970s to early 1990s experienced less favourable economic conditions, due to a high unemployment rate and the restructuring of the industrial economy. However, they benefitted from the 'Golden Spring' – 'Age' would overstate it – of the Italian welfare state. The shape of housing policies, the collapse of the rental market, the shift in housing demand from major cities to less expensive areas and the still-available opportunities for self-development pushed these cohorts into home ownership.

Finally, those entering their adulthood since the 1990s have had to cope with insecurity in the labour market and the retrenchment of the welfare state; not to mention real housing prices and rents that have been increasing dramatically.

However, the improvement in living and economic conditions since the end of World War II, the expansion of home ownership as a popular form of wealth and the structuring of welfare assets progressively increased the economic capacity of older people. Their capacity to support their offspring consequently increased over time, up until the end of the last century.

An empirical analysis of intergenerational housing-related transfers

Data and methods

The analysis presented is based on data from the survey *Famiglia e soggetti sociali*, carried out in 2003 by the Italian National Institute of Statistics. Retrospective data were collected on individuals' labour market participation and on major family events. Women who had been married at least once were also asked to provide information about their accommodation during the first or only marriage, and about any help received.

The analysis was carried out in three steps. First, some descriptive estimates of the timing of several steps in the transition to adulthood were calculated for both men and women. The purpose was to better illustrate some aspects of the intergenerational gaps discussed. Second, by focusing on marriage as an important stage in both family life and housing career, it was possible to describe the pattern of couples' accommodation at the time of marriage and its change over time. Different forms of housing-related support were examined. Third, from this selected sample, I focused on the couples that did not co-reside with their ascendants at the time of marriage. It was possible to analyse the role of parents' transfers in sustaining independent housing for their daughters, on a subsample of 8054 women.

A variable *type of accommodation and help received for housing* was derived by considering the original survey variables for co-residence with parents (at least one) versus independent accommodation and – for the latter – housing tenure, various ways of becoming a homeowner, and other possible forms of parental help. In the case of co-residence, it was not possible to distinguish whether spouses went to live in the parental home or parents went to live in the spouses' home.

A *region of birth* variable distinguishes between the north-west of the country, 'Third Italy' (the north-east and north-central regions), the 'South and Islands', and abroad. This partitioning accounts for different socioeconomic contexts, distinct patterns of migration and for different models of housing settlement. The north-west is the area of industrialization and urban expansion after World War II; Third Italy is the area of de-localization of labour and housing demand during the 1980s and 1990s; the South and Islands represent relatively underdeveloped areas, which experienced massive out-migrations after the war.

Seven birth *cohorts* were defined, using five-year intervals for individuals born in the period 1938 to 1972. This selection was a compromise between considering relatively young cohorts, the possibility of observing life-course events within each cohort and limiting sample selection issues. For the purpose of this work, it should be noted that selection effects might nevertheless influence what is observed for the younger cohorts. This caveat will be revisited in the discussion that follows, when relevant.

Turning to individual characteristics, *age at marriage* was considered to be an indicator of the position in the life course and a proxy for the couple's savings. *Educational level*, comprising five levels, was included as an indicator of previous parental transfers in terms of human capital. Finally, *number of siblings* was considered as an indicator of possible constraints on parents' capacity to provide support to each child.

As regards parental-level variables, *occupational class of origin* was derived from the original survey data on parents' employment when the interviewees were 14 years old. The EGP class schema (Erickson and Goldthorpe 1992) was followed, with some minor adjustments due to data constraints. This variable was expected to account for resources available to parents and for different degrees of control over various forms of capital. Finally, one further variable was used to describe the *proximity between the couple and the woman's parents* (or the nearest parent, if they were living in different places) at the time of marriage.

Generational gaps and nest-leaving

Tables 3.1 and 3.2 illustrate the main changes across the cohorts considered. The completion rate of higher (or further) education for men is more than doubled if one compares the older with the younger cohorts. These changes in educational attainment are even more pronounced for women. The median age at which young people take their first job increased by two years, for both men and women. The median age of nest-leaving also increased. In both cases the observed differences across cohorts are likely to be underestimated, as some individuals in the younger cohorts still had to make these transitions at the time of the interview.

Interviewees who had already left the parental home were asked about the main motive for that choice. Their answers are also reported in Tables 3.1 and 3.2. Taken together, marriage and cohabitation are the major motive. They account for 62–65 per cent of men's motives and for 80 per cent, and even more, of women's motives. Whereas marriage was almost the only option for the older cohorts, leaving the parental home for cohabitation has become more common for younger individuals. Differences persist between men and women with regard to the importance of marriage as a reason to leave the parental home. These differences can be attributed to gender-specific social norms and to differential participation in the labour market. The importance of moving out for study-related reasons increased, especially for women. The salience of the need for independence and autonomy also increased for both men and women, even though gender differences remain.

Finally, some descriptive statistics are reported for women, on several steps of their family career. They show a long-term trend toward postponement of marriage and of having a baby. The age of the first birth has increased and the total number of children has decreased. This long-term trend is apparent notwithstanding the possibility that what is observed for the younger cohorts could in part be the result of a selection effect. The above findings are consistent with previous research in the field (Barbagli *et al.* 2003, Buzzi 2007 and Pisati 2002, for instance).

Accommodation at marriage and parental help

Table 3.3 provides estimates for the accommodation of couples at the first or only marriage, and for family housing-related help. Notwithstanding social and cultural changes, marriage still typically tends to coincide with leaving the parental home, especially for women. Social norms also inform family help: parents are more likely to support their children if they are getting married rather than if they are starting a cohabitation (Mencarini and Tanturri 2006).

Three major trends are apparent. First, the importance of co-residence declined over time. Co-residence was a solution adopted by about one quarter of couples in

TABLE 3.1 Shifting demographics: selected indicators by birth cohort and sex – men.

	Birth cohort							
	1938–42	1943–47	1948–52	1953–57	1958–62	1963–67	1968–72
Average number of siblings	3.2	2.9	2.6	2.5	2.5	2.2	2.0
Completed higher or further education (%)	24.7	32.3	41.5	47.7	50.2	50.3	56.4
Never worked (%)	0.3	1.0	1.3	1.0	1.9	3.2	5.5
Median age at first job (if ever worked) (years)	18	18	19	20	20	20	20
Never left parental home (%)	1.8	2.7	4.3	6.7	8.6	15.2	30.4
Median age when left parental home (if ever left) (years)	25	25	25	25	25	26	26
Main motive for leaving the nest (if left)							
cohabitation (%)	0.5	1.1	1.1	1.5	2.5	6.6	10.1
marriage (%)	61.8	62.1	65.2	65.0	62.5	57.3	47.4
work (%)	18.7	19.9	15.1	15.5	15.9	16.2	19.9
study (%)	3.0	3.5	4.5	4.9	4.5	3.7	5.2
independence, autonomy needed (%)	3.6	3.5	4.1	4.9	7.2	8.0	9.0
other reasons (%)	12.4	9.9	10.0	8.2	7.4	8.2	8.4
all motives (%)	100.0	100.0	100.0	100.0	100.0	100.0	100.0
Sample size (all individuals in the cohort)	1483	1605	1684	1667	1766	1918	1854

Source: Author's own estimates from the ISTAT survey *Famiglia e soggetti sociali 2003*

TABLE 3.2 Shifting demographics: selected indicators by birth cohort and sex – women.

	Birth cohort							
	1938–42	1943–47	1948–52	1953–57	1958–62	1963–67	1968–72
Average number of siblings	3.1	2.9	2.6	2.6	2.4	2.2	2.0
Completed higher or further education (%)	16.9	25.7	34.7	45.1	53.0	54.8	63.1
Never worked (%)	29.2	28.3	25.6	21.7	19.7	21.3	21.5
Median age at first job (if ever worked) (years)	19	19	19	19	20	20	21
Never left parental home (%)	1.0	1.9	2.7	2.9	4.9	9.4	17.3
Median age when left parental home (if ever left) (years)	23	22	22	22	23	24	24
Main motive for leaving the nest (if left)							
cohabitation (%)	1.3	1.8	1.9	3.9	5.7	7.2	11.4
marriage (%)	83.1	80.8	82.1	78.6	78.0	73.9	66.8
work (%)	6.0	7.3	6.1	6.1	6.3	5.8	6.1
study (%)	2.3	2.5	2.9	4.2	4.0	5.0	6.6
independence, autonomy needed (%)	1.4	2.5	3.0	4.3	3.9	5.7	6.5
other reasons (%)	5.9	5.1	4.0	2.9	2.1	2.4	2.6
all motives (%)	100.0	100.0	100.0	100.0	100.0	100.0	100.0
Never married (%)	5.7	7	6.7	8.1	10.1	16.4	28.3
Median age at marriage (if ever married) (years)	23	23	22	22	23	23	23
Average number of children	2.1	2.0	1.9	1.8	1.7	1.5	1.0
Median age at birth of first child (if ever had one) (years)	25	24	24	24	25	27	27
Sample size (all individuals in the cohort)	1604	1625	1764	1791	1953	1996	1827

Source: Author's own estimates from the ISTAT survey Famiglia e soggetti sociali 2003

the eldest cohort and by only 11 per cent in the youngest. Decline in this type of accommodation is steeper for co-residence with the husband's parents than for co-residence with the wife's. The decreased relevance of patrilocality is due to the decline of specific farmers' settlement models, to women's increased levels of education and to their higher levels of participation in the labour market (Barbagli *et al.* 2003). In general, the decline of co-residence also marks a cultural and housing shift: sharing a dwelling between adult generations tends to be unacceptable nowadays.

Second, renting consistently declined across the considered cohorts, with the exception of an increased importance of this type of accommodation for those who experienced migration and who typically entered the housing market before its collapse: those in the 1943–52 cohorts. Finally, the relevance of both home ownership and rent-free dwellings also increased over time. Becoming a homeowner thanks to ascendants' financial help is a modality that increased more than other ways of entering this tenure.

It was possible to consider family help as a whole, including co-residence, the various types of transfers for home ownership and provision of rent-free dwellings. The last two rows of Table 3.3 show that at least one third of the spouses' housing solutions involved some help from their parents, when considering women born after 1953. This figure is higher for the younger cohorts but this may depend on a possible selection effect: housing independence is postponed in the absence of family support. It should be noted that this complementary explanation does not contradict, from a substantive point of view, one of the main theses of this study: the increased dependence of housing autonomy on family support.

Housing-related transfers for autonomous accommodation

A further step in the analysis consisted in investigating the sole intergenerational transfers oriented to the attainment of independent accommodation. For this purpose, couples co-residing with (at least one of) their parents were not considered, nor were the couples in which one of the partners already owned the dwelling when the spouses moved in.[2] Only transfers from the bride's parents were considered. This choice was largely due to constraints in data available for men. Previous research, carried out on a selected sub-sample from the same survey data, considered both men and women and might be informative on the possible effects of selecting women only: compared to sons, daughters are less likely to receive parental help (Poggio 2008).

In our sample 86.4 per cent of the brides received no help from their parents; 6.2 per cent received in-kind transfers, and 5.8 per cent financial help for home ownership; 1.6 per cent inherited their first accommodation at marriage. Estimates from a multinomial logistic regression modelling these outcomes are presented in Table 3.4. The purpose of this modelling exercise was to depict possible patterns in housing support, according to the type of help provided. The last column provides summary statistics for the selected sample.

TABLE 3.3 Couples' accommodation at marriage and housing-related transfers received from their parents, by bride's birth cohort.

	Cohort						
	1938–42	1943–47	1948–52	1953–57	1958–62	1963–67	1968–72
Co-residence							
Co-residence with parents (bride's parents) (%)	8.3	7.5	5.3	6.4	5.6	5.6	4.9
Co-residence with parents-in-law (bridegroom's parents) (%)	18.3	13.4	12.3	11.1	8.7	6.7	6.0
Independent accommodation							
Home ownership with parental help:							
home inherited from parents (%)	1.6	0.9	0.8	1.2	1.1	1.4	1.9
home inherited from parents-in-law (%)	1.8	1.1	1.1	1.0	1.9	2.0	1.4
home given by parents (%)	0.9	0.7	1.3	1.5	2.3	2.3	1.6
home given by parents-in-law (%)	1.1	0.8	0.7	1.1	1.2	1.7	2.1
received financial help from parents (%)	0.8	0.7	1.0	1.2	2.0	3.8	3.8
received financial help from both parents and parents-in-law (%)	1.3	1.4	1.7	1.9	2.3	3.7	4.7
received financial help from parents-in-law (%)	0.4	0.6	1.1	1.6	1.4	2.4	1.4
Home ownership without parental help:							
home inherited from (given by, acquired with help from) others (%)	0.5	0.5	0.8	0.9	0.7	0.8	1.1
home built or purchased with own means (%)	8.3	9.5	10.0	10.5	11.5	11.7	12.8
home already owned by one of the spouses (%)	5.9	5.4	7.2	6.9	9.2	8.0	8.8
Free of rent:							
allocated by parents (%)	1.1	1.6	2.7	3.0	3.9	4.4	5.0
allocated by parents-in-law (%)	2.5	2.3	3.1	4.5	5.2	6.2	7.3
allocated by others (%)	1.7	1.3	0.9	1.0	1.8	1.3	1.1
Rented (%)	45.5	52.3	50.0	46.2	41.2	38.0	36.1
All (%)	100.0	100.0	100.0	100.0	100.0	100.0	100.0
Sample size	1512	1512	1645	1646	1755	1669	1310
Overall transmission from parents (%)	14.0	12.8	12.8	15.2	17.2	21.2	21.9
Overall transmission from parents or parents-in-law (%)	38.1	31.0	31.1	34.5	35.6	40.2	40.1

Source: Author's own estimates from the ISTAT survey *Famiglia e soggetti sociali 2003*

Coefficients are presented in their exponentiated form, as relative risk ratios (RRRs). The reference outcome is receiving no help. Modelled alternative outcomes are: having received in-kind help (a dwelling given or free of rent), financial help or having inherited the dwelling. Inheritance has been considered separately. Given its accidental character, this type of transfer cannot be planned and contracted, as happens with inter vivos transfers. Neither is it something people can usually rely on, when planning a marriage.

As expected, the probability of receiving a dwelling as an inheritance is not clearly structured. The only two exceptions are the effects of age at marriage – which is correlated with the age of the parents – and of the proximity between the spouses and the bride's (living) parent.

Both the region of birth and the cohort influence the probability of receiving housing related transfers at marriage: other things being equal, women born in the north-west and in Third Italy are more likely to receive housing help from their parents, compared to those born in the South and Islands or abroad.

The chances of receiving help have increased for the younger cohorts: in comparison to the older cohorts, the likelihood of receiving in-kind help more than doubles, on average, for women born after 1957, while the chances of receiving financial help more than double for women born after 1962, other things being equal.

The age of the bride influences the likelihood of receiving financial help – the older she is, the more likely she is to receive support – but not her chances to benefit from in-kind transfers. Having siblings reduces the probability of receiving parental support, especially the in-kind type.

There is a strong positive association between proximity to parents and the probability of receiving help from them. This is especially the case for in-kind forms of support. Conversely, the further the spouses settle from parents the less likely they are to receive housing-related transfers. A similar pattern is also apparent for the probability of receiving financial transfers. However, differences are definitely more limited in the latter case, and the significance of estimates lower. These differences between in-kind and financial transfers, in their association with proximity, suggest interpreting the relations between proximity and in-kind transfers as being based on location specific resources relevant for the transmission of home ownership (Poggio 2008).

Class of origin influences the likelihood of receiving parental housing-related transfers. Daughters from bourgeois families have a higher chance of receiving both in-kind and financial support (on average, 60 per cent higher) compared to daughters from the working class. In the case of in-kind help, differences are even greater between brides from the working class and those from the petty bourgeoisie (urban self-employed and farmers).

The analysis also shows that housing-related material transfers, especially the in-kind ones, are associated with educational level. Housing-related transfers tend to cumulate with previous investments in formal education.

TABLE 3.4 Relative risk ratios for the probability of receiving parental housing-related transfers for independent accommodation at the time of marriage (women ever married, born 1938–1972), by type of transfer – multinomial logistic regression model ($n = 8054$).

	Model						Summary statistics (%, means)
	In kind: no help		Financial: no help		Inheritance: no help		
	RRR	SE	RRR	SE	RRR	SE	
Region of origin							
North–west	1.47**	(0.21)	1.19	(0.16)	0.70	(0.19)	18.4%
Third Italy	1.29*	(0.17)	1.39**	(0.16)	0.71	(0.17)	27.1%
South and Islands (ref.)	—	—	—	—	—	—	50.3%
Abroad	0.92	(0.26)	0.57	(0.17)	0.47	(0.29)	4.2%
Cohort							
1938–42 (ref.)	—	—	—	—	—	—	12.1%
1943–47	1.05	(0.30)	0.80	(0.21)	0.51	(0.18)	13.4%
1948–52	1.60	(0.42)	1.05	(0.26)	0.38**	(0.14)	14.8%
1953–57	1.80*	(0.49)	1.16	(0.29)	0.67	(0.21)	14.9%
1958–62	2.25**	(0.60)	1.47	(0.35)	0.59*	(0.18)	16.2%
1963–67	2.22**	(0.60)	2.54**	(0.58)	0.66	(0.20)	16.0%
1968–72	2.25**	(0.61)	2.60**	(0.60)	0.87	(0.27)	12.6%
Age at marriage (ref. mean, by 5 years)	0.91	(0.06)	1.25**	(0.06)	1.37**	(0.12)	24 years
Educational level							
University	1.70**	(0.33)	1.26	(0.23)	0.75	(0.30)	9.3%
Upper secondary/vocational	1.51**	(0.19)	1.41**	(0.18)	1.44	(0.32)	33.2%
Lower secondary (ref.)	—	—	—	—	—	—	32.5%

	Model 1		Model 2		Model 3		%
Primary school	0.71*	(0.14)	1.08	(0.20)	0.95	(0.27)	22.2%
No formal education	1.99	(0.70)	0.94	(0.50)	1.23	(0.61)	2.8%
Siblings (ref. mean)	0.91**	(0.03)	0.85**	(0.03)	0.94	(0.04)	2.6
Parents' occupational class							
Bourgeoisie	1.66*	(0.35)	1.56*	(0.28)	1.00	(0.42)	6.7%
Middle class	1.15	(0.21)	1.32	(0.20)	0.76	(0.25)	12.9%
Urban self-employed	1.97**	(0.28)	1.25	(0.18)	0.98	(0.28)	15.8%
Farmers	1.67**	(0.29)	0.97	(0.18)	1.01	(0.30)	13.3%
Blue collar workers (ref.)	—		—		—		33.0%
Agricultural labourers	1.42	(0.28)	0.84	(0.19)	0.84	(0.29)	10.0%
Missing information	0.65	(0.18)	0.86	(0.20)	1.59	(0.45)	8.3%
Proximity at marriage							
In the same building	9.49**	(1.20)	1.38	(0.31)	8.88**	(2.10)	7.5%
Within 1 km (ref.)	—		—		—		26.5%
More than 1 km but in the same town	0.46**	(0.07)	1.24*	(0.16)	0.88	(0.23)	26.6%
Less than 16 km	0.31**	(0.07)	0.99	(0.16)	0.54	(0.21)	13.8%
More than 16 km	0.19**	(0.04)	0.70*	(0.10)	0.32**	(0.11)	25.4%
Constant	0.02**	(0.01)	0.03**	(0.01)	0.03**	(0.01)	—

Source: Author's own estimates from the ISTAT survey *Famiglia e soggetti sociali 2003* * $p < 0.05$, ** $p < 0.01$

Concluding remarks

The intention of this chapter has been to examine two interconnected topics. The first is the delayed transition to adulthood in Italy, with a focus on housing independence and on external economic constraints from the labour and the housing markets. A second aim has been to consider Italy as a case study for a discussion on the complex interplay between generational inequality, intra-cohort cleavages and social inheritance, which is inherent to family intergenerational housing-related transfers.

Great variability exists in the opportunities that the market and the welfare state have offered to young people in Italy since the end of World War II. Younger cohorts have experienced increasing economic difficulties, due both to a greater labour market uncertainty and the retrenchment of the welfare state. Different housing-related constraints are also evident. Real housing prices and rents have almost doubled since the 1990s. The substantial abdication of the welfare state from the responsibility of providing a decent level of social protection in the housing domain left young people dependent on market processes and on family wealth.

Housing provision has become more and more market driven. Insecurity of home ownership, due to possible mortgage defaults, is still a marginal phenomenon but is emerging as a new social risk, especially for younger generations and immigrants (Poggio 2012). Finally, the social requirement of an early entry into home ownership for young people – due to the lack of 'acceptable' alternatives in the rental sector – has become particularly demanding in this context, if one cannot rely on family help. The changing features of the labour and housing markets affect the first phases of the family life course and are also likely to have long-term consequences. They can undermine welfare and private asset-building, as both participation in pension schemes and access to home ownership have become more problematic.

Intergenerational gaps exist and changes that have occurred in the housing domain have contributed to structuring them. However, it has been argued that other intra-cohort cleavages maintain their salience and that the impact of generational inequality varies across social strata. Further, some re-stratification takes place via family intergenerational housing-related transfers and should been taken into account. Some evidence has been provided – albeit limited to help received by women when getting married – on the importance of these transfers and on their social stratification. This leads into the second aim of this chapter and to the attempt to shed some light on the various factors at work and the different cleavages.

Individuals with low levels of education and/or from the working class are more affected by globalization and by its induced social and economic changes in the labour and in the housing markets. Being a foreign or domestic migrant – a condition that also typically coincides with being a young adult – tends to imply different disadvantages, as a result of being a new entrant into the local housing market and of being less likely to be supported by parents because of distance. Migrants are also typically discriminated against by housing policies.

However, some social strata may benefit more than others from compensatory private intergenerational transfers: individuals from the upper class and the petty bourgeoisie, and those with a high level of education. From previous research we also know that sons are more advantaged than daughters.

From this perspective, both the importance of generational inequality and the salience of intergenerational transfers should be reconsidered. There is no doubt about the fact that, at an aggregated level, generational inequality is a relevant issue. The dependence of young people on their parents' resources remains as a general problem of social citizenship for younger citizens. Similarly there is no doubt about the partial compensatory effects of private intergenerational transfers, when considered at an aggregated level. However, looking at these processes in more detail allows a better examination of who loses and who gains, within a given cohort, vis-à-vis globalization *and* housing-related intergenerational transmission. The latter seems more likely to contribute to the widening of – rather than compensating for – existing social inequalities.

Finally, and for the purposes of this discussion, considering in the analysis both generational inequality and intergenerational transfers may also help in reconciling the two research perspectives that have been introduced. In the analysis of the life chances of younger generations it is important to distinguish the enhanced capabilities of certain social strata from the reduced capabilities of others. Within the general context discussed, it is possible to schematically distinguish two polar positions, as an example. On the one hand, there are young people who are experiencing atypical employment as a way to explore different possibilities in the labour market, especially if they aspire to qualified and remunerative positions. They postpone definitive professional choices, as they tend to do in other domains relevant for the transition to adulthood, as an element of freedom. Housing-related transfers – even in simple terms of reasonable expectations – and other forms of family support can be associated with the preconditions for such capabilities.

On the other hand, there are young people who are experiencing unprotected employment as they simply have no alternatives. They are also at risk of being trapped in atypical employment. They postpone new family formation because of the lack of resources that are socially required for that purpose. They cannot rely on family housing support, and so they have to face high housing costs; or – if they can – available family resources might be specifically localized and could represent a constraint in relation to opportunities in different local labour markets. Considering these two profiles within the same framework of young peoples''disadvantages' will probably lead to erroneous conclusions. The topic is complex but it certainly deserves further and more systematic investigations.

Acknowledgements

I am grateful to the editors and to the other contributors of the book for the useful discussion we had at the City University of Hong Kong meeting in May 2011, and for their valuable comments received on a previous version of this chapter.

This work is partially based on a secondary analysis of data from the ISTAT survey *Famiglia e soggetti sociali 2003*. All the faults are mine.

Notes

1 These findings seem to contradict evidence from Bernardi and Nazio (2005). In fact, the two studies adopted two different measurement criteria: in the latter study those working without any contracts were considered separately.

2 Because of missing information on the way they had acquired their home. Couples in which both the parents of the bride were not alive at the time of marriage were also excluded. Finally, some cases were excluded because of missing information on the region of birth.

References

Allen, J., Barlow, J., Leal, J., Thomas, M. and Padovani, L. (2004) *Housing and Welfare in Southern Europe*, Oxford: Blackwell.

Attias-Donfut, C. and Arber, S. (2000) 'Equity and solidarity across the generations', in S. Arber and C. Attias-Donfut (eds) *The Myth of Generational Conflict*, London: Routledge.

Attias-Donfut, C. and Wolff, F. C. (2000) 'The redistributive effects of generational transfers', in S. Arber and C. Attias-Donfut (eds) *The Myth of Generational Conflict*, London: Routledge.

Baldini, M. and Poggio, T. (2012) 'Housing policy toward the rental sector in Italy: a distributive assessment', *Housing Studies* 27(5).

Ball, M. (1990) *Under One Roof: Retail Banking and the International Mortgage Finance Revolution*, New York: Harvester-Wheatsheaf.

Barbagli, M., Castiglioni, M. and Dalla Zuanna, G. (2003) *Fare famiglia in Italia. Un secolo di cambiamenti*, Bologna: il Mulino.

Barbieri, P. and Scherer, S. (2009) 'Labour market flexibilization and its consequences in Italy', *European Sociological Review* 25(6): 677–692.

Bernardi, F. and Nazio, T. (2005) 'Globalization and the transition to adulthood in Italy', in H.P. Blossfeld, E. Klijzing, M. Mills and K. Kurz (eds) *Globalization, Uncertainty and Youth in Society*, Oxon, UK and New York: Routledge.

Bernardi, F. and Poggio, T. (2004) 'Home ownership and social inequality in Italy', in K. Kurz and H. P. Blossfeld (eds) *Home Ownership and Social Inequality in Comparative Perspective*, Stanford: Stanford University Press.

Buzzi, C., (2007) 'La transizione all'età adulta', in C. Buzzi, A. Cavalli and A. de Lillo (eds) *Rapporto giovani. Sesta indagine dell'Istituto IARD sulla condizione giovanile in Italia*, Bologna: il Mulino.

Castles, F. G. and Ferrera, M. (1996) 'Home ownership and the welfare state: is Southern Europe different?' *South European Society and Politics*, 1(2): 163–184.

De Santis, G. (2008) 'La donna è mobile (e l'uomo anche)', *Neodemos*, 23 July. Online. Available at: <http://www.neodemos.it/index.php?file=onenews&form_id_notizia=227> (accessed 15 December 2011).

D'Alessio, G. and Gambacorta, R. (2007) 'L'accesso all'abitazione di residenza in Italia', *Questioni di economia e finanza*, 9, Rome: Banca d'Italia.

Erickson, R. and Goldthorpe, J. H. (1992) *The Constant Flux: A Study of Class Mobility in Industrial Societies*, Oxford: Clarendon Press.

Esping-Andersen, G. (1990) *The Three Worlds of Welfare Capitalism*, Cambridge: Polity Press.

Facchini, C. and Villa, P. (2005) 'La lenta transizione alla vita adulta in Italia', in C. Facchini (ed.) *Diventare adulti. Vincoli economici e strategie familiari*, Milano: Guerini e associati.

Ferrera, M. (1996) 'Il modello Sud-Europeo di welfare state', *Rivista italiana di scienza politica* 1: 67–101.

Forrest, R. (2008) 'Globalization and the housing asset rich', *Global Social Policy* 8(2): 167–187.

Guiso, L. and Jappelli, T. (1996) 'Intergenerational transfers, borrowing constraints and the timing of home ownership', *Temi di Discussione*, 275, Rome: Banca d'Italia.

ISTAT, National Institute of Statistics (2010) 'La vita quotidiana nel 2009', *Informazioni*, 5, Rome: ISTAT.

Kemeny, J. (1981) *The Myth of Home Ownership: Private Versus Public Choice in Housing Tenure*, London: Routledge and Kegan Paul.

Mencarini, L. and Tanturri, M. L. (2006) 'Una casa per diventare grandi. I giovani italiani, l'autonomia abitativa ed il ruolo della famiglia di origine', *Polis* XX(3): 405–430.

Mills, M. and Blossfeld, H.P. (2005) 'Globalization, uncertainty and the early life course: a theoretical framework', in H.P. Blossfeld, E. Klijzing, M. Mills and K. Kurz (eds) *Globalization, Uncertainty and Youth in Society*, Oxon, UK and New York: Routledge.

Mulder, C. H. and Billari, F. C. (2010) 'Home-ownership regimes and lowest-low fertility', *Housing Studies*, 25(4): 527–541.

Naldini, M. (2003) *Family in the Mediterranean Welfare States*, London and Portland, OR: Frank Cass.

Pisati, M. (2002) 'La transizione alla vita adulta', in A. Schizzerotto (ed.) *Vite ineguali. Disuguaglianze e corsi di vita nell'Italia contemporanea*, Bologna: il Mulino

Poggio, T. (2008) 'The intergenerational transmission of home ownership and the reproduction of the familialistic welfare regime', in C. Saraceno (ed.), *Families, Ageing and Social Policy: Generational Solidarity in European Welfare States,* Cheltenham, UK and Northampton, MA: Edward Elgar.

—— (2009) 'Le principali dimensioni della disuguaglianza abitativa in Italia', in A. Brandolini, C. Saraceno and A. Schizzerotto (eds) *Dimensioni della disuguaglianza in Italia: povertà, istruzione e salute*, Bologna: il Mulino.

—— (2012) 'The housing pillar of the Mediterranean welfare regime: relations between home ownership and other dimensions of welfare in Italy', in R. Ronald and M. Elsinga (eds) *Beyond Home Ownership: Housing, Welfare and Society*, London: Routledge, 51–67.

Sartori, F. (2007) 'La vita con la famiglia di origine', in C. Buzzi, A. Cavalli and A. de Lillo (eds) *Rapporto giovani. Sesta indagine dell'Istituto IARD sulla condizione giovanile in Italia*, Bologna: il Mulino.

Schizzerotto, A. (2002) 'Lavori protetti e non protetti', in A. Schizzerotto (ed.) *Vite ineguali. Disuguaglianze e corsi di vita nell'Italia contemporanea*, Bologna: il Mulino.

Spilerman, S., Lewin-Epstein, N. and Semyonov, M. (1993) 'Wealth, intergenerational transfers, and life chances', in A. B. Sørensen and S. Spilerman (eds) *Social Theory and Social Policy: Essays in Honor of James S. Coleman*, Westport, CT: Praeger.

Tosi, A. (1995) 'Shifting paradigms: the sociology of housing, the sociology of the family, and the crisis of modernity', in R. Forrest and A. Murie (eds) *Housing and Family Wealth: Comparative International Perspectives*, London and New York: Routledge.

4

THE HOUSING TRANSITIONS OF YOUNG PEOPLE IN AUSTRALIA

Change, continuity and challenge

Andrew Beer and Debbie Faulkner

Australian society has experienced profound economic, social and political change over the last four decades as the nation has deregulated its economy, continued to receive large numbers of immigrants and experienced significant deindustrialisation. Many of these changes have ushered in a new set of processes that have served to mediate the relationship between housing and the life course of individuals and households in Australia. Economic liberalisation that began in the mid-1980s has resulted in a more affluent, but less equal, society while changes in social policy – including the introduction of 'no-fault divorce' in the 1970s, higher rates of participation in higher education, and new forms of income support – have changed household dynamics. At the same time, Australia's demographic structure has been transformed by a combination of processes, including the structural ageing of the population (Hugo 2003), shifts in household composition (Beer 2008a) and ongoing growth in one- and two-person households. These broad societal processes have affected the relationship between households and their housing in many and profound ways: they have contributed to a greater emphasis on housing as a con-sumption good within Australian society; they have resulted in the marginalisation of some groups within the housing market; and seen housing affordability emerge as a major political and policy challenge (Beer and Faulkner 2011). Critically, the relationship between individuals and their housing over their life course has, in many cases, experienced a step change. There is now greater uncertainty within the housing market and the trajectories of individuals and households are now less predictable than in the past. Every stage in the life cycle has been affected by these changes, including childhood and the early adult years.

This chapter considers the relationship between housing and life course in the years between youth and middle age in the Australia of the twenty-first century. It examines this issue from the perspective of broader changes taking place in the relationship between households and their housing. It argues that identifiably new relationships are emerging in the early years of adulthood, but that established patterns of housing consumption have retained their prominence for many younger adults. Moreover, the chapter argues that the increased complexity of housing market pathways and experiences for this cohort has confounded much analysis. The chapter begins by considering the insights offered by the established literature on housing careers and housing histories. It argues that in the twenty-first century there is a strong case for arguing that the relationship between housing and the life course is better thought of as a series of transitions that may, or may not, have an identifiable direction and pattern of movement. The chapter then moves on to consider some of the key debates around the housing of young people in Australia and draws upon survey data collected in 2006–07 to shed light on both new and enduring processes within the housing market experiences of this group.

Housing careers, housing histories and housing transitions

For more than four decades academic research has paid considerable attention to the relationship between housing and the life course, although interest in the topic has waxed and waned over time. Conventionally, this relationship has been expressed as a 'housing career', which can be most easily understood as the sequence of housing an individual or household occupies over their life course. Over time, other terms have been used to describe and understand this set of relationships, including 'housing histories', 'housing biographies', 'housing sequences' (Clark *et al.* 2003) and, most recently, 'housing pathways' (Clapham 2005).

The concepts of housing careers, housing pathways and housing histories first received widespread attention within the academic literature in the 1970s and early 1980s (Forrest 1987; Kendig 1984; Payne and Payne 1977; Pickvance 1974). This body of research noted that there was a strong correlation between stage in the life cycle and the type of housing an individual occupies. Households, it was claimed, progress through the housing market in response to their changing demographic, economic and social circumstances. Households were seen to simultaneously ascend three discrete but related ladders: an employment career; a life-stage progression (implicitly raising children); and a housing career. The pattern of housing consumption was also seen to reflect local housing market conditions, as the specific circumstances in any place – such as the cost of housing, the type of stock available and tenure structure – influenced outcomes. Importantly, this body of research recognised that housing careers reflected the balance of constraints and opportunities that direct households into particular niches within the public housing sector or the private market.

In Australia the concept of a housing career has been used to explain the strong correlation between the type of dwelling a household occupied and its stage in the life cycle. In a landmark study in Adelaide, South Australia, Kendig (1981) examined the housing careers of those who moved during 1975–76. The principal focus of this research was the drivers that underpinned relocation from one dwelling to the next. Importantly, Kendig tested the common assumption that nearly everybody follows the same housing progression or 'career'. It is usually supposed that young adults with their own income leave the family home to rent a flat and enjoy the single life. After marriage, both partners work and economise on rent so they can save a deposit to buy a house in which they will rear their children. Although a few move later to bigger houses before their children grow up or to own their flat after children leave home. It is usually assumed that most households remain in their first owned home into old age, enjoying the low costs and security of outright ownership.

(1981: 1)

One way of understanding and reflecting upon the different ways of examining the interaction between life course and the housing market is to consider how these issues have been represented in the past. Kendig, Paris and Anderton (1987) argued that a conventional housing career could be conceptualised as a ladder. This perspective on housing careers implies an upward movement through the housing market, while allowing for the possibility of slipping 'backward'. The 'housing career ladder' implies a start point and a destination, but also assumes a hierarchy of tenures, and a household structure amenable to both entry into home ownership and the eventual achievement of outright occupation.

Badcock and Beer (2000) used the imagery of 'snakes and ladders' to represent an alternative perspective on movement through the housing market in Australia. They argued that 'it is no longer good enough to presume that home ownership is an escalator for everyone, or to assign home owners to a class position and leave it at that' (p. 9). They argued that 'not everyone enjoys the fruits of capital accumulation' (Badcock and Beer 2000: 10). More recently, the work of Clapham (2005) and others has added a degree of finesse to our understanding of how individuals interact with the housing market. Other recent research has also generated an enhanced appreciation of the diversity of directions and outcomes people experience as they navigate their way through the housing market, with Clark *et al.* (2003), in particular, highlighting regional variation in housing outcomes. This more sophisticated understanding reflects our appreciation of increased diversity within society and the life course of individuals (Figure 4.1).

Beer, Faulkner and Gabriel (2006) concluded that over the last 40 years the relationship between housing and the life course had been fundamentally trans-formed. Their conceptualisation highlighted greater complexity in the life course, with an enhanced life span, periods of giving – and receiving – care, and both entry into and exits from marriage; multiple tenures over an individual's life; increased life expectancy; and a much more variable relationship between income and expenditure as circumstances vary both domestically and with respect to participation in the labour market. Beer and Faulkner (2011) noted employees in post-industrial societies are more likely to be made redundant than equivalent workers 40 years previously (Beer 2008b) but are also more likely to work past the age of 65 (Figure 4.2). Others receive sufficient financial rewards from paid work to either retire early

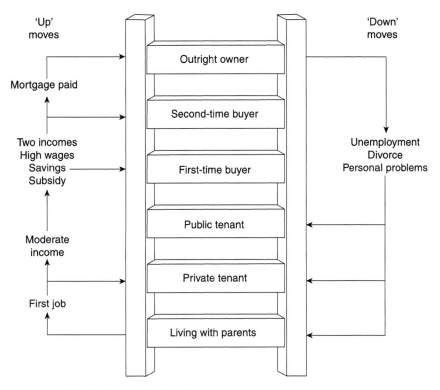

'Up'
moves

Mortgage paid

Two incomes
High wages
Savings
Subsidy

Moderate
income

First job

Outright owner

Second-time buyer

First-time buyer

Public tenant

Private tenant

Living with parents

'Down'
moves

Unemployment
Divorce
Personal problems

FIGURE 4.1 The Snakes and Ladders board game.
Source: based on Kendig, Paris and Anderton, 1987 p.30

or purchase a second or even third home for their own use (Paris 2011). Often these 'second homes' are in another region, another nation or even another continent. Some, of course, have enjoyed sufficient wealth to both leave paid work early and seek multiple residences. For younger people, entry into the housing market has become more difficult as a consequence of rising housing costs, greater insecurity in the labour market, the tightening of lending criteria since 2008 and increased competition for housing from older generations (Beer and Faulkner 2011). Overall, this perspective recognises that advanced economies such as Australia in the twenty-first century can now be characterised as 'risk' societies (Beck 1992; Giddens 1984) with new social dynamics that require individuals and households to carry an increasing share of the burden of uncertainty and a much higher level of differentiation between individuals than evident previously. Importantly, young people are more exposed to risk than older generations.

Beer and Faulkner (2011) have argued that the ability to move through the housing market and realise one's preferences is determined by five dimensions of the personal economy of the household. That is, there is a life-stage dimension that is congruent with conventional accounts of housing careers; a dimension that reflects position within the labour market and the economic resources a household can call

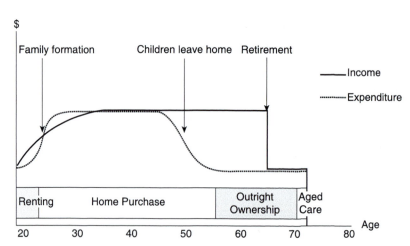

Industrial Australia

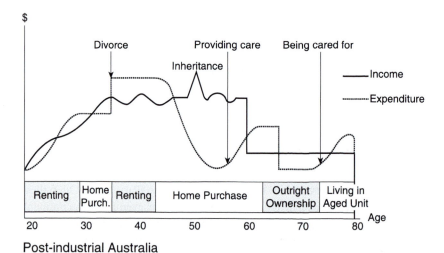

Post-industrial Australia

FIGURE 4.2 Changed life histories and changing housing careers.

upon; while health, disability and wellbeing is the third driver of housing outcomes. This dimension acknowledges the prevalence of disability and ill health within society and its profound impact on housing outcomes for individuals. Tenure *per se* is seen to be a fourth factor influencing the capacity to move through the housing market and recognises that a prior history in one tenure or set of circumstances – for example, crisis accommodation or home ownership – may open up possibilities for housing not otherwise available. Finally, lifestyle values and aspirations represent a fifth, and very influential, set of drivers of housing outcomes and appear to be more prominent in the twenty-first century than for earlier generations.

Each of these dimensions can be seen to exert an influence, potentially or in reality, on housing decisions at any point in time and this in turn leads to the

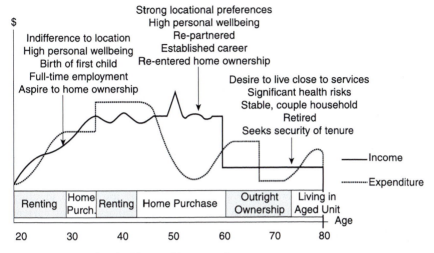

FIGURE 4.3 Housing decision making over time.
Source: Beer and Faulkner, 2011, p. 35

conclusion that individual housing decisions reflect the relative balance and standing of each (Figure 4.3). Early in the life course, for example, demographic factors such as marriage and the birth of a child may be an important influence on decisions taken about housing, but position in the labour market, and the type and quality of housing aspired to will be important also. In mid-life, demographic factors may have relatively little impact on housing decisions, but tenure may exert a greater influence through the accumulation of housing wealth that has now opened up a greater range of housing options. These changes are better thought of as a set of 'transitions' rather than a housing 'career', because while households and individuals grow older, across the population as a whole a percentage of changes in housing arrangements are regressive, while others reflect no advance.

The use of the term 'housing transitions' is supported by data on the reasons why people moved through Australia's housing market over the period 1996 to 2006 (Beer and Faulkner 2011). These data suggested that while there was a great deal of activity in the housing market, few households could be thought of as participating in an observable housing career. We therefore conclude that the term 'housing transitions' better reflects the movement of individuals and households through the housing market over time and across the life course. This term implies change but does not suggest a single source or destination. Moreover, the term is entirely consistent with the findings of work by Seelig *et al.* (2005) on the housing consumption patterns of income support recipients in Australia. They found considerable mobility within the housing market, but this activity was marked by an ongoing directionless 'churn', rather than purposive steps along a housing career ladder.

'Housing transitions' suggests a focus that is not on the housing career, but on the framework within which housing decisions are made and the cumulative impact of those decisions. This frame of reference is one where *some* individuals are increasingly unconstrained by financial and demographic imperatives and not all individuals start on an equal basis. Importantly, the processes of transition through the housing market have cumulative impacts and are affected by all five dimensions outlined above. For example, the housing decisions of younger Australians over the next decades will, in part, reflect their experience of the Global Financial Crisis, the structures of the households they were raised in and their level of educational attainment.

Younger Australians and housing in the twenty-first century

So far this chapter has considered a new way of understanding the relationship between housing and the life course in Australia, and by implication in other developed economies. It is important to ask, what are the changes affecting current and future generations of young people? Some parts of the answer to this question are already known, as there is a notable body of published research on the housing of younger people in Australia and comparable societies, but other dimensions of this question remain unknown or poorly understood.

Key changes affecting younger persons and their capacity to traverse Australia's housing system are evident in almost every dimension of social and economic life in Australia. Increased participation in education – secondary and tertiary – is one of the most important drivers, with the Australian Government setting a target of 40 per cent of persons aged under 35 holding a first degree by 2025. Rapidly escalating housing costs have been a second driver of change in the housing of younger Australians. More than one million households across Australia are affected by housing stress (Yates 2007; Yates and Milligan 2007), with the greatest incidence in the private rental market, in which young people are concentrated. High rental costs impede entry into owner occupation and effectively thwart the aspirations of some households.

Demographic processes have also affected the housing transitions of younger Australians, some of which reflect the households from which they come, rather than their own preferences. Fully 42 per cent of marriages in Australia end in divorce (Hugo 2003) and approximately one third of all children are raised in a household with one or more step-parents (Beer, Faulkner and Gabriel 2006). Young people from such households may have different patterns of entry and initial engagement with the housing market when compared with their peers from more traditional families, and marital dissolution is commonly identified as one of the triggers of youth homelessness in Australia (McKenzie and Chamberlain 2003). At the other end of the social spectrum, increased affluence within Australian society has meant that a growing number and percentage of young people come to the housing market from relatively affluent households, which in turn influences their housing expectations and behaviours. Changing demographic patterns amongst younger households have added further complexity to their interaction with the housing market. Key trends have included falling marriage rates and delays in the arrival of children post-household formation.

A new perspective on the relationship between younger persons and their housing in Australia is available from the *Housing 21 Survey*. This survey was undertaken from late November 2006 through to the end of January 2007 at a national level. The *Housing 21 Survey* was developed to shed light on the housing transitions of Australians in the twenty-first century and was implemented as a random sample, statistically significant at the level of individual states. Across Australia some 2600 interviews were completed, with participants aged from 16 to 85 occupying all tenures. The survey was undertaken as a Computer-Aided Telephone Interview (CATI) and recorded a 40 per cent response rate (Beer and Faulkner 2009). The *Housing 21 Survey* collected a wide array of data on demographic structure, current housing, movement between 1996 and 2006, tenure, employment, attitudes to housing, the presence of a disability in the household and location.

The value of the *Housing 21 Survey* for the analysis of the housing decisions and trajectories of younger Australians is reflected in the data on the reasons why individuals moved from one dwelling to the next over the period 1996–2006. Figure 4.4 presents all the reasons given for moving through the housing market over that ten-year period, regardless of the number of moves undertaken by the individual household, and it is clear that there is significant differentiation between the youngest households – those aged 18–24 – those aged 25–34 and the total population of respondents. When compared with the other groups, persons aged 18–24 were more likely to move dwelling because housing costs were too high, because they had been evicted (11 per cent of all moves) or as a consequence of a relationship change. Those aged 25–34, by contrast, were over-represented amongst moves that related to increasing size of the family, and the purchase of a home. This group, however, was much more similar to the general population in their reasons for moving than the younger group. This in turn underlines the value of a disaggregated analysis of younger housing consumers and, where practicable, subsequent analysis in this chapter will distinguish between the two groups.

It is worth noting that persons aged 25 to 34 are the most mobile group within Australia's housing market (Figure 4.5) and they were the only age cohort to record two or more moves as a modal response. Minnery and Zacharov (2007) noted from their qualitative analysis of the housing transitions of the 25 to 34 year cohort that

> The early housing pathways of the younger group were in many cases very chaotic – with moves around many dwellings and types of accommodation.
>
> *(2007: 29)*

One focus group participant of this age group from Launceston noted that 'I've moved trillions of times' (Minnery and Zacharov 2007, p. 34). Much of this movement appeared to be involuntary and driven by changing relationships, unstable households (such as group housing), the demands of education and employment opportunities, as well as returning to the family home. The frequency of movement through the housing market for younger Australians reflects their tenure, their

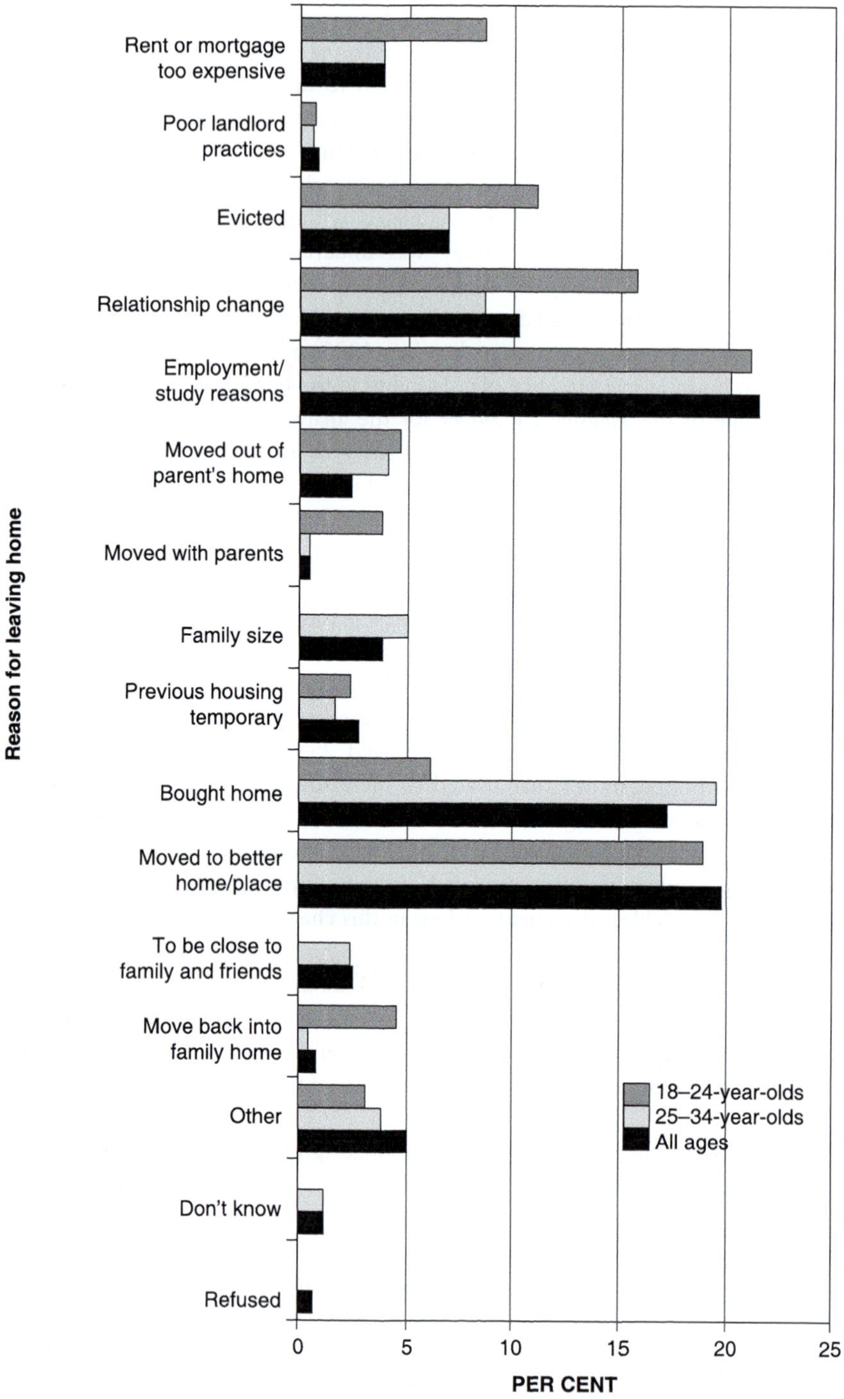

FIGURE 4.4 Reason for moving through the housing market, 1996–2006.

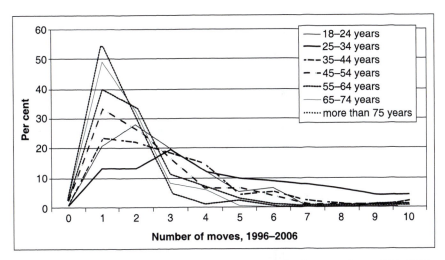

FIGURE 4.5 Number of moves through the housing market by age cohort, 1996–2006.
Source: Housing 21 Survey

engagement with higher education, their position within the labour market and the formation and dissolution of relationships.

Leaving the family home

In the past, leaving the family home to enter a long-term relationship – usually entry into marriage – was the point at which an individual's housing career commenced. Marriage and 'setting up home' was an unambiguous and socially sanctioned transition to independence. While this demographically determined transition to independence in housing remains important for the younger age groups, its importance has declined significantly over recent decades. There is growing evidence also of younger persons leaving the parental home for relatively short periods, only to return on one or more occasions. In some instances, younger people appear to return to the family home on an almost permanent basis. There is a need to reconsider the transition to independence in housing for younger people in Australia: where once 'moving out' of home was a binary phenomenon – you either lived in the family home or you had irrevocably left – it is now a period of change marked by steps forward and backward that could extend over some time (Figure 4.6).

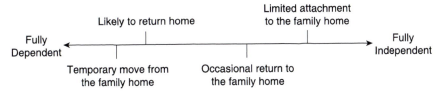

FIGURE 4.6 The transition to independence.

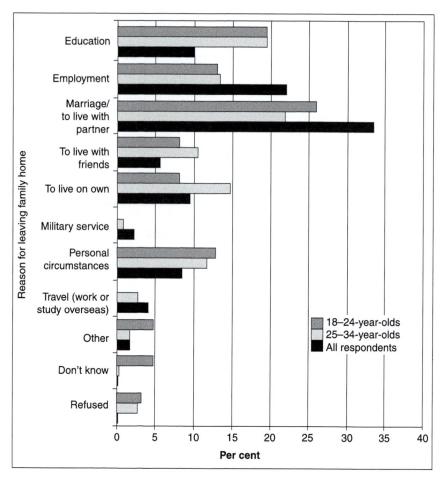

FIGURE 4.7 Reason for leaving the family home by age.
Source: Housing 21 Survey

Figure 4.7 presents data from the *Housing 21 Survey* on the motivations behind first moving from the family home for persons aged 18–24, those aged 25–34 and all respondents to the survey. It is clear that across all age groups marriage or to live with one's partner remains the single most important reason for moving out of the parental home. However, education-related moves were far more significant for the younger cohorts when compared with all respondents, with just under 20 per cent of those aged 18–24 and those aged 25–34 leaving the family home for this reason. By contrast, employment-related movement out of the family home was much less frequent amongst younger Australians when compared with the population as a whole. Clearly, education, and especially higher education, has been substituted for employment in the lives and housing experiences of younger Australians.

Persons aged 18–24 were more likely than those aged 25–34 to have moved out of the parental home in order to marry or cohabit with their partner. This suggests that relationship formation is an important reason (just over one quarter of all cases) for a relatively early move to independent living and housing. At the same time, approximately 12 per cent of young people moved to independent living because of 'personal circumstances', which commonly reflects conflict with parents. Finally, it is worth noting that persons aged 25–34 were more likely than either the younger cohort or the total population of respondents to have moved out of the parental home in order to 'live on their own'. This suggests that many in this cohort may have completed their education while remaining in the family home, and then chosen to move to independent living upon securing employment.

It is often argued that younger people remain in the family home for an extended period when housing costs are higher. Data on the median age of first leaving home in Australia lend some support to this hypothesis (Figure 4.8). Australia has an urban settlement that is characterized by metropolitan primacy, with the state capitals accommodating the lion's share of their state population – often 70 per cent or more of the population total. More than 40 per cent of the nation's population lives in Sydney and Melbourne alone. Importantly, New South Wales (NSW) and Victoria – home to the largest metropolitan centres – had higher median ages for first leaving the parental home – 19 and 20 respectively, compared to 18 in South Australia, Western Australia, the Northern Territory and Tasmania and 17 in Queensland. While the differences are not great, they do suggest that higher housing costs are affecting the housing decisions of younger Australians.

The birth of children and links to housing transitions

Marriage and the birth of children have conventionally been seen as pivotal markers of the move from rental accommodation to home purchase in Australia (Neutze

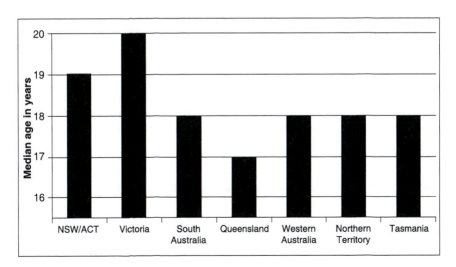

FIGURE 4.8 Median age of first leaving home, persons aged 18–34.
Source: Housing 21 Survey

and Kendig 1991) and it is important to question whether this relationship holds in the twenty-first century. The available evidence suggests that non-demographic factors are increasingly central to movements within housing markets. The evidence from the *Housing 21 Survey* on the impact of the birth of children on housing transitions is equivocal because, when asked, few households suggested that the arrival of children was their primary reason for moving from one dwelling to another through the period 1996 to 2006. In addition, if we consider the dwellings currently occupied, only 21 per cent reported changes to their household due to the arrival of one or more children. On the other hand, amongst respondents aged 18–54 almost 70 per cent of home-purchasing households reported the presence of one or more children in their home and 57 per cent of all households accommodating children were home purchasers. These data suggest a link between family formation and home purchase, but cannot throw light on the strength or direction of this relationship.

Through the *Housing 21 Survey* it is possible to calculate the time between first entry into home ownership and the birth of the first child. These data were calculated for all respondents who had entered home purchase and where the eldest child in the household was under 20 years of age. They showed that fully 67 per cent of the 610 respondents who had entered home ownership at some stage in their life and also had children did so prior to the year of the birth of their first child. Some 36 per cent entered home purchase in the five years prior to the arrival of their first child, 10 per cent purchased in the year their first child was born and 13 per cent entered home purchase in the five years after the arrival of their firstborn. In aggregate, fully 60 per cent of households to enter home ownership did so in the period five years before and five years after the arrival of their first child. The year the first child was born was also the most common year for entering owner occupation.

Overall the data support the contention that the arrival of children remains an important driver for many households to enter home purchase and that, while it remains a significant influence, the increasing proportion of older households within the housing stock, the impact of relationship breakdown and lower fertility rates amongst women has reduced its visibility within the housing market. For the vast majority of respondents – regardless of tenure and income – having children motivated them to seek stable and secure housing for their family. For those who could afford it, this meant entering home ownership and having control over their housing environment and its location.

Labour market status and housing market position

In the late 1990s Winter and Stone (1998, 1999) argued that home ownership rates amongst young people in Australia were falling because of a phenomenon they referred to as 'marginal attachment to the labour market'. That is, they noted the increasing tendency for younger Australians to be unable to find full time and/or permanent work, but instead were engaged as contract or casual employees. The authors observed that across the economy as a whole labour market security had declined and that there had been an increased 'casualisation' of the labour force. Winter and Stone (1998) argued that the connection between life course and position within the housing market had weakened and that role in the labour market now determined an individual's housing circumstances, both at a single point in time and through the life course as a whole.

The *Housing 21 Survey* has the capacity to shed light on the impact the form of employment has on housing outcomes for persons of all ages. Data on the relationship between the nature of employment and tenure for young adults is presented in Figure 4.9, and is drawn from 138 households in which two adults were resident and the survey respondent was aged between 18 and 34. Households were divided into two: in the first group – the smaller of the two – no resident adult held a permanent contract of employment. In the second group at least one adult, and potentially both, possessed an ongoing job. It is important to acknowledge here that self-employed persons have been excluded from this analysis because it is not clear that they have either a 'marginal' or 'secure' attachment to the labour market, though there is a high level of home ownership for this group, even at this age. What is clear from the data, however, is that there is a strong relationship between the form of employment and tenure for households in the younger age cohorts. Those with permanent employment were twice as likely to be home owners and three times as likely to be home purchasers as those where no adult member of the household held full time work. Households where the respondent was aged 18–34 and neither

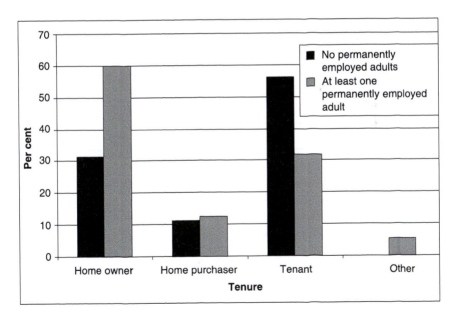

FIGURE 4.9 Tenure of two-person households in which respondent is aged 18–34, by employment status of the household.
Source: Housing 21 Survey

adult held a permanent position were concentrated in rental housing. The results, therefore, are broadly supportive of the Winter and Stone (1998) hypothesis and suggest that the absence of permanent, secure employment is a substantial impediment to entry into owner occupation for younger Australians.

Home ownership and younger Australians

Over recent decades there has been concern at an apparent fall in the rate of entry into home ownership in Australia, with Yates (1999) noting that Australians aged under 34 are much less likely to have entered home purchase than either their parents or grandparents. Baxter and McDonald (2004) developed an alternative perspective on the apparent falling rate of entry into home purchase, arguing that younger Australians are postponing, rather than cancelling, entry into home ownership. Their analysis of the *Negotiating the Life Course Survey* suggested that most households achieve owner occupation by age 44. This is an important issue for Australian governments and civil society, because the structure of income support in older age assumes high levels of home ownership (Castles 1998).

Most Australians who become owner occupants enter home purchase rela-tively early in their adult lives, with 67 per cent of respondents to the *Housing 21 Survey* doing so by age 30 (Figure 4.10). These data, however, relate to all of the approximately 1900 respondents who had entered home purchase prior to 2006, regardless of their age when the survey was conducted. The data presented in

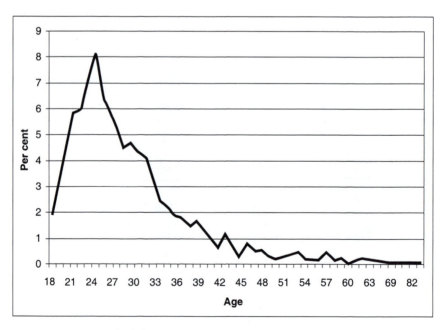

FIGURE 4.10 Age at which home purchase entered, all respondents.
Source: Beer and Faulkner, 2011, p. 70

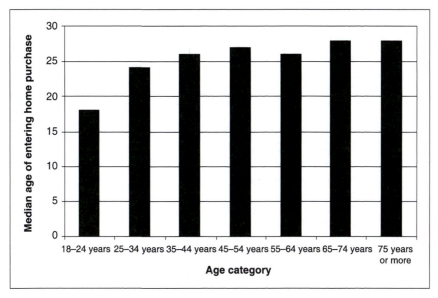

FIGURE 4.11 Median age of first home purchase for those who have achieved home purchase, by age group.
Source: Housing 21 Survey

Figure 4.11 draws our attention to the fact that, amongst those who have achieved home ownership, there was relatively little variation across generations in the median age of entry into the tenure. Indeed the younger age cohorts show a slightly lower median age than the older groups, but this reflects the incomplete nature of data for this cohort, with those who will purchase later in life not yet evident in the reported data.

The data presented in Figure 4.11 suggests that the median age for entry into home ownership for those who have achieved this tenure has declined slightly over the past 40 years. A more important question, however, is the percentage of each cohort to enter home ownership by a particular age, and especially ages 34 and 44, the traditional and emerging thresholds for measuring the rate of recruitment into owner occupation.

The *Housing 21* data permitted the calculation of the age at which the respondent first entered home ownership, and for the total population (including persons currently tenants) 51 per cent had taken out their first mortgage by age 30 and 16 per cent of those aged 18–24 were already home buyers. The more critical data is the percentage of each cohort to become home purchasers or owners at a benchmark date and Figure 4.12 reveals that the results contradict the conventional interpretation that younger cohorts have found it more difficult to enter home purchase than older groups did at the same age. For those aged 25–34, fully 56.7 per cent had entered home purchase by the age of 30, compared with 56.8 per cent of the 35–44 cohort, 52.6 per cent of the 45–54 group, 53.9 per cent of those aged 55–64, 50.8 per cent of the cohort aged 65–74 and 41.9 per cent of those

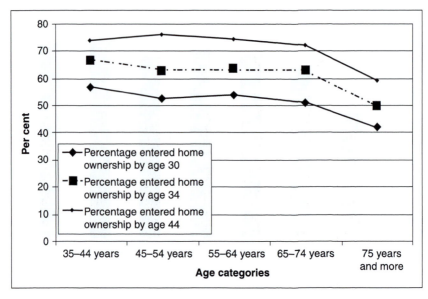

FIGURE 4.12 Percentage of the population to have entered home purchase at age 30, 34 and 44, by cohort.
Source: Beer and Faulkner, 2011, p. 71

aged over 75. Similar trends are evident at the other benchmark ages of 34 and 44 years, and it is worth noting that the percentage of households to have entered home purchase by age 44 is broadly comparable between 35–44-year-olds and 45–55-year-olds, even though the majority of the former group had not achieved that age at the time the survey was conducted. Put simply, the *Housing 21* data show that more Australians have been able to enter home ownership at younger ages over recent decades.

The introduction of the First Home Owners Grant (FHOG) in 2000 contributed to early entry into home purchase, with Wood *et al.* (2003) showing that the FHOG 'brought forward' home purchase decisions for a significant number of households. Kupke and Marano (2002) concluded that, for those households able to secure the FHOG, the timing of home purchase was determined by access to the grant. However, the FHOG alone does not explain the younger ages for entry to home purchase because of the relatively modest level of assistance provided and the high rates of entry to home purchase amongst those currently aged 35 to 44. While the overall finding appears to be at odds with earlier analyses (Baxter and McDonald 2004; Yates 1996), it is consistent with the outcomes we would expect within a liberalising housing market and an increasingly prosperous economy. Earlier generations were confronted by the need to save for an extended period in order to secure a home loan, had lower household incomes and had higher rates of entry into public housing. Moreover, some groups, such as women, were effectively excluded from entry into the housing market by discriminatory lending and employment practices (Watson 1988).

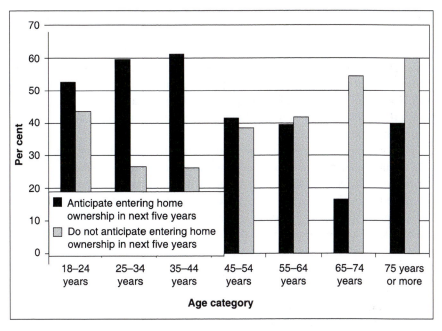

FIGURE 4.13 Expectation of entering home purchase, by age category.
Source: Housing 21 Survey

It is important to examine why the conclusions on entry into home ownership by age from the *Housing 21 Survey* appear to be at odds with the results of earlier research. Critically, the data discussed here report the age at which the respondent entered home ownership, regardless of their current tenure. A significant proportion of individuals and households who entered home purchase subsequently left the tenure. Earlier research based on secondary data analysis simply considered the age of the population at a point in time – for example the 1996, 2001 or 2006 Census – and their current tenure, regardless of whether they were previously an owner occupant. The *Housing 21* data show that, when compared with earlier generations, younger Australians today are both more likely to enter home purchase and more likely to exit from that tenure. The challenge for public policy into the future, therefore, may be assisting people to retain owner occupation following divorce, rather than increasing the rate of entry.

There is clear evidence that the aspiration to home ownership remains strong amongst younger Australians. Baum and Wulff (2003) examined the aspiration to home ownership amongst young renting households in Australia. They concluded that there was a decline in home purchase expectations amongst 25–34-year-olds between the late 1970s and early 1990s. While expectations may have fallen, anticipated rates of entry into home purchase remain high. The *Housing 21* data suggest that fully 60 per cent of 25–34-year-old respondents currently living in rental housing believed they would enter home purchase within the next five years (Figure 4.13). It is important, however, to give weight to Baum and Wulff's (2003) observation that the expectation of entry to home purchase has a low predictive capacity. On the other hand, the data speaks to the respondent's perception of the barriers to home purchase and how easily they believed these hurdles could be overcome. Subsequent events would have seen many of the expectations of younger people realised, with the Global Financial Crisis in 2008 and 2009 resulting in reduced interest rates and house prices that have fallen in the long term. By contrast, it was the older age groups that did not believe they would enter home purchase within the next five years.

It has been speculated that intergenerational transfers of wealth may assist current and future generations of younger Australians into home ownership. As other chapters in this volume show, such processes are important in other parts of the developed world. In Australia, however, the practice of giving assistance with housing costs appears to have had very little impact on the accommodation of younger households. While 88 respondents to the *Housing 21 Survey* (22 per cent of households aged under 34 in owner occupation) reported they had received monetary assistance, only 10 households received a gift and in all instances the value of assistance received was worth less than $1,000. Just two households received a loan from parents, and no households received a loan guarantee or inherited a house. Critically, then, younger generations of Australians are largely left to their own devices – generationally – when it comes to entering home ownership. In part this is a product of an under-developed tradition in Australia of assisting younger households to enter home ownership, the fact that many parents would still be repaying their own mortgages when their children entered the home purchase market, and the increasing propensity of older Australians – potentially the grandparents of home purchasers – to consume their housing wealth in later life (Oldsberg and Winters 2005).

As might be anticipated, few younger households reported significant wealth holdings of their own (Figure 4.14). Clearly, many respondents aged 18–24 were unable to estimate the wealth of a household headed by their parents, but across the board, all young people held less wealth than the population as a whole, and the youngest cohort held the least wealth. There was a significant concentration of wealth holdings valued between $50,000 and $99,000 amongst the 25–34 year age group, much of which would be held as equity in their home.

Impediments to home ownership

Wood *et al.* (2003) argued that poor housing affordability in Australia had a measurable impact on recruitment into home ownership and that the rate of entry into the tenure fell as the cost of purchasing rose relative to renting. Figure 4.15 shows that, for households where the respondent was aged 18–34 years, renting was more affordable than home purchase and while 57 per cent of tenants paid less than 20 per cent of their household income in rent, home purchasers were over-represented relative to tenants amongst purchasers paying 20 to 40 per cent of income for their housing. Some 42 per cent of purchasing households paid between 20 and 40 per cent of income for their housing, compared with 26 per cent of

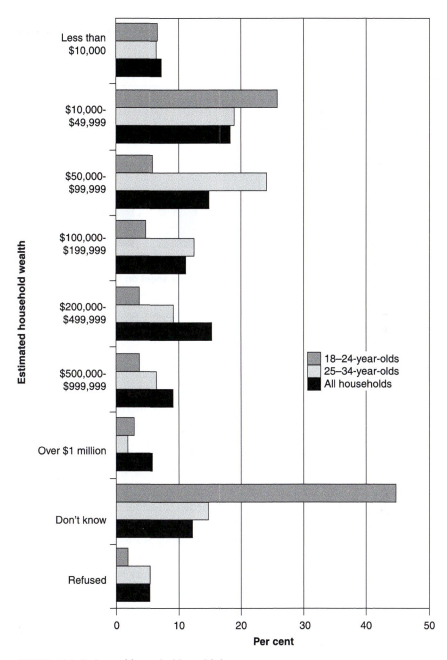

FIGURE 4.14 Estimated household wealth by age.
Source: Housing 21 Survey

tenants. Younger tenants had a bimodal distribution with respect to housing afford-ability, being concentrated in both affordable housing and in the least affordable housing, where they were paying 50 per cent or more of their income for housing.

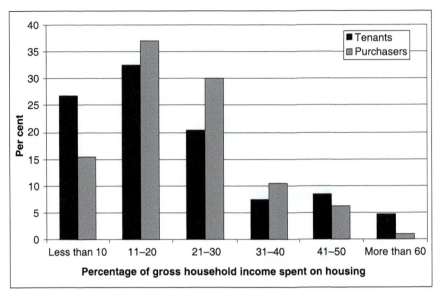

FIGURE 4.15 Housing affordability for tenants and purchasers aged 18–34.
Source: Housing 21 Survey

This finding is consistent with Census-based studies of the incidence of 'extreme housing stress' (Baker and Beer 2007).

Interest rate movements and higher house prices in Australia have placed greater pressure on home purchasers than in the past. This has resulted in speculation that increasing numbers of Australian home purchasers will default on their mortgages and fall out of home ownership, never to return. This issue was explored through the *Housing 21 Survey*, and, as Figure 4.16 shows, for both the younger age groups and the total population of respondents, few respondents left owner occupation because of cost pressures or as a consequence of the impact of unemployment. Instead, relationship breakdown was the single most significant reason for falling out of home ownership for the sample as a whole. The second and third most important reasons for leaving home ownership across the sample as a whole were employment-related movement and temporary relocation into rental housing while the owner extended or renovated their existing home. It is clear that for the Australian population as a whole the termination of relationships plays a substantial role in driving people to leave owner occupation and enter rental housing.

Conclusion

This chapter has examined the housing transitions of younger Australians. In many ways it is inevitably a truncated discussion because the housing transitions of a significant percentage of this group remain unformed. The analysis has focused on

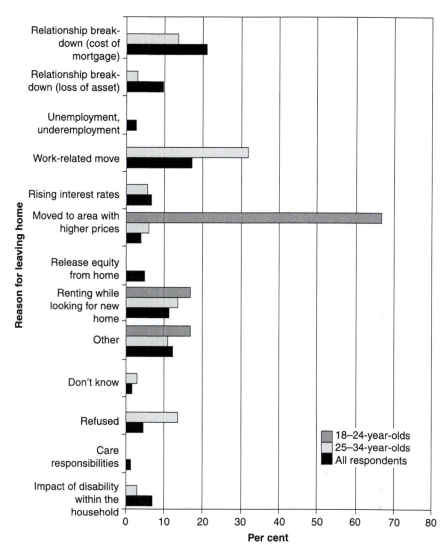

FIGURE 4.16 Reasons for leaving owner occupation and shifting to rental housing, by age cohort.
Source: Housing 21 Survey

two critical issues within Australian public policy and academic debate: the ability of young people to enter home purchase (and the common perception that entry to home purchase has become more difficult for young adult Australians) and the idea that significant numbers of young adults remain in the family home. The discussion has shown that young Australians are entering home purchase younger than their parents or grandparents and that while the percentage of 25–34-year-olds enumerated as home purchasers at the Census has fallen, this is a reflection of their inability to remain in the tenure, rather than enter owner occupation at all. This insight leads to a fresh understanding and set of policy prescriptions focused on assisting households at risk to maintain their tenure. The research has also shown that the majority of 25–34-year-olds live in conventional family households. Most of this cohort (88 per cent) left the family home by age 24, and while some may return to the family home for one or more periods, it is not a large-scale phenomenon and is largely invisible (at just 3 per cent) among the households for this age group.

It is often said that there are lies, damn lies and statistics. Despite the evident limitations of quantitative analysis, such analysis can shed useful light on the changing relationship between younger households and their housing. In many ways, the analysis here presents a much more complex picture than some previous scholarship would have us accept. The absence of an identifiable 'housing career' for Australian households means that both the academic and policy communities need to re-examine deeply held assumptions and, in the case of the latter group, policy prescriptions. The analysis presented in this chapter suggests that the challenge of maintaining home ownership in Australia is far greater than that of entry to home purchase. This leads to the conclusion that there may be a need to redirect resources, including the First Home Owners Grant. Divorce and relationship breakdown clearly have an enormous impact on the housing circumstances of affected households and it is also evident that consumption motivations are driving the Australian housing market in new directions and in new ways. Younger Australians are both part of the making of this new Australian housing market and simultaneously affected by it. We can only conclude that the lifetime housing experiences of those Australians currently aged in their 20s will differ substantially from those already in their 40s. We can already see some of the dimensions of this change, but others will unfold over time in response to ongoing social, economic and political changes.

References

Badcock, B. and Beer, A. (2000) *Home Truths: Home Ownership and Housing Wealth in Australia*, Melbourne University Press: Melbourne.

Baker, E. and Beer, A. (2007) Developing a workable model of housing need: applying geographical concepts and techniques to a problem of public Policy, *Applied Geography*, 27: 165–180.

Baum, S. and Wulff, M. (2003) *Housing Aspirations of Australian Households*, Final Report, AHURI: Melbourne.

Baxter, J. and McDonald, P. (2004) *Trends in Home Ownership Rates in Australia: The Relative Importance of Affordability Trends and Changes in Population Composition*, Final Report, AHURI: Melbourne.

Beck, U. (1992) *Risk Society: Towards a New Modernity*, Sage: London.

Beer, A. (2008a) *Housing: Mirror and Mould for Australian Society*, Occasional Paper, Academy of Social Sciences: Canberra.

Beer, A. (2008b) Risk and return: housing tenure and labour market adjustment after employment loss in the automotive sector in Southern Adelaide, *Policy Studies*, 29(3): 319–330.

Beer, A. and Faulkner, D. (2009) *Twenty First Century Housing Careers and Australia's Housing Future*, Final Report No. 128, AHURI: Melbourne.

Beer, A. and Faulkner, D. (2011) *Housing Transitions through the Lifecourse: Needs, Aspirations and Policy*, Policy Press: Bristol.

Beer, A., Faulkner, D. and Gabriel, M. (2006) *Twenty First Century Housing Careers and Australia's Housing Future*, Positioning paper and literature review, Australian Housing and Urban Research Institute: Melbourne.

Castles, I. (1998) The really big trade off: home ownership and the welfare state in the new world and the old, *Acta Politica*, 33(1): 5–9.

Clapham, D. (2005) *The Meaning of Housing*, Policy Press: Bristol.

Clark, W., Deurloo, M. and Dieleman, F. (2003) Housing Careers in the United States, 1968–93: Modelling the Sequencing of Housing States, *Urban Studies*, 40, 1 143–160.

Forrest, R. (1987) Spatial mobility, tenure mobility and emerging social divisions in the UK housing market, *Environment and Planning A*, 19: 1611–1630.

Giddens, A. (1984) *The Constitution of Society*, Polity Press: Cambridge.

Hugo, G. (2003) Australia's ageing population, *Australian Planner*, 40(2): 109–118.

Kendig, H. (1981) *Buying and Renting: Household Moves in Adelaide*, Australian Institute of Urban Studies: Canberra.

Kendig, H. (1984) Housing careers, life cycle and residential mobility: implications for the housing market, *Urban Studies*, 21(3): 271–283.

Kendig, H., Paris, C. and Anderton, N. (1987) *Towards Fair Shares in Australian Housing*, Report prepared for the National Committee of Non-Government Organisations, International Year of Shelter for the Homeless, Highland Press: Canberra.

Kupke, V. and Marano, W. (2002) *The Implications of Changes in the Labour Market for the Ownership Aspirations, Housing Opportunities and Characteristics of First Home Buyers*, Final Report, AHURI: Melbourne.

McKenzie, D. and Chamberlain, C. (2003) *Homeless Careers: Pathways Into and Out of Homelessness*, Salvation Army: Melbourne.

Minnery, J. and Zacharov, R. (2007) *The Quality of Housing Careers*, Southern Research Centre: Adelaide.

Neutze, M. and Kendig, H. (1991) Achievement of home ownership amongst post war Australian cohorts, *Housing Studies*, 6: 3–14.

Oldsberg, D. and Winters, M. (2005) *Ageing in Place: Intergenerational and Intrafamilial Housing and Transfers in Later Life*, Final Report, AHURI: Melbourne.

Paris, C. (2011) *Affluence, Mobility and Second Home Ownership*, Routledge: Abingdon, UK.

Payne, J. and Payne, G. (1977) Housing pathways and stratification: a study of life chances in the housing market, *Journal of Social Policy*, 23: 125–156.

Pickvance, C. (1974) Life cycle, house and residential mobility: a path analytic approach, *Urban Studies*, 11: 171–188.

Seelig, T., Hoon Han, J., O'Flaherty, M., Short, P., Haynes, M., Baum, S., Western, M. and Jones, A. (2005) *Housing Consumption Patterns and Earnings Behaviour of Income Support Recipients Over Time*, Positioning paper, AHURI: Melbourne.

Watson, S. (1988) *Accommodating Inequality. Gender and Housing*, Allen and Unwin: Sydney.

Winter, I. and Stone, W. (1998) *Social Polarisation and Housing Careers: Exploring the Interrelationship of Labour and Housing Markets in Australia*, Working Paper No.13, AIFS: Melbourne.

Winter, I. and Stone, W. (1999) Home ownership: off course? in J. Yates and M. Wulff (eds), *Australia's Housing Choices*, University of Queensland Press: Brisbane.

Wood, G., Watson, R. and Flatau, P. (2003) *A Microsimulation Model of the Australian Housing Market with Applications to Commonwealth and State Policy Initiatives*, Final Report, AHURI: Melbourne.

Yates, J. (1996) Towards a reassessment of the private rental market, *Housing Studies*, 11: 35–51.

Yates, J. (1999) Decomposing Australia's Home Ownership Trends, 1975–94, in J. Yates and M. Wulff, *Australia's Housing Choices,* Queensland University Press: Brisbane, pp. 27–42.

Yates, J. (2007) *Housing Affordability and Financial Stress*, NRV3 Research Paper 3, AHURI: Melbourne.

Yates, J. and Milligan, V. (2007) *Housing Affordability: A Twenty First Century Problem,* Final Report, AHURI: Melbourne.

5

THE LIVING ARRANGEMENTS OF JUST-MARRIED YOUNG ADULTS IN TAIWAN

William D. H. Li

Introduction

In many contemporary societies the co-residence of parents and their adult children seems to be far from uncommon although leaving home is also an important stage in the children's transition to adulthood. In Taiwan, as in other Chinese societies, traditional filial piety has been critical for the living arrangements and welfare of the elderly, in which living with adult children has been the main type of living arrangement (Yan *et al*. 2003; Yi and Chu 1993). In other words, young adults may still co-reside with their parents when they get married, as traditional Chinese culture favors the elderly living with children (Hermalin *et al*. 1990; DaVanzo and Chan 1994), and the elderly are supposed to be taken care of by the younger generation.

Nevertheless, Taiwan has experienced a dramatic industrialization process over the last 40 years, in which the family structure along with other social institutions has changed significantly. With the growth of the nuclear family, the household structure has been transformed dramatically. When the younger generation gets married, the culture whereby they are supposed to live with their parents is no longer as strong. On the other hand, with the changing economic structure under the modernization process, employment and economic conditions seemingly foster the independence of the youngsters, so that they are free from the traditional rules regarding living arrangements.

Previous research has indicated that marriage or entering into a strong commitment with a partner has been one of the major determinants of parental home leaving (Flatau *et al*. 2007), but the evidence in Taiwan reveals a reverse development. The traditional agricultural multi-household family appears to remain popular in the now highly urbanized Taiwanese society. Thus, this chapter seeks to examine the following research questions:

1. What is the extent of co-residence of parents and married children?
2. What factors are related to the co-residence of those parents and married children?
3. What does this reveal in terms of the nature of current housing access in Taiwan?

A brief literature review on young adults leaving the nest and on their housing arrangements will be provided. This will be followed by an empirical analysis of the living arrangements of young adults in Taiwan when they get married. A birth cohort dataset related to the young adults' current living arrangements will be examined to show and explain the nature of housing access for young adults. First, information regarding the housing and the living arrangements of young adults will be briefly given.

Housing and young people in Taiwan: a brief account

Table 5.1 provides a snapshot of the housing stock based on tenure in Taiwan. As previous studies have revealed, unlike those countries with highly state-regulated housing provision, it is the market that has been the major provider. The role of the state in housing has been minimal. Home ownership has been a predominant feature of housing tenure. The percentage of homeowners increased from less than 80 percent in 1990 to 83 percent in 2000. On the other hand, the private rental sector has been in decline. The government's social provision of rented housing is nearly non-existent as the state favors a fiscal policy such as an interest rate subsidy to support the housing market (Chen and Li 2012).

As has been indicated, financial resources constitute one of the most important factors in being a homeowner (Blaauboer 2010; Dieleman and Everaers 1994), and the market for home ownership is subject to households' financial ability. Thus, as younger adults have relatively limited resources, the rate of home ownership among them is lower than for those in their 40s, 50s and 60s or older. On the contrary, rented accommodation and other informal living arrangements are very popular among young adults.

It was not long ago that the traditional Chinese family system was the dominant form, in which a married son, especially the eldest son, was supposed to live with

TABLE 5.1 Housing stock by tenure.

	Percentage of households		
	Own	Rent	Other
1990	79	13	8
2000	83	10	7

Source: 1990, 2000 Population and Housing Census, DGBAS, Executive Yuan

TABLE 5.2 Housing situation of newly wedded couples from two birth cohorts.

Housing	Birth cohort (%)	
	1953–63	1964–76
Parents/relatives	51	61
Rent	29	16
Parents bought	5	8
Buy	10	12
Other	5	3

Source: PSFD

the parents in an agricultural society. The rapid process of industrialization since the 1950s has, however, had a major impact on household structures and the nuclear family has become the main household type. Nevertheless, the changing household structure does not denote the non-existence of a traditional legacy. Table 5.2 shows the different types of living arrangements for newly married couples in two birth cohorts. For both cohorts, Taiwan was already an industrial society when they got married. However, as can be seen, living with parents was still the main type of living arrangement. Over half of the 1953–63 birth cohort lived with parents and/or relatives when they got married. About 40 percent of the cohort formed their own family by living independently from parents. Among them, most looked for housing in the rental sector, and only 10 percent went straight into home ownership.

The 1964–76 birth cohort shows an interesting trend in terms of living arrangements. Unlike modernization theory, which would suggest that the nuclear family would be popular and would be the substitute for the traditional agricultural multigenerational family type, the proportion of young married couples living with parents and being supported by their parents in respect of housing has actually been increasing. Over 61 percent were living with and being supported by parents and close relatives. Less than 20 percent of those in the cohort were renting and living independently from the parental home and 8 percent did not live with parents but lived in houses provided by their parents. Although 12 percent became homeowners, the majority of those young couples received family support with regard to housing when they got married. This has become much more common among those in the younger birth cohort.

Living with parents or relatives seems to be a popular alternative for young married couples, and further, it is not at all a temporary housing arrangement. Table 5.3 records how long those married couples lived with their parents. Among the 1964–76 birth cohort, those living with parents for more than 4 years comprised 47 percent of the total when the data were collected in 2003. In other words, for young married couples in Taiwan, living with parents appears to have become one of the major kinds of living arrangement. Clearly, it has been shown that

TABLE 5.3 Time spent living with parents and relatives among newly wedded couples.

Time living with parents or relatives	Cohort (%)	
	1953–63	*1964–76*
0–2 years	22	36
2–4 years	11	17
4+ years	67	47

Source: PSFD

while home ownership within the housing stock continues to increase, there has been a decrease among those young adults living independently when they get married.

The literature reveals that the desire for autonomy, privacy and independence stemming from marriage is the main reason why a young adult leaves home (Jacob and Kleinert 2008). The findings above, however, provide the main question for this chapter, namely: Who are those young married couples living with parents? Why do they do so? Finally, and most importantly, what relationship does this arrangement have with the characteristics of access to housing in Taiwan's society?

Literature review

As the nuclear family has been a dominant household type in Western societies, the patterns and factors related to young adults leaving home have been clearly documented (see, for example, Goldscheider and Goldscheider 1989). Several theoretical perspectives and frameworks have been provided in explaining the reasons for leaving home. The life course perspective assumes leaving home as being inevitable in order to build a new family life cycle stage. However, exchange theory focuses on decisions to move made by family members as depending on cost and benefit considerations (White 1994). Based on this perspective, this section will focus on the literature regarding costs and resources in relation to leaving home and living arrangements.

The resources available to young adults are closely related to living arrangements, which are in turn related to the economic characteristics of young married couples. There will, for instance, be a relatively higher cost associated with living independently or entering home ownership than there is with living with parents. Thus, those who marry at an earlier age with lower levels of education will have fewer resources for living independently. On the other hand, the timing of leaving home also seems to be related to constraints imposed by the wider social and economic context, such as a high unemployment rate among young adults (Aassve *et al*. 2002). Glick and Lin (1986) show how the economic situation, divorce and college enrollment have contributed to the increase in young adults living with parents. Murphy and Wang (1998) also found that the economic situation had contributed to the pattern of young adults leaving home. Recently, a tendency to delay leaving home has been found among European countries by Ward *et al.* (2006). Although the timing of leaving home continues to differ considerably among European countries, it has been observed that young couples are leaving home later compared to their counterparts a few decades ago. It has been suggested that the economic and wider social context, such as employment, education, housing prospects and parental support, are all factors related to these contemporary trends in leaving home.

As far as the resources of the parents are concerned, it has been shown that family structure and the socioeconomic characteristics of the family are related to young adults' leaving home (Aquilino 1990; Buck and Scott 1993). In addition, the residential relocation of young adults is related to the accessibility of family support. It has also been suggested that stress resulting from the parental homes being crowded, as indicated by the number of siblings, is a reason for moving out (Goldscheider and DaVanzo 1989). All of this shows that family resources are related to the pattern of young adults leaving home.

The provision of housing, as well as public policy, has also contributed to the living arrangements of young adults. Ineichen (1981) examined young married couples' living arrangements in Britain in the 1970s. He found that, under the structure of British housing provision at that time, there was a clear social class division between those entering the owner-occupied sector and those entering the council housing sector. The factors that differed between these two groups included fertility, the age of getting married, income, occupational status and the wife's occupation. Berrington and Murphy (1994) also examined the factors related to young adults' living arrangements in Britain. Using the Labour Force Survey, they found that there was an increasing tendency for young adults to live outside the parental home, which was certainly closely related to the options available for young adults. Higher social class young adults were more likely to live independently than those from the lower social classes.

Ermisch (1999) used panel data from the first half of the 1990s to examine the patterns of young adults' departure from and return to the parental home in the UK. Various factors such as house prices and the economic resources, both of the young adults and their parents, contributed to the living arrangements of young adults. Clark and Mulder (2000) also found that factors such as the structure of the housing market, regional factors and resources, especially those of the young adults, are closely related to their level of access to housing. More recently, Newman (2008) showed how emergent flexible employment in the recent labor market reforms combined with high levels of owner-occupied housing has contributed to the delay in young adults leaving parental homes.

Nevertheless, among Asian societies as elsewhere, leaving the parental nest has also been related to cultural norms regarding living arrangements. Traditionally, the elderly in East Asian societies have resided with their married sons, since the son is responsible for caring for the elderly (Kono 2000; Ng *et al.* 2002; Kim and Rhee 1997; Kamo and Zhou 1994). As various scholars have argued, staying with the parents has been a culturally preferred norm and the family bond a distinctive characteristic of East Asian societies (Goodman *et al.* 1998). However, amidst the rapid socio-economic changes taking place, family relationships are being modified among the East Asian societies. Recent studies of elderly care have indicated that the intergenerational familial bond has not been as strong as that presumed to exist in traditional culture.

A growing literature regarding the failures of the East Asian familial welfare model reveals the erosion of cultural norms in supporting parents (Cheung and Kwan 2009). Although several scholars have discussed the characteristics of the familial welfare system in South East Asian society (see, for example, Aspalter 2006), this system has been undergoing dramatic change. Young people nowadays are much freer to leave home. For instance, in China, there is evidence of increasing poverty among the elderly as the role of the younger generation in supporting old people declines (Saunders and Lujun 2006). In Hong Kong, Ng, Phillips and Lee (2002) found that the traditional role of the family in caring for parents ('filial piety') has been weakening in a rapidly modernizing society. Some elderly people living alone and some of those not living with children were found to be receiving less support, both emotionally and financially, from their adult children (Chou and Chi 2000), and they needed to keep working to support themselves (La Grange and Lock 2002).

For those among the younger generation who are living with the elderly, the status and power relations between the two generations do not involve, as culturally presumed, the youngsters' subordination to the elderly. The young have a more equal status, as the ideal culturally privileged status of the elderly has been in decline. In Singapore, seniors in the family have been found to provide services in exchange for financial support from the younger generation (Verbrugge and Chan 2008). In Japan, the traditional preference of the elderly for living with their children has also recently begun to be shaken (Kono 2000). Living with their children has become a strategy of the elderly whereby they will leave housing assets to cohabiting children in exchange for nursing care (Izuhara 2002).

Clearly, the current living pattern of young couples cannot be adequately interpreted based simply on a cultural perspective. Living with parents is in decline. In Taiwan, it was not long ago (1973) that 83 percent of parents lived with at least one married son (Freedman *et al.* 1994). By 2000, this percentage had fallen to below 60 percent, alongside the growth of various other living arrangements. Hsu *et al.* (2001) used cross-sectional data collected in 1984, 1990 and 1995 to examine the changes in attitudes toward supporting parents in Taiwan. It was found that supporting parents through co-residence has been in decline. Married children are now less likely than before to live with their parents. The recent increase in the population of elderly people living alone in Taiwan also reveals that fewer children would like to have their elderly parents living with them. The domestic role of the elderly in supporting the household has become a critical reason for their living with their children's family – rather than a traditional culture in which the elderly are supposed to be supported by their children – a similar trend to those revealed in other Asian societies. Elderly females are more likely to live with their children's family (Yeh and Lo 2004). This may partly be because elderly females are likely to have fewer resources, and also because elderly females are much more functional in providing domestic household services. The bond of filial piety among the younger generation in Taiwan has also recently been weakening. Lin *et al.* (2011) found elderly women to be heavily dependent on emotional support from their children. Nevertheless, for those not living with their children, less support has been provided by children, either emotionally or financially.

It was not long ago, in 1989, that the Senior Citizen Condition survey (SCC) revealed that over 58 percent of the elderly relied mainly on their children for financial support. The percentage of elderly receiving support from their children had fallen to 47 percent in 2005 (those in the sample without children were excluded). The other 37 percent of the total elderly population were reported to be self-supporting, and another 15 percent were supported through the government's public assistance program. It is thus evident that the support provided by children to the elderly has been in sharp decline (Ministry of Interior 2006).

From this review of the literature on leaving home and young adults' living arrangements, we can conclude that various factors are closely related to their living arrangements. First, those factors involved in young adults becoming independent are important in relation to their leaving home. Second, the resources available for co-residence with parents also affect living arrangements. In terms of housing, the number of siblings will be related to the living space available for newly married young couples who choose to stay in the parents' home. Finally, the social and economic context, especially in regard to the housing market, will affect young adults' living arrangements.

Culturally speaking, young married couples were not supposed to leave the parents' house, as the extended family formed by two generations or more has traditionally been a popular living arrangement. However, if, as a growing literature suggests, there is a weakening of filial piety this would seem to suggest that the younger generation is less likely to be bound by cultural tradition in living arrangements. With a growing number of married couples from the younger age cohort living with parents when they get married, an interesting question thus arises: Why are these young, just-married couples living with their parents, and who are they? Is this a culturally related decision?

Data, research design and variables

The Panel Study of Family Dynamics (PSFD) dataset compiled by Academia Sinica in Taiwan provides a unique opportunity to examine young, newly married adults' living arrangements. The PSFD is a large-scale panel survey which was first conducted in 1999, with several follow-up surveys conducted separately to collect different birth cohort data. For the purposes of this chapter, the data on those born between 1964 and 1976 are used for the analysis. The survey of the first wave, of the 1964–74 birth cohort, was conducted in 2003 and contains a wide variety of information about the family background of the respondents, their housing situation and the household resources when they got married.

Research variables

According to the literature mentioned above, four dimensions are examined in relation to young adults' living arrangements when getting married: the social and economic characteristics of the young adults, parental resources, the housing market and cultural norms regarding living arrangements when getting married. The dependent variable is their living arrangements when they are married. In terms of the social and economic characteristics of young adults, age, education and the job category of both husband and wife when they got married are included in the dataset. These are important variables in relation to the young couple's resources. Regarding living arrangements, the PSFD collects detailed information about young adults' living arrangements by using the recall question: *Where did you live when you got married?*

The dataset also provides valuable information about the parents of the young adults, such as ethnicity, education and the employment of the interviewees' (and their spouses') fathers, which is also included in the analysis. In terms of the housing situation, the number of siblings is taken into account as the previous literature has indicated that housing space is related to living arrangements.

The third dimension relates to the general economic context when the young couple got married. Two variables were created: first, the unemployment rate in the year in which the young couple married; second, the annual rent price index, which is used as an indicator for house prices.

The PSFD also provides information about cultural attitudes in relation to living arrangements. One question has been picked out: *Do you think it is important that a married son should live with his parents?* The answer is given on a continuous scale from 1 (very unimportant) to 5 (very important).

The general demographic characteristics of young adults are listed in Table 5.4. A total of 724 cases in the birth cohort for 1964–76 are examined. General information about the social and economic characteristics of the husband and wife are provided, along with information about their fathers. In terms of living arrangements, over 61 percent of the sample is living with parents or relatives, 8 percent had their house bought by their parents, 12 percent bought their own houses and 16 percent of young couples rented in the private sector. Clearly, the majority of newly wedded young adults enjoyed family support in regard to their housing.

Research design

A key aim of this chapter is to examine the factors related to young adults' living patterns with special reference to those who received parental support for their housing. Thus, answers to the question *Where did you live when you got married?* have

TABLE 5.4 Summary of research variables in the sample ($N = 724$).

Variable	1964–76 cohort (%)
Husband's job type	
Professional	19.8
Semi-professional	7.6
Sales, service or white collar	31.1
Skilled or non-skilled worker	40.4
Not in labor market	1.1
Wife's job type	
Professional	16.3
Semi-professional	32.8
Sales, service or white collar	25.8
Skilled or non-skilled worker	19.4
Not in labor market	5.7
Living arrangements	
Parents/relatives	61.2
Rent	16.1
Parents bought	7.5
Buy	12.4
Other	2.8
Husband's father	
Taiwanese	76.5
Hakka	9.7
Mainlander	10.8
Other	3.0
Wife's father	
Taiwanese	71.3
Hakka	11.0
Mainlander	10.0
Other	7.7
Husband's father's job	
Professional	11.0
Semi-professional	7.7
Sales, service or white collar	21.6
Skilled or non-skilled worker	57.9
Not in labor market	1.8
Wife's father's job	
Professional	8.8
Semi-professional	4.4
Sales, service or white collar	22.8
Skilled or non-skilled worker	62.6
Not in labor market	1.4

Source: PSFD

TABLE 5.5 Comparison of couples living with parents with others, 1964–76 birth cohort.

	Chi-square tests between two groups
Husband's education★★	15.928, 4 df, p = .003
Wife's education★★	14.561, 4 df, p = .006
Husband's job type★★	19.687, 4 df, p = .001
Wife's job type	6.069, 4 df, p = .194
Husband's father's ethnic category	0.833, 3 df, p = .842
Wife's father's ethnic category★	6.399, 3 df, p = .094
Husband's father's education	5.189, 4 df, p = .268
Wife's father's education	11.091, 4 df, p = .26
Husband's father's job	4.198, 4 df, p = .380
Wife's father's job	4.450, 4 df, p = .348
Husband's siblings	5.332, 4 df, p = .255
Wife's siblings	6.932, 4 df, p = .140

Source: compiled from PSFD ★ $p < 0.1$, ★★ $p < 0.01$

been recoded into two groups. One consists of those living with parents (those living with close relatives, parents-in-law and those living in a house bought by parents), and the other group includes those who rent or buy houses when they get married.

Table 5.5 provides information on the young couples, comparing those living with parents and those living independently. The results show that there are statistical differences between the two groups in terms of the husband's education, wife's education, the husband's job type, and the wife's father's ethnic category.

For those living with parents, the level of educational qualifications is more likely to be lower, for both husband and wife. In addition, the husband's occupation is more likely to be that of skilled or non-skilled worker. In terms of parental resources, neither the education nor the employment of the husband's or the wife's fathers are statistically significant in relation to young couples' living arrangements. It is the resources of young couples which seem to be critical to the living arrangements. Young couples with comparatively limited resources are more likely to live with the parental family.

The results appear therefore to support the previous findings that the resources of young adults are critical for their living arrangements when they get married. The more highly educated are more likely to live independently. In terms of parental resources, the statistics reveal that the resources of the wife's father's side of the family differ between these two groups. Due to the patriarchal arrangements in Taiwanese society the married couple is traditionally supposed to live with the husband's family. This result seems to support the view that the wife's resources, including those from her family, are important to the living arrangements. This issue can be further explored by applying logit models.

Logistic results and discussion

To understand the factors contributing to the living arrangements of young adults, a number of logit models were applied. Independent variables for the models were chosen based on the young adults' and their parents' social and economic characteristics. Several models were provided to examine these factors in predicting living arrangements and these are presented in Table 5.6. Model 1 reveals that the

TABLE 5.6 Bivariate logit analysis of the differences between living with parents and other arrangements (living with parents = 1, others = 0), 1964–76 birth cohort.

Explanatory variables	Model 1	Model 2	Model 3	Model 4
	Exp(B)	Exp(B)	Exp(B)	Exp(B)
Husband's age	0.961	0.931**	0.924**	0.931**
Wife's age	0.930**	0.936**	0.927**	0.930**
Husband's job type				
Professional (r)	—	—	—	—
Semi-professional	1.57	1.962*	2.024*	2.109*
Sales, service or white collar	1.386	1.346	1.376	1.388
Skilled or non–skilled	1.942**	1.863**	1.934**	1.900**
Not in labor market	3.326	958816628.031	885253900.972	964312245.309
Wife's job type				
Professional (r)	—	—	—	—
Semi-professional	0.787	0.669	0.691	0.665
Sales, service or white collar	0.887	0.897	0.897	0.881
Skilled or non–skilled	0.834	0.648	0.659	0.68
Not in labor market	0.932	0.527	0.509	0.484
Husband's father				
Taiwanese (r)	—	—	—	—
Hakka	—	1.268	1.27	1.272
Mainlander	—	1.358	1.365	1.487
Other	—	1.145	1.225	1.314
Wife's father				
Taiwanese (r)	—	—	—	—
Hakka	—	1.001	1.007	0.909
Mainlander	—	1.04	1.067	1.028
Other	—	5.191**	4.919**	3.66
Husband's father's job				
Professional (r)	—	—	—	—
Semi-professional	—	1.538	1.513	1.357
Sales, service or white collar	—	1.365	1.388	1.298

(continued)

TABLE 5.6 (continued)

Explanatory variables	Model 1	Model 2	Model 3	Model 4
	Exp(B)	Exp(B)	Exp(B)	Exp(B)
Skilled or non-skilled	—	1.084	1.072	0.984
Not in labor market	—	1.063	1.05	0.769
Wife's father's job				
Professional (r)	—	—	—	—
Semi-professional	—	0.717	0.75	0.735
Sales, service or white collar	—	0.669	0.68	0.636
Skilled or non-skilled	—	0.96	0.99	0.917
Not in labor market	—	0.667	0.667	0.656
Unemployment	—	—	1.134	1.114
Rent price	—	—	—	0.998
Living preference	—	—	—	1.321**
Constant B	3.407	4.183	4.247	3.551
Sample N	724	724	724	724
−2 Log Likelihood	798.293	666.45	664.749	651.906
Nagelkerke R^2	0.076	0.125	0.129	0.157

Source: SCC (r) – reference category, $*$ $p < 0.1$, $**$ $p < 0.05$

wife's age when getting married is negatively related to living with parents when only the social and economic characteristics of young couples are considered in the model. Further, those males with professional jobs when getting married are less likely to live with their parents compared with their counterparts who consist of skilled and manual workers. In Model 2, when parental resources are included in the equation, it is shown that those getting married at a younger age are more likely to live with their parents in the cases of both males and females. In addition, those males with better employment, such as those who are professionals when they get married, are more likely to live independently compared to those who are blue-collar workers. The wife's father's ethnicity is also related to living arrangements.

In Model 3, when the unemployment rate is included in the model, the results seem quite similar. The ages of the young couple and the husband's job are related to the decision regarding living arrangements. In Model 4, when the housing rent price and the cultural attitudes toward living with parents are added to the model, the results show that the ages of getting married for both husbands and wives are related to living arrangements, which is similar to the previous model's results. Nevertheless, the cultural attitude of young couples regarding whether it is important to live with parents is related to their living arrangements. Those with a positive answer to the statement that a married son should live with his parents are more likely to live with parents.

How do we explain the results? They present quite a complicated picture compared to the previous findings. These results seem to suggest that living with parents is closely related to both the resources of young adults and traditional cultural norms. Younger couples with fewer resources are more likely to live with parents, and those who prefer to live with parents are also more likely to live with parents. Nevertheless, it is difficult to believe that, among these couples, the traditional Chinese culture of living with parents is still a dominant value, given its weakening influence in Chinese societies (Logan and Bian 1999; Cheung and Kwan 2009).

I would argue that those young couples who choose to live with their parents do not do so based on traditional culture, but rather based on the resources available to them from living with parents. Various types of resources are made available in this way: parents provide a variety of nonmaterial assistance and financial support for their adult children (Goldscheider, Thornton, and Yang 2001). In Taiwanese society, some parents work for their adult children for no return by providing domestic services, including babysitting the grandchildren. Emotional closeness to children through co-residing with children has been an important element in life satisfaction among the Taiwanese elderly (Lin, Chang, and Huang 2011). For the young married couple, it seems reasonable to stay with the parents, as there is not a great deal of familial obligation, cost or contribution required in this arrangement.

More importantly, housing plays an important role, as living independently without parental support is becoming more difficult for young couples due to rising house prices. Along with the rising cost of housing, housing price-to-income ratios in Taiwan between 2005 and 2011 have risen from 6.29 to 9, meaning that house prices have risen from 6.29 to 9 times the average household income. The price-to-income ratio is even higher in Taipei city; in 2011, it was 16 times the average household income. Although a significant amount of mortgage subsidy is provided by the government for first-time buyers, the cost of buying is high. For these young couples, it seems clear that they would be better off living with parents than living independently in the rental sector, as the cost of housing is well beyond their means.

Conclusion

There has been little discussion in previous research about the living arrangements for young adults in Taiwan, and the factors that produce variations in their living arrangements when they get married have not been examined in the recent literature. Still less attention has been paid to the housing decisions of young adults within the current social and economic context. In this chapter, several factors, including housing and cultural influences, as well as the resources of young adults and their parents, have been taken into account. These have been drawn together to examine the living arrangements of young adults in Taiwan.

Unlike previous findings, in which marriage has featured as a critical factor for young adults leaving the parental home, the young adult cohort data reveal a reverse pattern of living arrangements, with more young people dependent on their parents compared to the older birth cohort. The results from examining the factors related to living with parents show that the resources of young adults are closely related to living independently. Those getting married at an older age and those with higher economic status are more likely to live outside the parental home. Those living with parents are more likely to receive parental support than those living independently, and benefitting from parental support is the main reason why young adults live with parents when they get married.

More importantly, this chapter has found that the housing market does play an important role in the living arrangements of young adults. Associated with the growth of home ownership, more young adults are choosing to live with their parents rather than to live independently. Sharing housing with parents has become a major living arrangement for young people when they get married. The family has thus become a major provider of accommodation for young adults in the current housing situation in Taiwan.

Acknowledgments

The author is grateful for grant support from the National Science Council (grant code: 100-2410-H-259-066) and valuable comments from the symposium on 'New generational fissures? Shifting demographics, economic change and the housing trajectories of young people', May 19–20, 2011, City University of Hong Kong, Hong Kong.

References

Aassve, A., Billari, F. C., Mazzuco, S. and Ongaro, F. (2002) 'Leaving home: a comparative analysis of ECHP data', *Journal of European Social Policy*, 12(4): 259–275.

Aquilino, W. S. (1990) 'The likelihood of parent-adult child coresidence: effects of family structure and parental characteristics', *Journal of Marriage and the Family*, 52(2): 405–419.

Aspalter, C. (2006) 'The East Asian welfare model', *International Journal of Social Welfare*, 15: 290–301.

Berrington, A. and Murphy, M. (1994) 'Changes in the living arrangements of young adults in Britain during the 1980s', *European Sociological Review*, 10(3): 235–257.

Blaauboer, M. (2010) 'Family background, individual resources and the homeownership of couples and singles', *Housing Studies*, 25(4): 441–461.

Buck, N. and Scott, J. (1993) 'She's leaving home: but why? An analysis of young people leaving the parental home', *Journal of Marriage and the Family*, 55(4): 863–874.

Chen, Y. and Li, W. D. (2012) 'Neo-liberalism, the developmental state and housing policy in Taiwan', in B.-G. Park, R. Child Hill and A. Saito (eds), *Locating Neoliberalism in East Asia*, London: Blackwell.

Cheung, C. and Kwan, A. (2009) 'The erosion of filial piety by modernization in Chinese cities', *Ageing and Society*, 29: 179–198.

Chou, K.-L. and Chi, I. (2000) 'Comparison between elderly Chinese living alone and those living with others', *Journal of Gerontological Social Work*, 33(4): 51–66.

Clark, W. A. V. and Mulder, C. (2000) 'Leaving home and entering the housing market', *Environment and Planning*, 32: 1657–1671.

Clark, W., Deurloo, M. and Dielemann, F. (2003) 'Housing careers in the United States: modelling the sequencing of housing careers', *Urban Studies*, 40: 143–160.

DaVanzo, J. and Chan, A. (1994) 'Living arrangements of older Malaysians: who co-resides with their adult children?' *Demography*, 31: 95–113.

Dieleman, F. and Everaers, P. (1994) 'From renting to owning: life course and housing market circumstances', *Housing Studies*, 9(1): 11–25.

Ermisch, J. (1999) 'Prices, parents, and young people's household formation', *Journal of Urban Economics*, 45(1): 47–71.

Flatau, P., James, I., Watson, R., Wood, G. and Hendershott, P. H. (2007) 'Leaving the parental home in Australia over the generations: evidence from the household, income and labour dynamics in Australia (Hilda) survey', *Journal of Population Research*, 24(1): 51–71.

Freedman, R., Thornton, A. and Yang, L. S. (1994) 'Determinants of co-residence in extended households', in A. Thornton and H. Lin (eds) *Social Change and the Family in Taiwan*, Chicago: The University of Chicago Press.

Glick, P. C. and Lin, S.-L. (1986) 'More young adults are living with their parents: who are they?' *Journal of Marriage and the Family*, 48(1): 107–112.

Goldscheider, F. K. and DaVanzo, J. (1989) 'Pathways to independent living in early adulthood: marriage, semiautonomy, and premarital residential independence', *Demography*, 26(4): 597–614.

Goldscheider, F. K. and Goldscheider, C. (1989) 'Family structure and conflict: nest-leaving expectations of young adults and their parents', *Journal of Marriage and the Family*, 51(1): 87–97.

Goldscheider, F. K., Thornton, A. and Yang, L.-S. (2001) 'Helping out the kids: expectations about parental support in young adulthood', *Journal of Marriage and the Family*, 63: 727–740.

Goodman, R., White, G. and Kwon, H.-J. (1998) *The East Asian Welfare Model: Welfare Orientalism and the State*, London: Routledge.

Hermalin, A. T., Chang, M.-C., Lin, H.-S., Lee, M.-L. and Ofstedal, M. B. (1990) 'Patterns of support among the elderly in Taiwan and their policy implications', *Comparative Study of the Elderly in Asia*, Research Report Series, No. 90-4, Michigan: University of Michigan Population Study Center.

Hsu, H.-C., Lew-Ting, C.-Y. and Wu, S.-C. (2001) 'Age, period, and cohort effects on the attitude toward supporting parents in Taiwan', *The Gerontologist*, 41(6): 742–750.

Ineichen, B. (1981) 'The housing decisions of young people', *British Journal of Sociology*, 32(2): 252–258.

Izuhara, M. (2002) 'Care and inheritance: Japanese and English perspectives on the "generational contract"', *Ageing & Society*, 22: 61–77.

Jacob, M. and Kleinert, C. (2008) 'Does unemployment help or hinder becoming independent? The role of employment status for leaving the parental home', *European Sociological Review*, 24(2): 141–153.

Kamo, Y. and Zhou, M. (1994) 'Living arrangements of elderly Chinese and Japanese in the United States', *Journal of Marriage and the Family*, 56(3):544–558.

Kim, C. and Rhee, K. (1997) 'Variations in preferred living arrangements among Korean elderly parents', *Journal of Cross Cultural Gerontology*, 12(2): 189–202.

Kono, M. (2000) 'The impact of modernization and social policy on family care for older people in Japan', *Journal of Social Policy*, 29(2): 181–203.

La Grange, A. and Lock, B. Y. (2002) 'Poverty and single elders in Hong Kong'. *Ageing & Society*, 22: 233–257.

Lin, J.-P., Chang, T.-F. and Huang, C.-H. (2011) 'Intergenerational relations and life satisfaction among older women in Taiwan', *International Journal of Social Welfare*, 20(s1): S47–S58.

Logan, J. R. and Bian, F. (1999) 'Family values and coresidence with married children in urban China', *Social Forces*, 77(4): 1253–1282.

Ministry of Interior (2006) *Report on the Senior Citizen Condition Survey 2005*, Republic of China, Taipei: Executive Yuan (text in Chinese).

Murphy, M. and Wang, D. (1998) 'Family and sociodemographic influences on patterns of leaving home in postwar Britain', *Demography*, 35(3): 293–305.

Newman, K. S. (2008), 'Ties that bind: cultural interpretations of delayed adulthood in Western Europe and Japan', *Sociological Forum*, 23: 645–669.

Ng, A. C.Y., Phillips, D. R. and Lee, W. K. (2002) 'Persistence and challenges to filial piety and information support of older persons in a modern Chinese society: a case study in Tuen Mun, Hong Kong', *Journal of Aging Studies*, 16: 135–153.

Saunders, P. and Lujun, S. (2006) 'Poverty and hardship among the aged in urban China', *Social Policy & Administration*, 40: 138–157.

Verbrugge, L. M., and Chan, A. (2008) 'Giving help in return: family reciprocity by older Singaporeans', *Ageing & Society*, 28: 5–34.

Ward, T., Calers, H. and Matsaganis, M. (2006) *Is It Too Difficult for Young Adults to Become Autonomous?* Research note, Directorate-General Employment, Social Affairs and Equal Opportunities, Unit E1 – Social and Demographic Analysis, European Commission.

White, L. (1994) 'Coresidence and leaving home: young adults and their parents', *Annual Review of Sociology*, 20: 81–102.

Yan, S., Chen, J. and Yang, S. (2003) 'Living arrangements and old-age support', in M. K. Whyte (ed.) *China's Revolutions and Intergenerational Relations*, Ann Arbor: University of Michigan Press.

Yeh, J. S.-C. and Lo, S. K. (2004) 'Living alone, social support, and feeling loving among the elderly', *Social Behavior and Personality: An International Journal*, 32(2): 129–138.

Yi, C. C. and Chu, C. R. (1993) 'The changes of Chinese family structure and function: a comparative study of Chinese society among Taiwan, Hong Kong, China, and Singapore', in C.Y. To (ed.) *Western Social Science Theories in Chinese Societies*, Hong Kong: The Chinese University of Hong Kong.

PART II

Housing affordability and youth housing trajectories

6

YOUTH HOUSING AND EXCLUSION IN SWEDEN

Mats Lieberg

Introduction

Sweden as a welfare state has historically been considered strong, with an ambitious housing policy. However, since the early 1990s there has been a decrease in housing subsidies and a rolling back of the welfare state (Birgersson 2009). These changes have been associated with rising house prices and costs, which have worsened young adults' chances on the housing market. This chapter examines the effects of housing on the lives of young Swedish people, with the aim of providing an overall picture of young people's housing situation in Sweden. The current housing situation and future housing expectations of young people 20–27 years old living in Sweden are analysed and discussed. The difficulties and obstacles facing young people are described and the mechanisms leading to marginalization and exclusion from the housing market are identified. The topic of exclusion is dealt with by studying a group of marginalized young people receiving social welfare benefits. The chapter concludes with a discussion on various proposed solutions which could help to improve the situation of young people in the housing market.

The chapter is based on three kinds of scientific material: (1) a survey of literature and secondary data sources available, including research reports, scientific articles, statistical information, national and government reports, official documents and reports or practical examples; (2) a quantitative study from 1997, repeated in 2009, based on a random sample of 2000 young people aged between 20 and 27, who were interviewed about their present housing situation, their housing history and their preferences for future housing; and (3) a qualitative study from 1997, based on semi-structured in-depth interviews with 15 adolescents and ten social workers, which examined the housing situation among a group of marginalized young people.

Sweden in an international perspective

From an international point of view, young people in Sweden have access to a high standard of housing as regards quality and spaciousness (SOU 1996; SCB 2008a). Young people in Sweden also tend to leave their parental home at an earlier age compared to their peers in other parts of Europe, especially compared to those living in the Southern and Eastern parts of Europe. Housing standards are similar throughout Sweden, whether young people live with their parents or independently (Lieberg 1997a). Homelessness and temporary accommodation, for example young people's hostels or institutions, are rare (Socialstyrelsen 2006). A long and stable Swedish housing policy with high state subsidies has contributed towards this trend.

Sweden and other societies in EU-Europe can be characterized as 'modern-modernizing' societies (Bendit *et al.* 1999). They are mainly service economies in which structural and technological changes give rise to social and cultural moderni-zation processes. Most of these societies, including Sweden, can be characterized by a growing complexity and diversity, resulting in difficulties and insecurities for different groups of the population, especially young people.

Contemporary developments in different life spheres and age levels within these societies have been successfully interpreted within the wider theoretical context, with the concepts of 'individualization' and 'social differentiation' (Beck 1992) playing important roles as analytical descriptors. 'Individualization' refers to long-term processes of social change and describes the continuous decline in the norma-tive power and resilience of social milieus and cultural traditions which accompanies socio-economic and technological development (Bendit *et al.* 1999: 20). Young people's housing situation as well as the processes of 'leaving home' or 'staying in the parental home', further discussed in this chapter, must be interpreted and understood in this wider context.

Recent data collected from the Eurostat Labour Force Survey show that, in the EU in 2008, 46 per cent of all young adults aged 18–34 still lived with at least one of their parents (EU-Communities 2009). The proportion of young adults aged 18–34 living with their parent(s) varies from 20 per cent or less in Sweden, Denmark and Finland, to 60 per cent or more in Bulgaria, Slovenia and Slovakia. It exceeds 50 per cent in 16 Member States. In France, 48 per cent of young people aged 18–30 live at home, in Spain 78 per cent. Unlike the Scandinavians and the British, the Spanish do not consider this a major problem.

It is interesting to see that, while in the northern EU countries very small changes are documented during the last twenty years, in the southern part of Europe a significant growth in the rate of those living in the parental home was recorded (EU-Communities 1996, 2009). Different hypotheses have been put forward to explain these changes: in Southern and Eastern Europe a general shortage of affordable housing, combined with difficulties in entering the labour market, as well as important changes in values connected to family tradition and culture, are the main explanations, while in Scandinavia and northern Europe the prolongation of the youth phase is often mentioned as the main explanation for longer periods of time remaining in the parental home. A Finnish study supports the assumption that a sharp slowdown in growth, coupled with high unemployment rates, makes it more difficult for young people to afford 'independent' living (Harala 1996). The consequences of this may include effects on young people's professional careers and on establishing their own way of life, and delayed childbirth.

Housing conditions for young people in Sweden

Recent research indicates that the position of young people in the Swedish housing market is becoming increasingly difficult (Bergenstråhle 2009; Enström 2009). Many young people would like to have their own home, but a combination of the situation in the housing market and the lack of a steady income has resulted in them either being forced to remain in the parental home or having to find a dwelling with less secure tenure (Lindén 2007). The cost of living in Sweden has increased substantially over the last ten years, mainly due to lower state subsidies and increased construction costs (Turner 1997; Enström 2009). The number of smaller, cheaper flats has decreased drastically (SOU 1996). Many landlords are intensifying demands on their tenants, even insisting on a steady income, a 'healthy' bank account, a clean credit record, etc. In addition, the current level of youth unemployment in Sweden is the highest since the depression in the 1930s. According to the Statistics Sweden (SCB 2008a), the open rate of unemployment among young people aged 20–23 reached 20 per cent in November 2008. A further 5 per cent can be added for those engaged in one or other of the labour market's programmes for the unemployed. Few people anticipate any radical changes within the next few years. Since 2002 there has been almost complete stagnation in the construction of new housing as a consequence of unemployment and decreased state subsidies.

Housing and the Swedish welfare state

Housing has played an important role in Swedish welfare politics for a long time, and has been closely associated with the Swedish welfare state. Housing has been regarded as the right of the individual, based on his or her needs and preferences. In many respects this ambitious housing policy has not been able to prevent increasing segregation, and in some places extremely impoverished housing environments (Nordin 2007).

Movement of people between different areas, migration from the countryside to the city and increasing immigration created segregated residential areas during the 1970s and 1980s (Musterd and Andersson 2006). Wealthy households gradually left these areas to move to better homes in other areas. The Million Program areas were drained of resource-rich groups, which found new abodes in 1980s detached and semi-detached housing areas. Poor families and immigrants were left behind in the suburbs. Many of these also moved within and between suburbs in an endeavour to find the right place in the 'new' community. There developed an ethnic and social/economic segregation as a result of which children and young people grew up in widely different situations, some in secure and stable conditions, others in a fractured and uncertain social environments (Wirtén 1998). This social uncertainty became a greater burden for economically and socially deprived groups than for others.

A combination of a new tax and funding system for housing and substantially reduced state subsidies has contributed to increased housing costs, especially as regards construction of new housing (Birgersson 2009). This situation has undoubtedly had an effect on young people trying to enter the housing market.

This re-structuring of society meant changes in relations not only between private households and the local community, but also within families. Many marriages and civil partnerships broke down and new family constellations were formed. Many of the young people interviewed had experiences of family break-up and its consequences, in the form of a constant struggle to be accepted by or to accept new family members – stepfathers and stepmothers, new siblings, etc.

Data from a recent study suggest that family background has now become an important factor in determining young adults' housing situation (Enström 2009). Young adults with parents who are owner-occupiers and whose fathers have a university degree seem to have become more likely to buy their housing. The results also indicate that growing up with a single parent – a factor that has been shown to put children at risk – now also seems to have become a constraint on choice in the housing market. The results of this study indicate that the housing opportunities of young adults may have become a matter of class affiliation (Enström 2009: 2).

The 1990s in Sweden have been described as a period of fundamental change. Sweden's entry into the international community and the integration of the Swedish economy and politics with the European market prepared the ground for a new situation in the housing sector. Simultaneously, one of the pillars of the 'Swedish model', i.e. full employment, collapsed, and Sweden has now joined the ranks of other European countries with high unemployment figures. There is every reason to believe that this will seriously affect the distribution of income, increase poverty and create an increasing tendency towards social marginalization.

The structure of the housing stock

Of the almost 4,000,000 homes in Sweden, about 75 per cent have been built since World War II. The joint housing stock has seen a substantial decrease in the number of small flats (SCB 2008a). Demolition and renovation have resulted in a diminishing number of single-room flats and other small flats lacking kitchen facilities since 1960. The number of two-room flats with a kitchen and bathroom decreased from 59 per cent to 34 per cent during the period 1960–1990. In addition, structural changes in households and family building have resulted in the number of single-person or two-person households increasing from just over 47 per cent to 71 per cent during the same period. As a result, competition for flats is very high (Boverket 2007; Birgersson 2009).

Flexibility in the housing market is currently relatively low. This especially affects young people, in particular those under 25 years of age who are not seeking newly built flats. These young people depend on established households moving on up the 'housing ladder', thereby releasing cheaper flats onto the housing market.

About half (54 per cent) of Sweden's households live in blocks of flats. The remainder live in small or single-family houses. When it comes to forms of tenure, 41 per cent of Swedish households own their own homes, 40 per cent rent and 16 per cent live in owner-occupied properties (SCB 2008a). The typical Swedish pattern is for small or single-family houses to be owned by individuals, while blocks of flats are owned by public associations or housing co-operatives. Large flats are found in small housing developments and small flats are found in blocks of flats. There are obvious regional differences in the housing stock. In sparsely populated areas, 95 per cent of the housing stock consists of small houses, whereas in metropolitan areas this figure is 30 per cent and in other urban areas it is 45 per cent (SCB 2008a).

Actors in the housing market

In recent years, there have been a number of changes in the Swedish housing market and its actors (Boverket 2007). The aim has been to deregulate the market and to gradually transfer the responsibility for building and housing to landlords and households (Birgersson 2009). The consequence of this is that government and municipal responsibility for housing has changed and diminished.

The earlier role of *the state* as regards norms, standards and levels of ambition has disappeared, or rather moved on into the hands of other actors in the field. Building legislation has been rewritten. The rules and regulations that previously applied to state grants have become more general in character. This has opened the door to new possibilities for building houses with different forms, standards and quality. This can allow young people to gain access to cheaper and somewhat less traditional housing.

Housing benefits have been the responsibility of the state since 1994. The state has also decided to cut interest allowances. This has led to an increase in the cost of new-builds and house renovation over the last few years.

The municipalities have also experienced changes in housing policy. Since 1993, they no longer have to provide a housing programme and there are no longer any housing departments. The individual landlord now has to advertise vacancies. In principle, this means that housing goes to the household which best suits the owner of the property. The municipalities are only responsible for the weakest groups in society – those on social benefits or in need of special support or care as regards housing.

The landlords have been given a freer hand in finding their tenants. By shifting the security of tenure, landlords can more easily give notice to troublesome tenants. On the other hand, tenants have been given a longer time to pay rent arrears before being evicted.

TABLE 6.1 Percentage of young people in different types of housing according to age, 2009.

Accommodation type	Age group (%)		
	20–23 years	24–27 years	20–27 years
Living with parents	33	8	21
Independent home	42	73	57
Student accommodation	9	4	7
Sublet	8	9	9
Living with friends	4	2	3
Other	4	4	3
Total	100	100	100

Source: SKOP, national survey, 2009

How do young people in Sweden live today?

The results of the 2009 national study showed that 21 per cent of young people in the age group 20–27 still live in the parental home (Table 6.1). This is compared to 15 per cent in the 1997 study. However, there are certain differences between age groups. The majority of young people in the age group 18–19 (86 per cent) still live with their parents. Only a few (8 per cent) have gone as far as finding their own dwelling. Of those aged 20–23, 33 per cent live with their parents. Of the 24–27 age group, 85 per cent have their own home and 8 per cent live with their parents. The majority appear to leave home when they are about 21.

If we look more closely at how young people actually live and compare this with the preference profile, we find that the majority have had a fairly good start in life. As a rule, young people live in small, modern homes. Of all the young people aged between 18 and 27 who have left home and are neither married nor cohabiting, just over half (57 per cent) have their own home, comprising one room, kitchen and bathroom or less. A further 33 per cent live in a flat with two rooms, bathroom and kitchen and 16 per cent have a larger home. There are also differences between the individual age groups. Of the few 18–19 year olds who have left home and not yet started to build a family, 63 per cent have their own home with one room, bathroom and kitchen or less. Fifty-five per cent in the age group 22–23 and 45 per cent in the age group 24–27 live in a flat of one room, bathroom and kitchen or less. It is primarily university or college students who live in one room, with or without a kitchen (41 per cent). Many young people in this group have one room and a kitchenette. Those who are married or cohabiting with no children always live in a larger dwelling than those who are living on their own. However, it should be noted that 7 per cent of young people live in a flat with one room, bathroom and kitchen or less.

Nearly all young people live in well-equipped accommodation with toilet and bathroom (98 per cent), kitchen or kitchenette (97 per cent) and deep freeze (94 per cent). The majority of homes also have a TV (96 per cent) and a stereo (96 per cent). Many have computers (64 per cent), primarily the homes of young people attending university or college, or secondary school. More men than women have computers and more young people in the lower age groups than in the higher age groups. More young people living at home have computers than those who have left home.

The process of leaving the parental home

The results from the 1997 Swedish national study show that, when young people leave the parental home for an independent home, this is a step in their effort to gain independence and enter adulthood (Lieberg 1997b). The act of leaving home is determined by several factors: the young person's own economic resources (income, capital) are crucial. Extending education means that it takes longer before a young person can earn an income. This, in turn, delays a young person's ability to leave the parental home. This applies in particular to teenagers (at secondary school) and, to a certain extent, young people in their early 20s. Longer periods of study after secondary school have resulted in young people having to move abroad or to other parts of Sweden and therefore leaving home at an earlier age.

Viewed over a longer period of time, living in the parental home in Sweden has gradually declined. Up to the end of the 1960s, the severe housing shortage presented an obstacle for young people wanting to leave home (Boverket 2007). One million new homes were built during the ten-year period between 1965 and 1975 in the so-called Million Programme. During this time, the number of young people living in the parental home decreased considerably (Ungdomsstyrelsen 1996). The reason was the availability of an additional number of large flats, which presumably led to a lengthy chain of people moving home that resulted in smaller flats becoming available for young people.

Viewed over a shorter period of time, there has been an increase in the number of the youngest young people (teenagers) living in the parental home, but a decrease among the older group of young people (Table 6.2). In 2010, 89 per cent of teenagers were still living in the parental home, compared with 76 per cent in 1975. Even among 20–24-year-olds, it appears that living at home has increased during this period, whereas it has decreased or been more stable among those aged 25–29. Young women in Sweden generally leave their parental home at a lower age than their male peers. Up to age 25 differences span a range of 10 to 15 percentage points, but after 25 they inevitably become smaller. The 1997 study showed that at an age of 28 or more, 12.1 per cent of young men and 7.3 of young women still lived in the parental home. These gender differences represent a general pattern found in Swedish (Lindén 2007; Bergenståhle 1997, 2009) as well as international studies (Jones 1995; Bendit et al. 1999).

On the other hand, what was not so familiar in the past is a significant number (20 per cent) of those who have left home for some reason returning to the parental

TABLE 6.2 Percentage of young people in Sweden still living in the parental home, 1975–2010.

Age group	Percentage living in the parental home							
	1975	1980	1985	1990	1997	2000	2005	2010
16–17	95	97	98	97	98	98	99	98
18–19	76	77	80	79	88	87	88	89
20–24	37	34	35	30	37	38	39	43
25–29	10	8	8	6	9	10	11	12

Source: Central Bureau of Statistics, Population and Housing Register 1997 and Total Population Register 2010

home (Lieberg 1997b). This new phenomenon, sometimes referred to as 'boomerang kids', has started to become quite common in Sweden. A 'boomerang kid' is a term used to describe an adult child that has left home at some point in the past to live on their own and has returned to live in the parental home. This return can be due to completed studies, divorce or unemployment – or lack of affordable housing. In 2001, almost 25 per cent of all adult children living with their parent(s) in Sweden were boomerang kids. And a majority of them were boys. So, leaving home today is no longer a final process. Many young people, and especially young boys, return to their parental home not only once but many times during the 'extended period of youth'. It is therefore more relevant to talk about being 'on probation from home', than 'leaving home' (Jones 1995; Lieberg 1997b).

Leaving home for good possibly does not happen until the young person is much older. In addition, various contributing factors relating to changes in the structure of the modern family must be considered, for example many young people share their housing between their mother and father, who may live in different places and who may have entered a new relationship and started to build a new family (SCB 2008b). These factors show that leaving home is indeed a much more complex and lengthy process than before.

A considerable number of these young people have economic reasons for returning home, for example they have lost their job, or could not afford their independent home. Today a large number of young people living at home are waiting to enter the housing market as soon as it is financially possible. Research in Sweden and abroad has shown that the transition to adulthood and leaving home is complicated, largely influenced by the changing family structure and by issues concerning employment, study and independent living (Löfgren 1991; Lindén 2007; Enström 2009). Increased knowledge of the long-term effects of remaining at home is therefore an important issue for research.

It is unusual in Sweden for young people to remain living in the parental home once they have started to build a family. Further, young people do not normally leave home to live with a partner, but usually begin by first living independently for a short period of time. Remaining in the parental home is strongly related to the young person's position on the labour market. Figures from 1991 show that only 20 per cent of those gainfully employed still lived in the parental home, while 72 per cent of young people who were studying lived in the parental home (Löfgren 1991).

Mobility aspirations

A number of studies show that young people are a mobile group within the housing market. Like a pendulum, they swing between different, sometimes temporary, housing solutions – from living in the parental home to student accommodation, from staying with friends to sublets, etc. In 1996 the number of young people in the age group 20–29 registering a change of address was three times greater than the national average (Bergenstråhle 1997). It is extremely difficult to obtain data about the period between leaving home and finding an independent dwelling, usually at about 20–21 years old. According to the Population and Housing Register for 1990, about 66,000 young people out of a total of just over 1,000,000 (6.7 per cent) did not belong to a so-called household in that year. These young people were registered as living in a parish or property but did not actually live there, or they were young people with no permanent home or who did not want to divulge where and with whom they were living (Ungdomsstyrelsen 1996).

In response to the question 'Do you plan to leave home within the coming year?' a total of 38 per cent of young people aged 18–27 replied that they did. The majority (44 per cent) of these were in the 22–23 age group. When individual groups were studied, it was found that almost half the 20–21 year olds said they planned to leave home within the next year (Figure 6.1). In order to find out the exact frequency of leaving home, the young people were also asked how many times they had moved within the last two years. Naturally this varied according to age. In all, 66 per cent had left home at least once during the past ten years. Of this

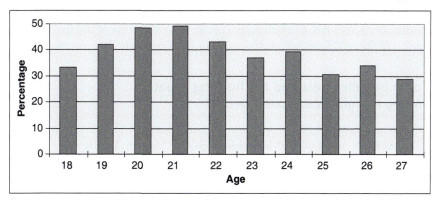

FIGURE 6.1 Proportion of young people planning to move within one year, 1996 (N = 2000).

66 per cent, more than a quarter had moved back home again three or more times. It would appear that young people are an extremely mobile group in the housing market.

Role of unemployment and other economic factors

A combination of developments in the labour market and access to smaller and cheaper dwellings is clearly controlling the possibilities for young people to leave home. In a situation of high unemployment and a housing market in recession, as has been the case in Sweden since the 1990s, the chances of young people finding an independent dwelling decrease. This in turn results in more and more of them being forced to remain in the parental home. Some have to return to the parental home for financial reasons, after having lived independently for some time. The national surveys show a strong link between a young person's position on the labour market and living at home. The number of young people living at home increases among the unemployed and decreases among the securely employed. Compared with those that have left home, to a great extent those young people still living at home are either in temporary employment or unemployed, or are engaged in a labour market youth training scheme. In all, 13 per cent of the young people in the 2009 survey regularly received financial support from their parents. This was especially common in the youngest age group, where 29 per cent received support. A large number of those young people receiving regular financial support from their parents were secondary school pupils (38 per cent), those living with their parents (24 per cent), those doing their national service (23 per cent) or those enrolled in some kind of government training scheme for the unemployed (22 per cent).

This indicates that many young people receive financial support and allowances to cover their living costs from different sources. Apart from housing benefits and rental support from their parents, young people can receive help to cover living costs from unemployment benefit or from regular financial support from their parents. A total of 36 per cent received some kind of financial assistance to cover housing costs. Very few received support from more than one of the five different sources of financial assistance mentioned in our questionnaire (Bergenstråhle 2009).

Youth homelessness and the housing situation among marginalized young people

According to a study by the Swedish National Board of Health and Welfare in 2010, there are about 30,000 homeless people in Sweden. This is approximately double the number found in a similar study in 2005 (Socialstyrelsen 2006). In addition, there is probably a large number of unknown cases, especially among young people who turn to various temporary and often non-contract housing arrangements. The homeless make up around 0.3 per cent of the Swedish population. Three quarters of the homeless are male and one quarter female, and there is an over-representation of people born outside Sweden. Very few have any work or salaried income, so many are dependent on benefits. Substance abuse and mental health problems are common among the homeless, but there are also homeless people without such problems.

A large proportion of the homeless (38 per cent) are in the age range 30–45 years and approximately 25 per cent are in the range 18–29 years. It is in these younger age groups and among women that the increase in numbers is greatest. In addition, there are unknown numbers of children who were not actually recorded in the investigation. Statistical data for Malmö, Sweden's third largest city, confirm that the increase in the number of homeless, with the exception of a few years in the beginning of the 2000s, has been constant in the past ten years.

During the 2000s, long-term dependency on benefits in Sweden has developed into something that does not affect only homeless people, substance abusers and dysfunctional families. Increasing unemployment and uncertainty in the labour market have resulted in more groups becoming dependent on the support of society (Salonen 1993, 2007). Despite this, those receiving benefits are still regarded as people who are unwilling or unable to support themselves, which in turn often contributes to feelings of consistently low self-esteem and a generally pessimistic self-perception.

The young people interviewed in 1997 as part of the qualitative study left the parental home earlier than others. Many of them had left home as 16- or 17-year-olds and lived in their own flat, often together with a boyfriend or girlfriend (Lieberg 1998). Leaving home so early is otherwise uncommon in Sweden. Only around 2 per cent of all young people of this age have left home. While their first home of their own was important for them, it was not always easy financially or socially. Many have had difficulties supporting themselves after leaving school which led to them losing their home. Girls often had difficulties in their relationships with older boyfriends. For many girls, having a boyfriend and moving in with him presented an immediate opportunity to move away from the family home. In particular, for girls without close female friends and without a job, a boyfriend represented an opening to a more adult and independent life. The boyfriend became their rescuer from childhood dependency on the family. It emerged in the interviews with these girls that the boyfriend was not always the man they had wanted, but their dependence on him made it difficult for them to end the relationship. The boyfriend was also not always the one they wanted to be the father of their future children. Despite this, some of them had babies at an early age, perhaps because their identity as a mother was important to them. Having a baby gave them the opportunity to alter the picture of themselves and their life, as they took on the new identity of mother and parent.

A new culture of unemployment is developing

Mass unemployment at the beginning of the 1990s and during the economic crisis in 2008–2009 has left its mark, although in recent years unemployment in

Sweden has been slowly decreasing. Between the lines there are glimpses of another truth – for the young, the group which experiences the greatest difficulty in finding work, the situation is still serious.

An investigation by Linköping University found that a new culture of unemployment is developing, especially among those young people who find it most difficult to enter the labour market (Hallström 1998). This culture is characterized by young people simply contenting themselves with state-run youth employment measures. They are unwilling to embark on long-term education and demand that society organize work and occupation for them. The decrease in youth unemployment in the past year has naturally altered the picture, but tragically there is always one group left out. The young people in the 1990s were the first in over 60 years to experience such a constrained labour market.

In our own data, there was a distinct contrast between the views of young people and officials interviewed as regards society's responsibility to organize work. This conflict probably also partly reflects the generation gap that exists in attitudes to work, with young people in Sweden appearing to resemble those in other European countries with high and permanent unemployment (Gabriel and Radig 1999). In such countries there is no parallel drawn between livelihood and work.

Future housing

As regards young people's housing demands in Sweden, it appears that traditional values steer demands for future housing. Today, young people's ideas about their future housing are not especially daring. A clear majority could certainly consider making a personal contribution to reducing housing costs. Specialist youth housing and 'eco housing' also appear to attract young people's interest. Otherwise, as regards maintaining a high standard of housing, it appears that the young people of today share the same values as past generations. This was indeed noticeable in the 1997 survey when it came to attitudes on future housing. A clear majority expressed a preference for having their own house with a garden, near the countryside. The question is whether Sweden is ever going to be able to afford such a high standard of housing again. Young people are not particularly interested in specific housing solutions. The majority said that the best way for young people to enter the housing market would be to reduce youth unemployment and thereby enable young people to pay their housing costs.

Final discussion

This chapter has shown that young people in Sweden tend to leave the parental home somewhat later in life than previously. The reasons for this are prolonged studies combined with increased housing costs and changes in the housing market. There is no evidence to indicate that this increase in young people remaining at home is the result of a change in attitudes among young people. Rather, it is the result of structural and economic factors. When there is high unemployment and an uncertain economy, many young people, and especially boys, choose to remain living at home, and an increasing number return home to live with their parents. 'On probation from home' or 'boomerang kids' is therefore a more appropriate expression than 'leaving home'. This is a new and important phenomenon that has not previously been included in Swedish research, since earlier studies concentrated on the final move from home and not the first move. The process of returning home appears to have been neglected because of difficulties of gaining access to the data and because leaving home has been assumed to be a one-off phenomenon. However, as returning home has become more common in recent years, in Sweden and in other countries, the process of leaving home may be considerably more complicated and lengthier than previously thought. It is also important to consider the differences between marginalized youth and the mainstream. Young people with social problems tend to leave the parental home much earlier than others.

These changes can be important in other ways, too. The national housing policy appears to be built on a model of economic rationality, which presupposes that young people will only leave home when they can afford to do so. Measures aimed at reducing the reasons for leaving home therefore automatically prolong the period in which young people live in the parental home. The effects of this are not especially apparent in Sweden as yet, but international research shows that many young people who leave home while quite young do so because of domestic conflicts, lack of space and difficulties in getting employment or studying in their home town (Coles 1995; Gabriel and Radig 1999; Enström 2009). Thus they often have no choice in the timing of leaving home. They are almost certainly not prepared to live in an independent home and they do not have the economic means for this. Although the situation in Sweden cannot be compared with the international situation, any developments that lead to youth exclusion in the housing market should be monitored. According to Jones (1995), the 'normative' pattern for moving home is largely built on economic rationality, while moving home because of marriage, work or studies is largely based on individual choice. The latter is therefore more sensitive to manipulation by different forms of state regulation and contributions.

This chapter shows that young people remaining at home and leaving home is a special area for research, and illustrates some of the related problems. It also shows the importance of continued research, not least as regards young people returning to live in the parental home and the increased economic responsibility on the family for young people who have reached the age of majority. Research should focus on ethnicity, gender, class and regional differences and on access to subsidies for different groups. Much research to date has focused on what the process means, mainly for marginalized and socially burdened households, so studies are needed on 'whole' families, without economic and social problems. Such studies should also examine the parents' viewpoint as well as young people's and view the young person's situation from both a family perspective and from a broader perspective within society.

When carrying out future studies about young people moving home, it must be made clear whether it is the first time of leaving home, the last time or a mixture of both. It is critical for young people seeking to free themselves from their parental home to set up home for themselves that good quality data are available to politicians and decision-makers. Cross-sectional studies that build on temporary households are therefore greatly limited, and comparisons with other studies should be avoided if the same definitions and methods of measurement are not used. The best results can be obtained from longitudinal studies, in which the same definitions and methods are used on many occasions to find trends and important changes in development, followed by deeper qualitative studies on a more individual level.

References

Beck, U. (1992) *Risk Society: Towards a New Modernity*. London: Sage.

Bendit, R., Gaiser, W., and Marbach, J.H. (eds) (1999) *Youth and Housing in Germany and the European Union*. Hemsbach, Germany: Leske + Budrich.

Bergenstråhle, S. (1997) *Ungas boende. En studie av boendeförhållandena för ungdomar i åldern 20–27 år.* (*Young people and housing. A study of young people's housing in the age groups 20–27.*) Stockholm: Boinstitutet.

Bergenstråhle, S. (2009) *Unga vuxnas boende – förändringar i riket 1997–2009* (*Young people's housing situation – national developments 1997–2009*), Rapport 1: 2009. Stockholm: Hyresgästföreningen.

Birgersson, B.-O. (2009) *Bostaden en grundbult i välfärden. En förstudie om levnadsvillkor och boende – del ett.* (*Housing as a fundamental of welfare. A pilot study on living conditions and housing – part 1.*) Stockholm: Hyresgästföreningen.

Boverket (2007) *Bostadspolitiken – Svensk politik för boende, planering och byggande under 130 år.* (*Housing Policy. Swedish politics for housing, planning and building over 130 years.*) Karlskrona: National Board of Housing, Building and Planning.

Coles, B. (1995) *Youth and Social Policy*. London: UCL Press.

Enström, C. (2009) *The Effect of Parental Wealth on Tenure Choice – A Study of Family Background and Young Adults' Housing Situation*, Arbetsrapport 2009: 1. Stockholm: Institutet för framtidsstudier.

EU-Communities (ed.) (1996) *Labour Force Survey*. Luxembourg: Eurostat.

EU-Communities (ed.) (2009) *Youth in Europe 2009*. Luxembourg: Eurostat.

Gabriel, G. and Radig, S. (1999) 'Housing support for young people at risk: a qualitative study', in R. Bendit, W. Gaiser and J. H. Marbach (eds) *Youth and Housing in Germany and the European Union*. Hemsbach, Germany: Leske + Budrich.

Hallström, B. (1998) *Arbete eller bidrag. En attitydundersökning bland arbetslösa ungdomar och ledande kommunalpolitiker.* (*Work or allowance. A study of attitudes among unemployed youth and local politicians.*) Rapport 1998: 2. Linköping: Linköpings universitet.

Harala, R. (1996) *Monitoring Youth Exclusion in Finland*. Helsinki: Statistics Finland.

Jones, G. (1995) *Leaving Home*. Buckingham: Open University Press.

Lieberg, M. (1997a) *Youth Housing in Sweden: A Descriptive Overview Based on a Literature Review*. Mälardalen University: Welfare Reseach Centre.

Lieberg, M. (1997b) *On Probation from Home: Young People's Housing and Housing Preferences in Sweden*. Mälardalen University: Welfare Research Centre.

Lieberg, M. (1998) *Bostäder och boende bland unga socialbidragstagare – en kvalitativ studie.* (*Dwellings and housing among young people with social allowances – a qualitative study.*) Mälardalen University: Welfare Research Centre.

Lindén, A.-L. (2007) *Hushåll och bostäder. En passformsanalys.* (*Household and housing. A correlation analysis.*) Lund: Sociologiska institutionen, Lunds universitet.

Löfgren, A. (1991) *Att flytta hemifrån. Boendets roll i ungdomars vuxenblivande ur ett siuationsanalytiskt perspektiv. (Leaving home. The role of housing in young people's transition to adulthood from a situation analytical perspective.)* Diss. Lund: Lund University Press.

Musterd, S. and Andersson, R. (2006) 'Employment, social mobility and neighbourhood effects: the case of Sweden', *International Journal of Urban and Regional Research*, 30(1): 120–140.

Nordin, M. (2007) 'Ethnic segregation and educational attainment in Sweden', in M. Nordin, (ed.) *Studies in Human Capital, Ability and Migration.* Lund: Nationalekonomiska institutionen, Lunds universitet, 107–132.

Salonen, T. (1993) *Margins of Welfare: A Study of Modern Functions of Social Assistance.* Lund: Hällestad Press.

Salonen, T. (2007) *Barnfattigdomen i Sverige. (Poverty among Swedish Children.)* årsrapport. Stockholm: Rädda Barnen.

Socialstyrelsen (2006) *Hemlöshet i Sverige 2005.* (Homelessness in Sweden 2005.) Stockholm: The Swedish National Board of Health and Welfare.

SOU (1996) *Bostadspolitik 2000 – från produktions – till boendepolitik. Slutbetänkande av bostadspolitiska utredningen. (Housing policy 2000 – from production to housing policy.)* Final committee report from The Housing Policy Report. Swedish Government Official Reports 1996: 156. Stockholm: Fritzes.

SCB, Statistiska Centralbyrån (2008a) *Boende och boendeutgifter 2006. (Housing and housing costs 2006.)* Stockholm: Statistics Sweden.

SCB, Statistiska Centralbyrån (2008b) *Ungdomars flytt hemifrån. (Leaving home.)* Stockholm: Statistics Sweden.

Turner, B. (1997) *Vad hände med den sociala bostadspolitiken? (What happened to the social housing policy?)* Stockholm: Boinstitutet.

Ungdomsstyrelsen (1996): *Krokig väg till vuxen. En kartläggning av ungdomars livsvillkor. (The winding road to adulthood. Mapping young people's living conditions.)* Youth Report 1996 part 1. Stockholm: Ungdomsstyrelsen (National Board for Youth Affairs).

Wirtén, P (1998) *Etnisk boendesegregering. (Ethnic housing segregation.)* Stockholm: The Institute of Housing Studies.

7

HOMEOWNERSHIP, COHORT TRAJECTORIES AND HONG KONG'S POST-EIGHTIES GENERATION

Ngai ming Yip

Introduction

The "post-eighties generation," referring to young people born after 1980, has emerged as a popular catchphrase in the media, both on mainland China and in Hong Kong. On the one hand, being raised in the 1980s when the Hong Kong economy had taken off, they share no experience of poverty, as their parents' generation did. On the other hand, they were hit by the worst economic recession since the Second World War when they entered the job market, and many have become rather disenchanted with the specious "tickets" to success associated with paper qualifications affected by inflation due to the rapid expansion of higher education in the 1990s. It is generally believed that such factors have combined to make this generation qualitatively different from their parents' generation, be it in attitudes to work, political inclination or life philosophy.

Housing stands out as one of the many difficult problems the post-eighties generation faces. Not only is housing central to their transition to independent adulthood, the post-eighties generation also finds their housing aspirations increasingly beyond reach. With prolonged education, increasing student debts and falling starting salaries against the backdrop of a property boom, young people are trapped between their aspirations to homeownership and their limited resources. Housing policy is also turning against them. Not only was the assisted homeownership scheme scrapped in 2002, removing an affordable route to homeownership for young singles with less resources, entry into public rental housing has been tightening up. All these factors act to exacerbate young people's housing problems.

Yet youth is a social construct and needs to be understood from a life-course perspective as well as in the cultural, social and comparative context. Whilst many issues young people face in Hong Kong are shared with their counterparts in the developed world, there are also marked differences between Hong Kong (and Asia) and the West. For instance, independent living for young people in Hong Kong is far less common than it is for their counterparts in north and west Europe. This is perhaps partly shaped by the income support system that has a strong bias towards families, but is largely the result of cultural norms. Housing is much more expensive relative to the incomes of young people, and publicly developed housing, which accommodates nearly half of the population, is also of profound importance.

This chapter will examine issues of housing of young adults in Hong Kong in their transition to adulthood, from the perspective of life-course analysis. It will look at the housing trajectories of young people using data on education, tenure and related attributes, within the social and economic context of the last three decades. A particular focus will be the interaction between housing, housing policy and households. The chapter starts with a description of the housing career and life approach to housing, which is followed by an analysis of the population census with respect to housing of different age cohorts, as well as the changing education, employment and living arrangements of young people. It will then examine the housing market and housing policy impediments to young people, and this will be followed by a review, based on data from in-depth interviews, of the changing social meaning of housing among young people. The chapter will conclude by identifying the specific social, economic and cultural factors that are at work in the creation of the housing problems of the post-eighties generation.

Housing careers and the life-course approach

The concept of housing careers emerged in the late 1970s (see, for example, Payne and Payne, 1977; Pickvance, 1974) to capture the idea of housing (tenure) mobility which appears to bear a strong association with the family life cycle as well as advancement in the workplace (typically that of the head of the household). The main thrust of the research was to offer an explanation as to how housing careers – for instance, entry into homeownership and progression through the housing market – responded to changes in the family career (family formation and change in composition) as well as occupational careers (promotion, retirement) (Clark *et al.*, 2003; Forrest and Kemeny, 1983; Saunders, 1990). The metaphor of a housing ladder has been extensively employed in visualizing such a progression. Despite variation in the "rungs" of the ladders in the literature to suit local context, a typical hierarchy of private renting, to public renting, and finally to homeownership is found in most such ladders (Kendig, Paris and Anderton, 1987; Beer and Faulkner in this volume).

Yet, with our growing understanding of "careers," the existence of standard and synchronized progression in family, occupation and housing followed by most people is evidently an over-simplification. Not only is regional variation in the housing market significant (Clark *et al.*, 2003), there is also substantial differentiation among homeowners in their progression in the housing market which cannot be accounted for by differences in earned income (Forrest and Murie, 1987). Structural changes in the housing and labour markets have blocked progression in the housing market and hence the notion of career in housing (Winter and Stone, 1998). Increasing social polarization and restructuring of housing policy have also pushed more households to the margins. For those households, housing career is an irrelevant concept. The idea of a housing career also offers little insight into the housing progression of people who are in and out of homelessness (Anderson, 2001). Despite the various attempts to improve the notion of career, such as the "snakes and ladders" metaphor (see Beer and Faulkner in this volume) or housing pathway (Clapham, 2002), they nevertheless have to compromise on the simple hierarchical notion the "ladder" is able to offer.

A more comprehensive conception of the dynamic interdependence of housing and other aspects of a household's life within a wider social and economic context is captured by the life-course approach. It is defined by Elder (1978, p.26) as "a concept of interdependent life patterns which vary in synchronization." It focuses on the meshing of individual careers within the family which are subject to internal family considerations as well as being influenced by external economic and social factors (Hareven, 1978). Life-course studies address the micro-macro and the macro-micro problem; that is, how structural conditions and how institutions impact on individual lives, and how outcomes impact on institutional and structural change (Mayer, 2000). In this respect, careers can be incorporated as a component of institutional time. Together with historical time (generations and cohorts) and individual time (life history, biography), these three aspects of the life-course, progressing in a sequence of stages or status configurations, are culturally and institutionally framed from birth to death (Heinz and Krüger, 2001).

Associated with the adoption of the life-course perspective is the destandardization of life experience (Brannen and Nilsen, 2002) as well as the decollectivization and individualization of life chances (Beck, 1994). Such processes in fact match the strand of neo-liberalist social policy which prevailed in the last two decades, and which emphases the responsibility of individuals and families in making decisions about the future. Yet it does not imply the total liberalization of life decisions, as the overall parameters of the welfare state still shape significantly the choices of individuals (Beck and Beck-Gernsheim, 1995). Nevertheless, it does lead to more diversified life experiences (Brannen and Nilsen, 2002)

Hence, housing for young people in Hong Kong has to be understood as the pattern of housing consumption in the transition from childhood to adulthood, framed by the individual, historical and institutional times of an individual. The rest of the chapter will elaborate on four aspects connected with the life-course of the post-eighties generation: the general demography and economic environment that shapes their life chances; cultural patterns of independent living; housing market and policy impediments which constrain their housing consumption and the resulting cohort trajectories of housing attainment; and finally the social meaning they attach to housing consumption.

Changing context and the uncertain future

As Furlong and Cartmel (1997) argue, despite the apparently more individualistic dimensions of life chances of young people nowadays, structural factors continue to play decisive roles in shaping their constraints and opportunities. Rapid economic growth is undisputedly the most prominent of these factors in the recent history of Hong Kong, and has changed the social landscape of the city completely. Hong Kong was able to achieve a continuously high rate of economic growth for nearly three decades, from the late 1960s to the mid-1990s. GDP in real terms grew annually at an average of 8.9% in the 1970s and 7.4% in the 1980s (Census and Statistics Department, undated). Hence, in 1997, the year when Hong Kong was about to experience one of its hardest and longest economic setbacks, GDP per capita at current US dollars had increased 28-fold since 1970 (World Bank 2011).

Increased affluence has created a fundamentally different milieu for the transition to adulthood for the post-eighties generation. Greatly improved fiscal capacity allowed the government to increase its investment in higher education in the late 1980s, which brought particular benefits to the post-eighties generation. Such expansion, apparently paralleling international trends at that time in equipping the work force for the upcoming structural transformation of the economy, in fact largely reflected the preparations of the colonial government for counteracting the projected brain drain in the wake of the return of sovereignty to China. With subsidized university places quadrupling in the early 1990s, the post-eighties generation was the first generation to take full benefit. In 2006, 28 per cent of young people aged 20 to 24 years old had completed or were receiving undergraduate training. This is higher than their elder counterparts at the comparable age range.

In fact, attainment in higher education for successive generations has improved over the years, and the post-seventies generation (people in their mid-twenties to mid-thirties in 2006) have gained more higher education if postgraduate qualifications are included. Although they started with a much lower level at the normal college leaving age, the improvement has apparently been made at a later age, probably as a result of the expansion of part-time postgraduate or undergraduate training. Respectively, 30 per cent and 33 per cent of people born during 1971 to 1974 and 1975 to 1979 were able to get qualifications at or beyond degree level (Figure 7.1). The 1971–74 birth cohort was able to improve the proportion of higher education attainment by 50 per cent in the ten years after the normal college leaving age. With similar projected trajectories, it seems that there is still room for an increase in the number of degree holders for the post-eighties generation.

Sparked by the Asian Economic Crisis, the continuous economic prosperity of three decades ended abruptly in 1997 and economic turbulence, marked by the outbreak of SARS and the economic tsunami, that continued for over a decade has dragged Hong Kong into economic uncertainty. Despite uncertainty being a normal feature of our daily lives (Furlong and Cartmel, 1997), the life chances of young people have nevertheless encountered unprecedented challenges. The combined impacts of structural factors, such as a contracting and deflationary economy amidst restructuring of the financial sectors, have shaped structural inequality, mediated through contingent individual decisions, in qualitatively different ways. As industries in Hong Kong moved their operations to China, displaced manufacturing workers were forced to shift to low-end service industry jobs which crowded

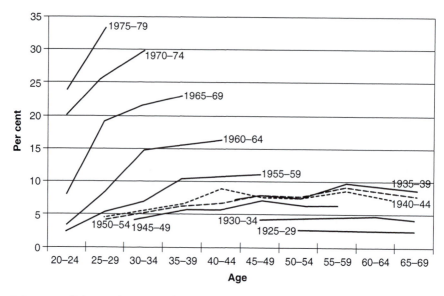

FIGURE 7.1 Cohort trajectories of higher education, 1981–2006.
Source: Author's reanalysis of the Population Census 1981–2006

young people out of the job market, particularly those with no qualifications. Hence, unemployment rates among younger workers were much worse than among their older counterparts. In 2009, 22 per cent and 16 per cent of workers aged 15–19 and 20–29 respectively were out of work – levels three to five times higher than that of the general population (Census and Statistics Department, 2010). Despite representing a substantial improvement over the worst year in 2003 (with 30 per cent and 19 per cent unemployment, respectively) (Census and Statistics Department, 2004), such high unemployment levels are still unprecedented in Hong Kong. For those young people fortunate enough to be in employment, their earnings were also much less than the average. Median income for workers aged 18–22 in 2006 was only 56 per cent of that of the general working population, a trend that has worsened since the early 1980s (Wu, 2010).

For the one third high achievers able to complete higher education, the currency of a degree has shrunk, compared to the situation a generation before. As Hong Kong develops its high-end service industry, it is the baby boomers who gain the most. In 2006, age cohorts born between 1965 and 1979 had the highest occupational attainment – one third were managers, professionals or semi-professionals, whereas only 17 per cent of the post-eighties generation were able to enter into such occupations. Although some of the post-eighties generation were still in higher education by 2006, as a result of a more extended period of education and training, their chances of getting a professional or managerial job is much slimmer. In fact, the expansion of professional and managerial jobs has been lagging behind the expansion of higher education (Wu, 2010). This suggests that it was more difficult for college graduates in 2006 to find a managerial or professional job than it was a decade earlier. Not only are job prospects apparently dependent on the historical time one joins the job market, over the last decade they have also been contingent on the timing of educational and job-seeking choices. For instance, teaching has long been a well-paid, secure job in Hong Kong, but with shrinking birth rates, many schools were being forced to close and teachers made redundant. With birth rates now rising again and numbers of cross-border students on the increase, teachers are in short supply. At the same time, an aging population and sudden epidemics (SARS, bird flu) have boosted the demand for healthcare workers. Yet the decision to enter into the professions has to be made years earlier. Of course, such unpredictability always exists, but in the last decade, increased globalization and more volatile economic cycles have amplified the long-term social and demographic fluctuations and made the social and economic environment more unstable, and hence more uncertain. Personal decisions made at a particular moment are thus more significant than before.

Cultural norms and independent living among young people

Leaving home to live independently is perhaps the most significant event connected with housing for young people. Not only does it alter the demand structure for housing, it also reflects changes in the institutional factors that underpin young people's independent living. Shaped by cultural norms and institutional factors, the patterns of co-residence with parents vary widely, even between different parts of Europe. For instance, while in Sweden less than one third (31 per cent) of young people aged 24 to 27 years old stayed with their parents in 1996 (Lieberg, 2000), 57 per cent of young people in Greece (Emmanuel, in this volume) in a comparable age group (24 to 28 years old in 1998) did likewise. Cultural norms exert a vital influence on life-course events. In Asia, young people who moved out of their parental homes were in the minority, compared with their counterparts in the West (Xenos *et al.*, 2006). Strong familial ties and the need for the family to provide child or elderly care in the context of inadequate state welfare, as well as other institutional influences, are some of the contributing factors.

In Hong Kong, despite the extremely crammed living environment, staying in the parental home until marriage is the norm – two thirds (67 per cent) of young people between 20 and 34 years old did so in 2006 and only 6 per cent lived alone. For young people aged 20 to 24, even fewer lived alone (2.5 per cent). Nearly all (91 per cent) stayed at home. The student population in this group should be high, and it is not uncommon for students to commute to college from home. This is a substantially higher level compared to young people in the West. And nearly half of those in their early thirties (42 per cent) still lived with their parents. Similar to the trend in the West, the proportion of young people living with their parents has in fact increased over the last fifteen years – between 1991 and 2006, an increase of 11 and 9 percentage points for those aged 20 to 24 and 30 to 34 years old, respectively, and even higher (14 per cent) for those aged 25 to 29.

TABLE 7.1 Young people living alone 1991–2006.

Year	Percentage of young people with higher education living alone			Percentage of all young people living alone		
	Age 20–24	Age 25–29	Age 30–34	Age 20–24	Age 25–29	Age 30–34
1991	4.0	7.9	8.4	2.7	4.5	5.0
1996	6.9	9.3	11.4	3.5	5.2	5.6
2001	2.2	7.7	10.2	2.0	5.5	6.3
2006	2.1	7.5	11.3	2.1	6.1	7.9

Source: Author's analysis of Census micro-data 1991–2006

A high level of co-residence with parents also prevails in other Asian countries, as observed by Xenos *et al.* (2006). In their 1980s study, the level in Hong Kong was exceptionally high. Home-leaving before marriage or leaving school was extremely rare for people between 20 and 24 in Hong Kong, compared to other Asian countries such as the Philippines or Thailand. A longer period in education and later marriage may be part of the reason, but high house prices were perhaps the main obstacle to young people living independently (Xenos *et al.*, 2006). Trajectories of the living arrangements of young people over the last three decades indicate that young people who have completed post-secondary education have been consistently more likely to live alone than their peers with lower levels of education (Table 7.1). With higher earning potential, people with higher qualifications may be able to support an independent apartment in Hong Kong, which is expensive relative to people's income.

Not only is the level of co-residence among young single people high, in 2006 over half (53%) of people in their early twenties who were married (only 4.5% of the relevant age group) also lived with parents. Both cultural expectation and high housing cost may be at work as pulling and deterring factors in shaping these co-residence outcomes. Without more detailed information it is difficult to be certain about the underlying factors, but the co-residence trend in Table 7.2 offers some hints. If cultural expectation is more dominant, we may expect a smaller difference in co-residence patterns between couples in different age groups. Yet whilst around a quarter (23 per cent) of married couples in their early thirties in 2006 stayed with their parents, over half (53 per cent) of young couples in their early twenties did likewise. This pattern has been quite consistent over the last decade and a half. The biggest jump in married couples living with their parents occurred after 1991. This matches the period during which the biggest post-Second World War housing boom made housing substantially unaffordable. It is perhaps these high housing costs that deterred married couples from living independently and younger couples, because of their more limited earning power, were more affected. But the proportion of married couples living with parents has apparently stabilized since 1996, despite falling house prices and improving mortgage terms.

TABLE 7.2 Young people living with parents.

Year	Unmarried young people living with parents (%)			Married young people living with parents (%)			All young people living with parents (%)		
	Age 20–24	Age 25–29	Age 30–34	Age 20–24	Age 25–29	Age 30–34	Age 20–24	Age 25–29	Age 30–34
1991	86	78	69	40	27	20	80	56	33
1996	89	80	72	51	33	23	84	61	39
2001	92	83	73	50	33	23	89	67	42
2006	93	82	69	53	33	23	91	70	42

Source: Author's analysis of Census micro-data 1991–2006
Note: Figures include people living with grandparents or parents-in-law

The housing market and the transition to adulthood

Since staying with parents is almost a cultural norm for young singletons in Hong Kong, leaving home is an event associated with marriage and is not perceived as an independent decision. It is therefore not surprising that housing for young people was never in itself a policy issue. As younger generations have become increasingly dependent on the market to fulfil their housing needs, policy discourse on housing for young people has been framed by the concern about affordability for first-time buyers.

The impacts of the neoliberal approach to housing policy on people's preference for homeownership in Hong Kong have been discussed elsewhere (see, for example, Forrest and Lee, 2003): younger generations are apparently more attracted to home-ownership than their older counterparts. Not only did age cohorts born after 1961 (the baby boomers) include more homeowners, they also became homeowners at an earlier age. Whereas only 13 per cent of householders in the 1955–59 age cohort were homeowners in their early twenties, this was true of nearly one third (30 per cent) of the 1965–69 age cohort. In fact, all age cohorts born after 1961 were able to achieve a homeownership rate of around 40 per cent by their early thirties (Figure 7.2). Even in the post-eighties generation (who were between the ages of 20 and 26 in 2006), the proportion of homeowners had already reached 29 per cent (not shown in Figure 7.2). There appears to be a consensus on homeownership as the desired tenure, particularly among younger cohorts.

While the rising desire among young people to buy is apparent, there is a huge variety of ways to realise such dreams in the context of an increasingly volatile and uncertain market. Similar to the experience elsewhere, rising housing costs have been experienced by most first-time buyers as a result of land scarcity and the relocation of risk by financial institutions (Lawson and Milligan, 2007). Real house prices in Hong Kong have more than doubled since the early 1980s (Rating and Valuation Department, various years). Although when measured in aggregate terms affordability has greatly improved compared with the last housing boom in 1997

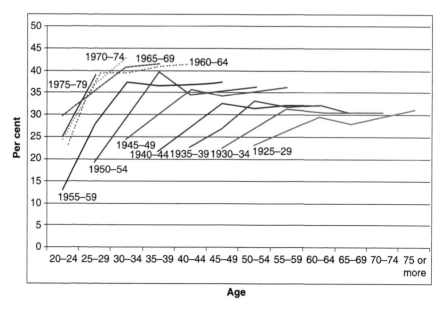

FIGURE 7.2 Cohort trajectories in private homeownership, 1981–2006.
Source: Author's reanalysis of the Population Census 1981–2006
Note: Owners under assisted homeownership schemes excluded

(Centaline, 2011), such improvement is largely a result of reduced mortgage costs. This has come about partly through the liberalization of the mortgage market and more innovative mortgage instruments, but mainly because of the low interest rate regime created by the quantitative easing monetary policy package of the US. This inevitably increases the risk for marginal homebuyers when interest rates resume their normal trend.

First-time buyers in Hong Kong also face a rather stringent wealth constraint in relation to downpayments. Normally, 30 per cent of the value of the flat is required for the downpayment, a major hurdle for home buyers. A household who earned the median household income in 2010 would have to save four years' worth of their total income to pay only the downpayment for a 50-square-metre flat at the average price. This seems, however, not to deter young homeowners. The homeownership rate among the 1971–74 age cohort increased by seven percentage points during the period 2001–2006 (when they were in their late twenties and early thirties) while for the 1975–79 cohort (only in their twenties), the rate nearly doubled in the same period (Figure 7.2). Given that this was also the period during which Hong Kong was experiencing a major market slump, this may reflect the improved affordability for those who had a steady income and were able to exploit bargain prices at the ebb of the housing cycle. Yet few young people in their twenties could save fast enough for the downpayment, given their typical wage levels. Hence, it is highly probable that these young homeowners were able to secure extra help from their resource-rich parents. The reproduction of structural inequality is evident at this juncture.

For people who cannot afford homeownership, private renting presents a viable alternative. Yet the private rented sector in Hong Kong is equally unaffordable. In 2006, only one in eight households(13 per cent) lived in the private rental sector. Young people who live independently are rare – only 11 per cent of private renters were in their twenties. Yet a reduction in the supply of new flats in the last decade has pushed up private sector rents to more than 50 per cent higher than five years before (Rating and Valuation Department, 2010). In fact, the difference between rent and mortgage outgoings has been narrowed to 10 to 20 percent for newly built flats. In reacting to the huge demand for private rental units, entrepreneurial landlords have adopted an innovative approach. Rather than simply providing a shared flat for multiple occupation to increase supply, they renovate the flats into self-contained en-suites. Despite their extremely small size, often only 10 to 15 square meters, such flats are extremely popular because of their relatively low rent levels and central locations. However, most of the "sub-divided" flats are being altered without official permission, as they are unlikely to comply with fire and health regulations. Recent casualties in fire tragedies have shown the existence of these fire risks and the government is taking action to tackle such illegally altered structures.

Housing policy impediments

Forrest in this volume argues that, in a society in which leaving home and marriage are simultaneous decisions, it is not surprising to find that it is not easy to get public support for housing for young people. Such sentiment is particularly prevalent in Hong Kong. The need of young people for independent living is often undermined. Single persons as a group have least priority, if they are eligible for housing assistance at all.

Assisted homeownership programmes (HOS), launched in the late 1970s as shared equity housing, have helped tens of thousands of first-time buyers to overcome the income and wealth constraints in home buying. However, the programmes only included households formed by "related" persons. Even young couples need to be legally married before they are eligible, and single persons were totally excluded. In fact, such schemes were targeted mainly at public tenants, who need to surrender their public housing units, and thus competition among non-public tenant first-time buyers has been keen. As waiting time for public rental housing used to be very long, so assisted homeownership scheme buyers who need to take the public tenant route tend to be in their middle age. Added to such groups are sitting tenants who bought their public rental flats when the sale of public rental housing was reintroduced on a large scale in late 1990s.

Hence, it is not surprising that assisted homeowners, who made up 16 per cent of the population in 2006, were largely people in middle to old age. The proportion of young people in this tenure is small. As shown in Figure 7.3, households whose heads were born after the 1970s are under-represented. In fact, the proportion of HOS owners dropped during the period 2001–2006 among those born after the 1960s. This is probably associated with the improved affordability for these groups

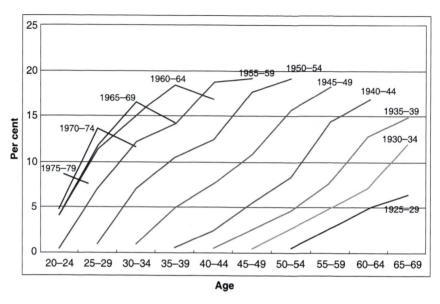

FIGURE 7.3 Cohort trajectories in assisted homeownership schemes, 1981–2006.
Source: Author's reanalysis of the Population Census 1981–2006
Note: Tenant Purchase Scheme included

in the private housing market, as it was no longer necessary to opt for assisted homeownership, which has always been their second priority. Practically none of the young householders in the sector live independently. Some of them formed independent nuclear families (sometimes having been pushed to reschedule their marriage plans) and many of them may just be "owners in name" who hold the title for their family as it is easier for owners who are young and have a stable income to get a mortgage.

Public rental housing is equally discriminatory towards young people, albeit that, unlike the assisted homeownership scheme, young people do have the right to make an application for rental housing. However, this is largely a by-product the Hong Kong Housing Authority's introduction of a housing scheme for single people in the 1990s, for which the main target was the single elderly. In the earlier years of its introduction, no age limits were set. This created little uneasiness as the number of single young applicants was very small. Concern grew, however, in the early 2000s. This was partly because the number of young single applicants was increasing rapidly, but perhaps it was largely a political gesture in response to the anticipated reduction in public housing supply, after a brief increase in supply during the first few years of the new Hong Kong Special Administrative Region Government.

From 2007 to 2010, applicants in the single, non-elderly queue increased 3.5 times more quickly than applicants in other groups, and in late 2010 this group constituted 42 per cent (HKHA, 2011) of the general waiting list (which has 145,000 households on it). This is a substantial increase from 34 per cent in 2007.

Amongst the single, non-elderly applicants, 44 per cent belonged to the post-eighties generation. In fact, nearly one quarter (24 per cent) of new applicants in 2010 were under the age of 30. These young, single applicants were also indirectly portrayed as undeserving of housing. Both the Hong Kong Housing Authority and the media emphasized, intentionally or otherwise, that a substantial proportion of these post-eighties applicants possessed postsecondary qualifications (40 per cent in late 2010), an apparent implication that they should not rely on the state to solve their housing problems.

To maintain the policy pledge of allocation within three years of application, at the same time as avoiding the need to increase public housing supply, single non-elderly applicants were taken out of the general waiting list system to form a separate queue in 2005. A "quota and point" system is applied, in which priority of allocation depends both on waiting time (12 points per year) and age of the applicant (three points per year). Younger applicants are in a disadvantaged position. An applicant of 18 years of age who has been in the queue for five years has the same score as a new applicant aged 38 (or needs to wait 11 years to equal the score of a new applicant aged 60). In mid-2010, the average score of singleton applicants under 30 was only 36, whereas the corresponding score for applicants over 50 was 125 (LCQ17, 2010). With an extremely limited quota for single non-elderly applicants – only 1593 in 2007 and 1948 in 2009 (HKHA, 2011), as against a total allocation to the waiting list of 18,700 and 20,875 (HKHA, 2008, 2010), respectively – applicants in the single non-elderly queue in fact needed a high score to secure a flat: an average of 138 (for those aged 31–40), 141 (41–50), and 147 (50 and over) (LCQ17, 2010). Thus in practice no applicant under the age of 30 was able to enter the public rental sector as an independent household.

Amongst applicants under the age of 30 in 2010, 90 per cent of them were still living with their family and thus had no urgent need for a home. About another one third (31 per cent) of applicants (HKHA, 2011) were over-qualified, as they earned more than the income limit (HK$9300 in 2010, which is more or less the median individual income for Hong Kong). Hence, given that their chances of getting a public flat in the short run are slim, their applications may instead signal the desire of young people for independent living. This is confirmed in surveys conducted by the Hong Kong Housing Authority. The overwhelming majority of applicants under the age of 30 (81 per cent in 2010) indicated a desire to live independently as the reason for applying for public housing, whereas many of the applicants over 30 years old were also concerned with improvement of quality of living and reducing their housing costs (Table 7.3).

Such a desire for independent living may have existed for a long time but has been suppressed because of high housing costs in the private housing sector – out of reach for most young people. Public housing is at least a hope that could be realized if they can wait long enough. Yet with a growing demand from young people for public housing, but with little chance of getting a public flat, there is an increased risk of stirring up further frustration among the already disillusioned post-eighties generation. In such a context, the idea of developing hostels for

TABLE 7.3 Reasons for applying for public rental housing.

Reasons for applying for public housing	Under 30 years (%)			30 years or over (%)		
	2008	2009	2010	2008	2009	2010
Want to live on my own / Want to split from existing household	80	73	81	54	56	63
High rent in present accommodation	13	14	12	32	27	30
Small living area in present accommodation	42	29	18	40	22	19
Poor living environment in present accommodation	11	4	4	21	13	10
Unemployment / Decline in income	10	6	3	24	16	7
Other	—	1	—	1	2	—

Source: HKHA, 2011
Note: Respondents were allowed to choose up to two items, so columns do not total 100%

working youth was put forward in a recent Policy Address (Policy Address, 2011). However, a welfare approach is to be adopted, in which a small number of hostel spaces will be offered by welfare agencies either from their current spare capacity or by building new hostels on land earmarked for "government, institution or community" development. The intention to avoid triggering a long-term housing commitment to young people is evident.

The changing meaning of housing consumption

Whatever the broad statistical trends in the past, it is important to understand and explore the social meaning of housing consumption for young people. How does housing fit into aspirations and expectations for future lifestyles? Exploring the social meaning of housing consumption will also provide insights into issues of housing affordability. The analysis that follows is based mainly on a small number of interviews with young people in Hong Kong, conducted as part of an ESRC project in 2007 (see the acknowledgements section at the end of this chapter) and one focus group with young people undertaken for this chapter in early 2011. The interviewees were split almost equally in terms of gender, and all had completed their postsecondary education. All were aspiring middle class, engaged in managerial or professional jobs. Four interviewees who were married at the time of the interview had bought their homes and the rest were staying with their parents. None of the unmarried interviewees lived independently. Several themes emerged in the interviews.

Independent living and proximity to parents

Perhaps in compliance with prevailing social norms, none of the interviewees had an expectation of (and they had not pursued) independent living before forming families of their own. This includes those who had experience of living independently, either in their college years or when working in other countries. However, reasons behind this are complex. Motives are mixed, and include feelings of mutual support and obligation to stay in the parental home, and the convenience of not having to do housework, as well as saving on living costs. Of course, high housing costs in Hong Kong are one of the most important hurdles to independent living. Most of the respondents living with their parents made regular contributions to the household, some even giving one third of their salary:

> My income is low and I cannot afford to live independently. In fact, although I lived in a student hostel when I did my undergrad, I do not fancy living on my own. I do not want to do housework. I work in the creative industry and usually have to work overtime. Staying in the parental home, which is located in the urban area, is more convenient to me.
>
> *Single women in her late twenties, living with her parents*

> I think it is natural to stay with parents before you marry. It is close to my workplace and saves travel time. I also make a contribution to my parents, one third of my salary, for my daily living expenses as well as there being a sense of responsibility. My mum says she will save part of it for my wedding. At the same time, I am also saving for my own home.
>
> *Single university graduate in his mid-twenties, living with his parents*

Yet neither of these interviewees thought they would live with their parents after marriage. This also matches the statistics from the previous section indicating that single young people seldom live independently, whereas childless married couples who lived with their parents (or in-laws) were also in a minority. However, if couples not living with parents have a choice, they prefer to live close by. Again, mutual support, practical or emotional, is their concern. If parents live nearby, family gatherings can be more frequent, parents can help the young couple with housework or child minding, and children will find it easier to attend to their elderly parents.

> I moved out after getting married but we bought a flat which is close to my parents. My parents can help to look after my baby boy and we often come back to my parents' home for dinner.
>
> *Research assistant in his mid-thirties with a PhD, married to a nurse*

Housing as investment and security

Nearly all interviewees had a rather traditional view of housing as a secure investment which would enhance their sense of security. Most of them were determined to buy when they found the time was ripe, though some had reservations about whether they could afford to buy the kind of flat they wanted. There was only one exception, a couple who ran their own business. They were renting privately but were reluctant to commit to buy, as they found it more profitable to invest money elsewhere – house price levels were too high to generate any handsome return:

> We have been looking for a flat to buy, around 800 to 1000 square feet, but they are too expensive. Not value for money to buy now. It is better to deploy the money for other investments which can be more profitable. I enjoy staying in rented accommodation.
>
> *Married woman in her early thirties who ran a business with her husband*

A few others regarded the prevailing price levels as too risky for owner occupiers. Yet they did buy properties for investment while they stayed in the parental home or in rental properties. Most of these investments were jointly held with other family members. However, nearly all the interviewees perceived housing in Hong Kong as not being good value for money, particularly those who had lived abroad for some years:

> I am staying in a rental accommodation with my parents, though I did live for a long time on my own while I stayed in the States. It is more spacious in the old property we are staying in. It is too risky to buy your home but properties are good investments. So I have bought two flats with my parents for investment.
>
> *Single man in his late twenties, a returning emigrant living with his parents*

Constrained choice and the ability to pay

A convenient location was the prime concern for all respondents when choosing where to buy. They wanted their homes to be close to their workplace or their parents, but at the same time near shopping and leisure activities. Since most people in Hong Kong use public transport, locations along the railway lines were their preferred choice. With a high priority on investment return, most of them would prefer a flat in the urban areas, where property appreciated more than in the suburbs.

However, all but two interviewees faced the dilemma of wanting a home they did not think they could afford. They were, in general, pessimistic about realizing their dream homes. Jobs are not as secure as before and there is also more uncertainty about the prospect of continuing income improvement. Hence, making decisions about a long term commitment like home buying is more difficult. Given that higher education in Hong Kong is getting expensive and a second degree, usually on a self-financed basis, is becoming essential for a good job, their ability to pay for their home is eroded by the burden of student loan repayments as well as the need to save for further studies. Although most of them did not expect help from their parents towards home buying, they would certainly not turn it down if it were offered.

> I am staying in a public housing flat with my brother. Quite spacious. Buying a flat is too expensive for me and I am satisfied with the 300 square feet we

have now. Maybe I'll buy when I get married but not until I pay back my
student loan and finish my master's degree

Male master's student in his late twenties

Concluding remarks

Two distinct features relating to housing are apparent in the transition of local
young people to adulthood. On the one hand, the overwhelming majority of young
people in Hong Kong stay with their parents until they marry; those who live independently are rare. On the other hand, the need for independent living has been
largely absent from policy debates. Cultural norms, notably familism, have been
widely perceived as the underlying driving force for young people to stay in the
parental home. It is perhaps the same force that pushes the housing needs of young
people off the policy agenda.

The life-course perspective offers valuable insight, allowing the the underlying
dynamics of housing for young people to be examined. From the life-course
perspective, life events can be understood as the outcomes of a complex interaction
between individual time, institutional time and historical time. With respect to
individual time, biographies of young people are no longer being dictated by life
stages that were fairly standardized for older generations. Education and employment,
as well as marriage and child rearing, are less standardized, and more uncertain and
risky. The interaction with institutional and historical time is also getting more
complicated. The patterns of co-residence and, conversely, independent living
are significant life events relating to housing for young people which can illuminate
such interaction, particularly against a local context.

Familism is indisputably a significant force in sustaining social development in
Hong Kong (Lau, 1978), as well as an important provider of social services, particularly in the time welfare state support was very limited. Yet it is not clear whether
it is the pulling force of familism that draws young people to stay at home or the
hurdle of high housing costs that hinders them from leaving. Indirect evidence at
least hints that some subtle changes have taken place in this interaction. The
individual time and biographical profiles would suggest that prolonged education
and an unstable job market have made young people financially less independent
and more vulnerable. This intensifies their dependence if they have to rely on their
more resource-rich parents. At the same time, housing is in general less affordable,
but a fluctuating housing market has offered more opportunities for young people
with more secure jobs or for those who can secure financial support from the
family. Hence individual time interacts with historical time (or the economic and
housing cycle) to produce greater levels of dependence on the family among young
people, hence leading to a higher level of co-residence.

Waiting in the queue for public housing, however, opens up the possibility of a
cheaper independent living alternative. The continuous upsurge of young people
on the waiting list signifies, at least to some extent, the explicit expression of a desire
for independent living. Hence, at the same time as their dependence on parents for

housing has increased, their demand for independent living has in fact been gradually growing. These seemingly contradictory developments are not paradoxical but reflect a central dilemma for most young people. As shown by responses from in-depth interviews, not only does the individual time of moving out of parental homes interact with the institutional time of cultural expectation, the historical time of ups and downs in the housing market also matters, as the asset value of the home they buy is another important consideration. Other more utilitarian considerations, concerning such things as housework and convenience, are also at work, and family linkage is still a significant factor, finding expression in their notion of "independence with proximity."

From our analysis on cohort trajectories, we observe that the baby boomers (people born in the 1960s) took advantage of the housing market and housing policy in attaining homeownership. It is in such a context that homeownership has emerged as a normative pattern for the life-course, and something younger generations aspire to. But economic turbulence in the last two decades, particularly the Asian Financial Crisis and the SARS epidemic, has made such housing futures very uncertain, especially for the younger cohorts. At the same time, differentiation among young people is increasing. Not only is there substantial variation in income and job prospects between and within professional and white collar occupations, and thus expanded gaps within the younger cohorts, family background also becomes significant where home buying is concerned. Intergenerational transfer is increasingly pivotal for young home buyers. From the cohort analysis of homeownership and occupational and educational attainment, there are clear signs of generational fissures between the baby boomers and the rest of the population. This is an important issue which helps to shed light on our understanding of the housing pathways of the young generation in the context of a rapidly restructuring economy and compressed economic cycles, as well as an increasingly divided social and political environment.

Acknowledgements

The research for this chapter is part of a broader project, *Housing the Post Eighties Generation: Attitudes, Aspirations and Future Trajectories*, supported by the Hong Kong RGC (No. 9041696). The chapter also draws on research funded by the UK Economic and Social Research Council, *Housing Assets and Intergenerational Dynamics in East Asian Societies* (RES-062-23-0187).

References

Anderson, I. (2001) *Pathways Through Homelessness: Towards a Dynamic Analysis*, Urban Frontiers Programme, University Of Western Sydney, Research Seminar, 27 March 2001. http://www.urbancentre.utoronto.ca/pdfs/elibrary/Anderson_Pathways-Homeless_.pdf (accessed 20 November 2011).

Beck, U. (1994) The reinvention of politics: towards a theory of reflexive modernisation, in U. Beck, A. Giddens and S. Lash, *Reflexive Modernization: Politics, Tradition and Aesthetics in the Modern Social Order*, Cambridge: Polity Press.

Beck, U. and Beck-Gernsheim, E. (1995) *The Normal Chaos of Love*, Cambridge: Polity Press.

Brannen, J. and Nilsen, A. (2002) Young people's time perspectives: from youth to adulthood, *Sociology*, 36: 513–537.

Census and Statistics Department (2004) *Quarterly Report on General Household Survey*, Hong Kong: Census and Statistics Department.

Census and Statistics Department (2010) *Annual Digest of Statistics 2009*. http://www.statistics.gov.hk/publication/general_stat_digest/B10100032011AN11B0100.pdf (accessed 10 August 2011).

Census and Statistics Department (undated) *Economic Development of Hong Kong over the Past 40 Years*. http://www.censtatd.gov.hk/FileManager/EN/Content_1064/A2_E.pdf (accessed 10 December 2011).

Centaline (2011) *Affordability Ratio Table*. http://hk.centanet.com/icms/template.aspx?series=174 (accessed 4 May 2011).

Clapham, D. (2002) Housing pathways: a post modern analytical framework, *Housing, Theory and Society*, 19(2): 57–68.

Clark, W.A.V., Deurloo, M.C. and Dieleman, F.M. (2003) Housing careers in the United States, 1968–93: modelling the sequencing of housing states, *Urban Studies*, 40(1): 143–160.

Elder, G.H. Jr (1978) Family history and the life course, in T.K. Hareven (ed.) *Transitions: The Family and the Life Course in Historical Perspective*, New York: Academic Press.

Forrest, R. and Murie, A. (1987) The affluent home owner: labour market position and the shaping of housing histories, *Sociological Review*, 35(2): 370–403.

Forrest, R. and Kemeny, J. (1983) Middle class housing careers: the relationship between furnished renting and owner occupation, *Sociological Review*, 30: 208–222.

Forrest, R. and Lee, J. (eds) (2003) *Housing and Social Change : East-West Perspectives*, London: Routledge.

Furlong, A. and Cartmel, F. (1997) *Young People and Social Change: Individualization and Risk in Late Modernity*, Buckingham: Open University Press.

Hareven, T.K. (ed.) (1978) *Transitions: The Family and the Life Course in Historical Perspective*, New York: Academic Press.

Heinz, W.R. and Krüger, H. (2001) Life-course: innovations and challenges for social research, *Current Sociology*, 49 (2): 29–52.

Hong Kong Housing Authority (HKHA) (2008) *Hong Kong Housing Authority Annual Report 2007*. http://www.housingauthority.gov.hk/hdw/en/aboutus/publication/haar0708/index.htm (accessed 9 August 2011).

Hong Kong Housing Authority (HKHA) (2010) *Hong Kong Housing Authority Annual Report 2009*. http://www.housingauthority.gov.hk/hdw/en/aboutus/publication/haar0910/index.html (accessed 9 August 2011).

Hong Kong Housing Authority (HKHA) (2011) *Operation of the Quota and Points System for Non-elderly One-person Applicants of Public Rental Housing*, Memorandum for the Subsidised Housing Committee of the Hong Kong Housing Authority, PAPER NO. SHC 8/2011. http://www.housingauthority.gov.hk/hdw/content/document/en/aboutus/ha/paperlibrary1/shc/shc0811.pdf (accessed 20 October 2011).

Kendig, H., Paris, C. and Anderton, N. (1987) *Towards Fair Shares in Australian Housing*, Report prepared for the National Committee of Non-Government Organisations, International Year of Shelter for the Homeless, Canberra: Highland Press.

Lau, S.K. (1978) *Utilitarianistic Familism: The Basis of Political Stability in Hong Kong*, Hong Kong: Social Research Centre, CUHK.

Lawson, J. and Milligan, V. (2007) *International trends in housing and policy responses*, Melbourne: Australian Housing and Urban Research Institute.

LCQ17 (1 December 2010). Allocation of public rental housing flats, Reply of the Government to Legislative Councillor Fred Lee Wah Ming. http://www.info.gov.hk/gia/general/201012/01/P201012010154.htm (accessed 5 September 2011).

Lieberg, M. (2000) *Youth Housing and Exclusion in Sweden*, Eskilstuna: Mälardalens Högskola. http://Mdh.Diva-Portal.Org/Smash/Record.Jsf?Pid=Diva2:213926 (accessed 3 January 2011).

Mayer, K.U. (2000). Promises fulfilled? A review of 20 years of life course research, *Archives Européennes de Sociologie,* 41(2): 259–282.

Payne, J. and Payne, G. (1977) Housing pathways and stratification: a study of life chances in the housing market, *Journal of Social Policy*, 23: 125–156.

Pickvance, G.C. (1974) Life cycle, housing tenure and residential mobility: a path analytic approach, *Urban Studies*, 11(2): 171–188

Policy Address (2011) *Policy Address of the Chief Executive, Hong Kong Special Administrative Region*. http://www.policyaddress.gov.hk/11-12/index.html (accessed 5 November 2011).

Rating and Valuation Department (various years) *Property Review 2010.* http://www.rvd.gov.hk/en/ doc/hkpr11/03A.pdf (accessed 10 December 2011).

Rating and Valuation Department (2010) *Hong Kong Property Review, 2010.* http://www.rvd.gov.hk/en/doc/PR_fullbook/PR2010.pdf (accessed 10 September 2011).

Saunders, P.R. (1990) *A Nation of Home Owners*, London: Unwin Hyman.

Winter, I. and Stone, W. (1998) *Social Polarisation and Housing Careers: Exploring the Interrelationship of Labour and Housing Markets in Australia*, Australian Institute of Family Studies, Working paper No.13. http://www.aifs.gov.au/institute/pubs /WP13.html (accessed 10 November 2011).

World Bank (2011) *World Development Indicators.* http://data.worldbank.org/data-catalog / world-development-indicators?cid=GPD_WDI (accessed 10 December 2011).

Wu, X. (2010). Hong Kong's Post 80 Generation: Profits and Predicaments, Hong Kong: Central Policy Unit. http://www.cpu.gov.hk/tc/documents/new/press/HK's%20Post%2080s%20Generation%20-%20Profiles%20and%20Predicaments.pdf (accessed 10 August 2011).

Xenos, P., Achmad, S., Sheng Lin, H., Keung Luis, P., Podhisita, C., Raymundo, C. and Thapa, S. (2006) Delayed Asian transitions to adulthood: a perspective from national youth surveys, *Asian Population Studies*, 2(2): 149–185.

8

YOUTH HOUSING PROBLEMS IN CHINA

Yapeng Zhu

Introduction

Economic reform and the opening up of China to the world have transformed its economy and social class formation. This is particularly the case in the housing field. In the past three decades, the Chinese housing system has undergone profound changes associated with the launch of housing reforms. As a result, the in-kind welfare housing provision system based on the work unit system in the socialist period has been replaced by a market-oriented housing system in which accessibility to housing largely depends on ability to pay. A majority of urban households have become homeowners. This has led to the expansion of an emerging middle class, which is considered both the result of the social engineering of the reformist state and a consequence of the opening up of the economy and emergence of a private housing market (Tomba 2004). Although there have been some studies on the consequences of housing reforms in China (for instance, Wang 2004; Wang and Murie 2000), there has been little research which explores systematically the impact of housing policy on young people in Chinese cities. This chapter seeks to fill this gap by examining the current housing conditions of Chinese youth and the various housing problems they face. Contrary to the conventional wisdom, which holds that the middle class benefit from economic reform, our findings suggest that, while pro-homeownership policy and housing marketization reforms have created rising wealth for some, there has been a serious housing crisis among Chinese youth. This includes even the most privileged social group, young civil servants. Young people in China are struggling with various kinds of housing problems as a result of escalating housing prices and unfavourable institutional arrangements.

Housing restructuring, changing governance and the creation of the youth housing problem

Housing reform in China aims to transform the socialist welfare housing system into a market-oriented one through housing commercialization, housing privatization and housing socialization. The trajectory of housing reform evolved incrementally. Starting in the late 1970s, piecemeal reforms and experiments were carried out in pilot cities. Drawing lessons from these experiments, waves of housing reform took place in 1988, 1991, 1994 and 1995. Various strategies were adopted, ranging from gradual rent rises, the subsidized sale of public flats, the establishment of the housing provident fund scheme, and restoration of the private housing market. While these measures contributed to housing commercialization and privatization, they helped little in terms of housing socialization and led to a dual track housing provision system. The coexistence of internal welfare housing provision in the public sector and the open market in the private sector distorted the housing system and aggravated housing inequalities between the public and private sectors, between different work units and even between employees within a work unit. A key factor was that work units entered the housing market as irrational actors, buying houses at market prices and distributing them to their employees as welfare (Bian *et al.* 1996).

In response to these thorny housing problems and the economic slump brought about by the Southeast Asian financial crisis, the central government initiated housing monetarization reform in 1998. The new reform sought to replace provision of in-kind welfare housing by offering cash subsidies in the public sector and integrating the two markets. This opened a new chapter in the housing reform process. Besides pushing forward housing commodification and privatization, the 1998 reform made a breakthrough in housing socialization. The relationship between work units and their employees was severed, as recommended by the World Bank (World Bank 1992).

However, the housing monetarization reform had differentiated impacts on different social groups. A distinctive benefit gap emerged between 'old people' and 'new people' within governmental departments and public institutions; between employees in governmental departments and public institutions, and workers in state-owned enterprises (SOEs); and between employees in the public and private sectors. This can be attributed to the policy design and poor implementation. In most regions, the reform was implemented mainly in governmental departments and public institutions. While SOEs were granted discretion to implement the same reforms, most of them found it financially impossible to do so due to poor performance. Employees in the private sector were totally excluded from the reform and had to meet their housing needs through their own means. In addition to huge gaps between the public and the private sector, and between workers in SOEs and cadres in governmental departments and public institutions, cadres were also differentiated into 'old people' and 'new people', subject to different policy arrangements (Lee and Zhu 2006; Zhu 2009). The differences in housing benefits within this privileged group were no smaller than those between the public and private sectors:'old people' were able to buy public flats at heavy discounts or received a comparatively generous lump-sum subsidy with which they could afford to buy private housing, whereas 'new people' were only eligible to receive a monthly housing allowance of a specific sum or a certain proportion of their wages over a long period. Overall, the allowance was set too low to rent a room, let alone to buy a property. The implementation was also poor and selective across the country (Zhu 2009). Roughly speaking, reforms for 'old people' were comparatively better implemented in most cities, while subsidizing 'new people' was carried out poorly, because of either insufficient resource or resistance from young employees, who preferred a flat to a cash allowance[1] (Zhu 2009).

The housing restructuring process has dramatically transformed China's housing system, urban development and housing governance. It has had significant social, macro-economic and spatial impacts (Adams 2009; Wang 2000; Wang and Murie 2000). First, the state withdrew substantially from its role in housing provision, confining its attention to low- and medium-income households, with most urban residents having to meet their housing needs through the market. Second, positioned as one of the mainstay industries, the real estate sector has monopolized housing provision and accounts for a substantial share of the national economy. Third, due to the pro-homeowning tenure policy, the housing market has been booming in terms of housing investment, housing consumption and house prices. Housing has become one of the most valuable household assets. Fourth, the state, and in particular local government, relies mainly on revenue from land lease and taxation and levies on the real estate and property exchange. There is widespread corruption related to land acquisition associated with big projects. Last, due to skyrocketing house prices, more and more urban residents are unable to afford to buy properties.

As explained earlier, there has been no specific housing policy for young people. And although at the beginning many young people welcomed the monetarization reforms as occasioning clearer property rights, more choice, more social justice, and a more optimistic future (Zhu 2010), most of them are now suffering from the overheated real estate market and rampant property prices.

The housing situation for Chinese youth in the twenty-first century

The restructuring of the housing system and changing housing governance has had a profound influence on Chinese youth. To many of them, housing is not only a necessity, but is also intimately related to falling in love, getting married, job preferences and general lifestyle. In short, housing is vital to youth.

Due to limited information, however, it is difficult to provide a comprehensive picture of the housing situation of young people in China. According to a survey of 'residential conditions of Chinese youth in major and medium cities' jointly conducted by Insight China magazine and Tsinghua Media Survey Lab in Beijing, Shanghai, Guangzhou, Shenzhen and other major cities in China (Ouyang 2011), less than 40 per cent of Chinese young people (25–35 years old) are satisfied with their living conditions, while one fifth are greatly dissatisfied with living conditions of less than 10 square metres per capita space. In terms of housing tenure, 38 per cent purchased commercial housing, 23 per cent were living in their parents' flats, 22 per cent were renting and the rest were either living in dormitories or welfare housing, or buying affordable housing. Among renters, 61 per cent rented a separate apartment while 26 per cent had to share a flat. The rest were renting in a group (Ouyang 2011). Unlike western counterparts, private renting is very much a 'residualized tenure' in China, with tenants having no sense of security and little sense of belonging to the city.

Notably, Chinese youth attaches extreme importance to housing. Owning a home is a prerequisite for getting married, for many young Chinese. More than two thirds of the respondents in the survey explicitly stated that they were not willing to rent a flat when they married, while only a third could accept entering marriage without owning a home. This finding is supported by the distributional pattern of home ownership. Half of the married couples owned a commercial flat, while only 14 per cent of singles did so (Ouyang 2011). In terms of planning for the near future, more than one third of respondents were planning to buy a home within three years.

The perils of youth's dream of owning a home

Affordability is a major problem for most young people in China. Two thirds of urban youth are suffering some kind of pressure due to high housing costs: 54 per cent of survey respondents said that they had to be economical in everyday life, 43 per cent felt worried, 40 per cent had cut back on leisure and entertainment, 30 per cent lacked a sense of safety and 25 per cent were fearful of losing their jobs. A quarter of the young respondents said they had postponed their marriage, and 21 per cent had delayed child rearing (Ouyang 2011). Also, due to the high living costs, nearly half (48.7 per cent) of those living in the first frontier of Chinese cities, such as Beijing, Shanghai, Guangzhou, and Shenzhen, felt that life would be more manageable if they moved to a smaller city. Squeezed by the housing problem, 'getting away' from Beijing, Shanghai and Guangzhou has become a reluctant choice for many young college graduates.

Migrant workers and their housing problems

In addition to well-educated white-collar young people who seek to own a flat, migrant workers are also plagued with a variety of housing problems. According to the State Statistical Bureau (State Statistical Bureau of the People's Republic of China 2010), there were over 145 million peasant workers, among them some 30 million who were working in urban areas with their whole families. Nearly two thirds (65.1 per cent) were male and only one third (34.9 per cent) were female. Most migrants were young: 42 per cent were aged between 16 and 25 and a further

20 per cent were in the 26 to 30 age band. In terms of their marital status, 56 per cent were married and 41.5 per cent were single. Their average monthly salary was only 1417 yuan (1 USD = 6.3788 CNY as at 29 November 2011). The majority of migrant workers relied on their employers for dwellings. One third were living in dorms provided by their employers, 10 per cent lived on working sites or in shanties and some 8 per cent were living in their production unit or where they were doing business. Around 17 per cent had to share a rental apartment and a similar proportion were renting individually. Less than 1 per cent of migrant workers had bought properties. In terms of living expenditure, more than half received free accommodation provided by their employers, 7 per cent received housing subsidies from employers for renting privately, while 42 per cent received neither dormitories nor housing allowances from their employers. Considering their extremely poor salary, on average they could only spare 245 yuan (representing more than 17 per cent of their salary) on accommodation. This meant that they had to tolerate extremely poor living conditions. In order to minimize living costs, it was common for several people (sometimes more than ten) to share a small single room (State Statistical Bureau of the People's Republic of China 2010).

A housing crisis for a privileged social class: the case of civil servants in Guangzhou

Guangzhou spearheaded the housing reforms in the late 1980s as a way of slowly shifting the economic burden of providing conventional welfare housing. As a result of successive housing reforms and rapid economic development, the living conditions of urban residents in Guangzhou has substantially improved. By the end of 2000, 10.95 million square metres of housing had been built and living space per capita in the city had increased from 3.82 square metres in 1978 to 13.32 square metres in 2000 (Liao 2001). Nonetheless, housing assets were unequally distributed and there were widespread housing inequalities for workers in different sectors and work units. In 2000, there were still 6306 households suffering from various kinds of housing problems and 255 households were living in extremely poor conditions, with per capita living space of less than 6 square metres (Liao 2001). Determined to improve the housing situation, Guangzhou city government began to implement a new housing allowance scheme in 1997, aiming to terminate the welfare housing distribution (Guangzhou People's Municipal Government 1998). However, the scheme had limited success. The welfare housing system was not actually dismantled until the end of 1999 because of strong opposition from the civil service. Indeed, there was a delay of almost a year after the government offically terminated the welfare housing system and replaced it with the Housing Monetarization Policy (HMP) in 1998. Such a slow pace of implementation actually provided opportunities for civil servants to catch the 'last train' of welfare housing provision, further aggravating the already unfair housing allocation.

Initially, housing monetarization reform involved mainly government departments, public organizations and the state enterprises (SOEs). The rationale was that since government departments and major SOEs formed the cornerstone of political stability, housing reform should take priority in these sectors to ensure smooth transition and implementation. In addition, the model was characterized by a differentiation between 'old people' and 'new people', ensuring that the 'old' civil servants would be well protected while 'young' people would be handled under a different system. In fact, whether civil servants belonged to the 'old' or 'new ' group was not dependent on their actual age. Those who joined the service before 29 September 1997 were regarded as 'old people', otherwise they were 'new people'. This line was arbitrarily drawn only because the decision to launch the new reform was made on that day. 'New people' were only eligible to join the housing allowance scheme, whereas the old group were granted autonomy to choose between the new scheme or to continue benefiting from the welfare housing system. Such a scheme served to create equality issues as 'old people' already enjoyed a relatively higher level of benefits.

The 'new' and young are only eligible to receive a monthly housing allowance ranging from 233 to 933 yuan for 25 years, based on their job seniority (see Table 8.1). Housing allowances increases if they are promoted. The level of housing allowance is determined in relation to house price, space entitlements, proportion of housing allowance backed by the government and timespan of subsidy provision (Cheng 1998). Its rationale is that the burden of civil servant housing must be borne by both the government and individuals, on the basis that a couple can use their housing allowance and ordinary savings to afford a small flat of 50 square metres in area, at 3500 yuan per square metre (Cheng 1998). The government normally undertakes to cover 80 per cent of the cost of the home purchase with the remainder borne by civil servants. The establishment of the housing allowance scheme demonstrates the government's efforts to change the housing distribution system and to reduce, if not eliminate, the problems of the old welfare housing system, such as unfair distribution and limited tenure choice. With the housing monetarization

TABLE 8.1 Level of housing allowance in Guangzhou.

Rank	Monthly subsidy (yuan)	Space entitlement (m²)
Junior staff	233	25
Manager	280	30
Vice-head	327	35
Head	373	40
Vice-director	420	45
Director	467	50
Vice-department	513	55
Department	607	65
Vice-mayor	747	80
Mayor	933	100

Source: Guangzhou People's Municipal Government 1998

reform in full force, work units were expected to cease providing in-kind welfare housing directly to their employees. Workers are expected to be able to garner sufficient home-purchasing power from the new subsidies policy together with personal or family savings, as well as whatever was saved in the housing provident fund. Ideally, young civil servants should be better off when compared to ordinary workers in terms of affordability, and hence more able to purchase housing.

The housing situation of civil servants in Guangzhou

Although the housing reform aims to help civil servants become homeowners, owning a home is a dream beyond the reach of most young civil servants. A survey conducted by the Bureau of State Land and Housing Administration of Guangzhou in November 2008, involving eleven government departments and 4643 civil servants, revealed enormous housing affordability problems even for young civil servants, who used to be one of the more privileged groups during the welfare housing era.

Being integral to China's provincial administration policy, most young civil servants are recruited from outside the province to ensure impartiality and to prevent the building up of local power bases. These young civil servants are mainly university graduates recruited in highly competitive open exams. More than half of those surveyed (61 per cent) were married and most of them were in their early thirties. Therefore, housing is undoubtedly one of their primary concerns. In terms of income, they have a stable and reasonably good salary with minor differentials across departments and administrative ranks. In 2009 the average monthly salaries for the group at the provincial, municipal and district levels were 3108, 4453 and 4300 yuan respectively.[2] Comparing the average salary of 3348 yuan in 2007, they evidently belong to the middle-income strata in Guangzhou. Since 2000, housing monetarization reform has been strictly enforced for all civil servants in Guangzhou and they therefore have to meet their housing needs through the market. According to the survey, many of them were facing affordability problem, as only 38 per cent had bought their first home. Compared to the homeownership rate of 91 per cent[3] in 2007, this social group had a lower rate. Figure 8.1 shows the relationship between the time of joining the civil service and the rate of homeownership. The homeowner rate for civil servants who joined after 2005 was only 14 per cent, reflecting with soaring housing prices in the city which made it more difficult for them to afford a flat.

Noticeably, civil servants in municipal and district government departments had a higher homeownership rate than those at the provincial level (see Figure 8.2). This is quite different from the situation in the in-kind housing distribution system, under which work units in higher administrative ranks always had better housing situations (Logan, Bian and Bian 1999), but congruent with the fact that the wage is higher in municipal and district government departments than at the corresponding provincial level. It reflects that salary has become a crucial factor in determining one's living conditions and tenure choice. To some extent, the logic of housing distribution has changed from a mechanism based on one's administrative rank and seniority to one based on market competiveness.

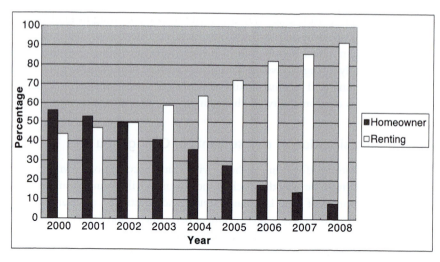

FIGURE 8.1 Housing tenure of young civil servants in Guangzhou.
Source: Bureau of State Land and Housing Administration of Guangzhou survey of housing situation of civil servants in Guangzhou City, conducted in November 2008

Renting as the major tenure

The majority of young civil servants in the survey housed themselves through renting (45 per cent) or sharing houses with their parents or friends (20 per cent).

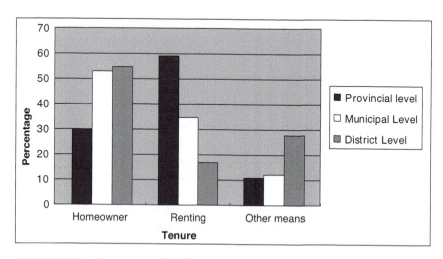

FIGURE 8.2 Housing tenure of civil servants in government departments at different levels in Guangzhou.
Source: Bureau of State Land and Housing Administration of Guangzhou survey of housing situation of civil servants in Guangzhou City, conducted in November 2008

Of the tenants, 73 per cent were renting public housing or dormitories while the remaining 27 per cent rented a private flat. Renters preferred living in the older districts, near to their workplaces. The average size of a rented flat was 36 square metres, with a monthly rent of 517 yuan. Clearly, access to makeshift accommodation provided by work units is the most important way for young civil servants to obtain housing, demonstrating the continuing role of work units in providing housing to their employees in the context of the booming housing market.

Overall, the housing conditions for new civil servants were quite poor, and they were not at all satisfied. Many of them were struggling to pay their mortgage under high financial pressure, eagerly expecting a salary rise, an increase in housing allowance levels or housing provident funds and other sources of financial support, such as interest rate subsidies for mortgages. Compared to 'old people', who bought their public flats at nominal prices, the new civil servants felt unequally treated. The asset gap between access to a small amount of housing subsidy for the young civil servants and access to housing benefits in kind was huge, and there seemed to be no sound reason for it.

Well educated, competent and qualified, this social group saw themselves, and were seen, as an elite in Chinese society. They had high expectations about housing and other life necessities. However, there was a sharp contrast between their high expectations and reality. In short, new civil servants in Guangzhou who began work after housing monetarization reform was carried out in 2000 were experiencing serious housing affordability problems. For many, irrespective of whether they owned or rented, housing expenditure accounted for a third to a half of their household income. Under such financial pressure, many of them had delayed marriage or having a family. The housing problems for this group are now so serious that the local authority is concerned that housing issues might affect the organizational stability of the civil service, and civil servants might abuse their power or use bribery to gain access to housing.[4]

The problem of housing affordability

House prices have climbed far higher than the buying capacity of ordinary wage earners, including civil servants. For example, house prices in Guangzhou have been rising since 2000 – from 3900 yuan per square metre in 2000 to 9346 yuan per square metre in 2009 (see Figure 8.3). With the rapid urban sprawl, house prices in the central area of the city have more than quadrupled. In contrast, over the same period salary rises in Guangzhou have been moderate. As Figure 8.3 shows, although both salaries and house prices have increased since 2000, housing prices have risen much more rapidly than salaries and disposable incomes, especially after 2005, when the housing market boomed and house prices rocketed. The widening gap between moderate household income rises and rapidly increasing house prices was the major reason for the poor purchasing power of ordinary local people, including civil servants. Even a senior official complained that house prices in Guangzhou were so high that he could not afford one square metre with two months' salary (Huang 2009).

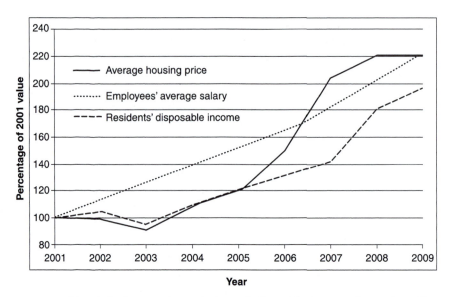

FIGURE 8.3 Trends in house prices, salaries and disposable income, Guangzhou City, 2000–2008.

Source: Guangzhou Statistical Yearbook 2001–2008; figures for 2009 are from the *Guangzhou Statistical Communiqué of National Economy and Social Development for the Year 2009*

Note: The average commercial house price is calculated as the total value of commercial housing sales contracts divided by the floor space of commercial housing sold.

Poor policy design

The housing affordability problems of young civil servants can also be attributed to flaws in the policy design of the housing allowance scheme. First, as outlined earlier, in 1997 policy-makers adopted a very standard house price of 3500 yuan per square metre as the basis for calculating housing allowances. In reality, in 1998 house prices for Economical Housing ranged from 3000 to 3500 yuan per square metre and the average commercial house price was 4400 yuan per square metre. The adoption of such a low standard housing price directly determined the low level of housing allowance and reflected the financial pressures on local government.

Housing affordability problems were further aggravated by the freezing of housing allowance levels for the past ten years, despite the fact that average house prices at the end of 2007 were three times the standard price set in 1997. In such circumstances, there is no doubt that most civil servants cannot afford to buy a flat in the market, irrespective of whether or not they receive a housing allowance. As housing allowances have not risen in line with property prices, their role in assisting homeownership has become negligible.

Second, the space entitlement was very small. This greatly reduces the effectiveness of the housing allowance scheme in supporting home purchase. In order to maximize profit, real estate developers in China tend to produce spacious, high-end flats which are far beyond the purchasing power of young civil servants. In recent years, the average flat size of newly built housing in the market has been more than 100 square metres, and the average second-hand flat size no smaller than 84 square metres – much bigger than the space entitlement stipulated in the housing allowance scheme. Thus, it would be difficult to find suitable flats on the market even if house prices were not rising. As it is, average house prices have increased by a factor of more than four the past ten years.

Third, the level of housing allowance was calculated based on the unit of the family, rather than individuals. This further reduced purchasing power. As stated previously, the housing allowance was calculated to enable recipients to be able to afford a suitably sized flat (according to rank) at the standard house price of 3500 yuan per square metre. However, this standard was based on the assumption that both members of a couple were eligible for the housing allowance scheme. In fact, a survey in 1998 of about 1600 civil servants found that in more than three quarters (76 per cent) of families only one person was eligible for the housing allowance scheme (Guangzhou People's Municipal Government 1998). This shows that, even in the ideal situation for which the housing allowance scheme was designed, most target families would still be unable to afford a flat. The 2008 survey of young civil servants indicated that 82 per cent received monthly housing allowance, but cases where both partners got a housing allowance accounted for only 27 per cent. These civil servants may have difficulty renting a single room, let alone buying a home.

Last, the timespan for housing subsidies is too long. In order to lessen the financial burden on the government, the fixed sum of housing allowance is spread over 25 years (300 months) and inflation is not taken into account. This makes it more difficult for participants to accumulate sufficient resources for mortgage purchases in a short period and reduces the effectiveness of this scheme in ameliorating the living conditions of the civil servants. Moreover, policy-makers did not consider the long transitional period before civil servants could afford to buy a flat. In fact, the housing allowance is barely sufficient to cover the costs of renting a flat

Poor implementation of the housing monetarization reform

Housing monetarization reform has been implemented mainly in governmental departments and public institutions. SOEs were given autonomy to decide whether they followed the same plan to solve housing problems in their work units. However, most SOEs cannot afford to provide housing subsidy and thus the housing monetarization reforms have been generally confined to government departments and public institutions.

By 2008, there were 10,323 civil servants in Guangzhou (8 per cent of all the civil servants) who had joined after 2000, when housing monetarization was carried out. This group had no opportunity to access welfare housing, unlike those who began their career earlier. These new civil servants had to meet their housing needs through the private market with the support of the cash allowances issued in relation to job rank (see Table 8.1). There were also about 190,000 employees in public institutions (*shi ye dan wei*), which were fully or partially supported by the state budget. These institutions were also covered by the same reform plan.

However, housing monetarization reform was poorly implemented, even in a comparatively wealthy city like Guangzhou. By the end of September 2008, some 19,000 civil servants had received cash allowances.[5] The situation in public institutions was much worse. Only 3773 public employees (of the 15,000 who joined after the reform) had received a housing allowance in the same period. There are two main reasons for the poor implementation: one is that civil servants have been reluctant to sever the relationship with their work units in relation to housing provision, which is the major objective of the housing monetarization reform. They prefer in-kind housing to cash subsidy, especially in conditions of rampant house price inflation. The second reason is that the level of housing allowance is so low that it is of little use in improving housing affordability. Even among those who had received monetary subsidies in the general population, including public employees and workers, the homeownership rate was only 40 per cent, slightly higher than the overall average rate of the sample of civil servants. This shows that the current housing allowance scheme has played a very limited role in improving housing affordability and access to homeownership.

In addition, the affordable housing project, a tailor-made scheme for providing housing to medium-income households, was poorly implemented. This is partly because the Chinese government attached too much importance to housing marketization and the possible benefits of the rapid development of the real estate sector. In Guangzhou, the municipal government did not provide Economical Housing until 2007, when local house prices had risen beyond the means of most ordinary families. As a result, young civil servants had no opportunity to buy subsidized housing. Moreover, central government made further adjustments and the target groups for Economical Housing were shrunk from medium-to-low income groups to low-income families. This policy adjustment deprived civil servants (and other middle income earners) of the possibility of purchasing state-subsidized Economical Housing. Without this channel for housing provision, it was more difficult for young civil servants to become homeowners.

Solving the youth housing problem: tensions between economic development, political stability and social equality

Differentiated housing benefits

Housing reform has involved a redistribution of vital interests for almost all urban citizens. Generally, housing reform has taken an incremental approach, following the principle of 'old people, old way; new people, new system'. While this mode of housing restructuring helped gain support for the reform and minimize possible resistance, it created a huge gap between 'old people' and 'new people' in terms of housing benefits. 'Old people' can enjoy the benefits of cheaper housing. Also, a very small number of 'old' employees who did not gain access to a flat will be entitled a large lump-sum subsidy, enabling home purchase. In contrast, 'new people' can get only a small housing allowance over a long time period, with reduced chances of owning a flat.

This huge wealth disparity, without any reasonable justification, has become a major constraint in policy formulation on tackling the housing problems of civil servants, let alone the excluded private employees. Given the immense welfare gap between civil servants and workers and between public and private sectors, specific policies to support privileged civil servants might arouse resentment. But without such interventions, there may be strong feelings of unfairness and discontent among the younger civil servants, and this could harm the solidarity of the civil service. This also involves political risks.

This difficult situation is further aggravated by the design and implementation of housing reform. As discussed above, China's housing reform programme has mainly targeted and been implemented in government agencies and public institutions. This involves a form of exclusion of workers in state-owned enterprises and collective enterprises, joint ventures and private enterprises, which account for about 80 per cent of urban residents. Housing monetarization reform has, in fact, only been carried out in a small number of well-run state-owned enterprises, where work units have been able to provide housing subsidies and contribute to the provident fund for their employees. Most state-owned enterprises and collective-owned enterprises have poor economic performance. They have difficulty paying salaries, contributing to the mandatory Housing Provident Fund[6] and Social Security Foundation, and needless to say optional housing subsidies. As a result, many 'old' workers are facing severe housing difficulties. To a large extent, the unfairness is a product of both the institutional inequalities in the socialist housing regime and the market mechanisms introduced in the reform period (Bian *et al.* 1996; Logan *et al.* 1999).

The housing problems in state-owned enterprises should be emphasized because, except for monopolized SOEs such as China Telecom, the general housing and economic situation of workers in SOEs is much worse than that of civil servants. Research shows that civil servants had been better housed than workers before the reform. With the launch of housing monetarization reform, housing problems in SOEs were aggravated because living standards and other social benefits depended entirely on the economic performance of the enterprises and the majority of enterprises performed poorly. In addition, state-owned enterprises laid off a great number of workers, which further exacerbated the housing difficulties for these new urban poor (Wang 2004). And workers who had suffered from the dismantling of the socialist welfare system during the market transition now had to bear the burden of the 'three new mountains' of education, health and housing, following retrenchment of public expenditure and reduced state provision. In contrast, civil servants continue to enjoy their privileged status in terms of job security and occupational welfare. They can also get housing subsidies and access the housing provident fund, which is financed from the public treasury. Hence, overall, they have more purchasing power than workers.

During this period of growing social tensions and social polarization, the government needs to consider the housing problems of all social groups. However, it is obvious that the government cannot tackle the housing problems of workers and civil servants in the same way as it did prior to the reform. Hence, there is a dilemma: if the government does not deal with the housing problems of civil servants, the resourceful civil servants will be discontented and this could undermine the regime; if the government takes steps targeted at only civil servants, it would be exposed by the mass media and provoke negative reactions from not only employees in the private sector, but also public employees and SOEs, which could undermine its legitimacy. In addition, the solutions should also take migrants into account. It is by no means an easy job.

A dilemma of economic development and social justice

China has now become the second largest economy in the world. However, the sustainability of the Chinese mode of development is in question. Despite the economic growth, a lot of problems have emerged, such as an energy crisis, regional disparities, environmental pollution and growing social polarization. In response to the negative impacts of the Southeast Asian Financial crisis in the late 1990s, the Chinese government ceased the in-kind housing distribution system and boosted the development of the real estate sector, which has been positioned as 'a new growth pole' of the Chinese economy. The Chinese economy is now over-reliant on this sector; 'kidnapped' by it, according to Yi (2004). The Chinese government has defined the housing problem as an economic rather than a social issue. This has led to an overheated property market and various problems in the housing field which necessitate governmental intervention. But even now, because sustained economic growth is crucial for the government, the state is still striking a balance between a stable economy and meeting the housing needs of medium-to-low income households. This is implicitly shown by the fact that regulatory measures to cool the housing market have been not effectively implemented in the past few years. While there was a rapid increase in public investment and development in 2011, a year that could be called 'a great leap forward' in public rental housing, housing schemes such as the social rental housing scheme and the Economic Housing scheme have been insufficiently financed (Liu 2011b).

Civic engagement, housing movement and social unrest

With the economic reforms, the Chinese political regime has changed over to so-called 'authoritarianism 2.0' (Mertha 2009). NGOs, social organizations and even individuals now have more opportunities to get their voices heard and exert some kind of influence in the policy-making process (Mertha 2009; Saich 2000; Zhu and Cheng 2011). In the housing field, access to privatized housing has become a discriminator between social actors. It has more weight in determining social status than income (Tomba 2004). Generally speaking, homeownership is a key symbol for the middle class. Many of them become 'house slaves' as mortgage payments account for a large proportion of their family income. There are still others who are eager to enter this category. Squeezed by the rocketing property prices, young people have launched a 'don't buy housing' movement in Shenzhen, and there are housing cooperative movements in the major cities in China. These social movements show high levels of dissatisfaction over a current housing policy which prioritizes economic growth over meeting the housing needs of ordinary people and assures the monopoly role of the profit-maximizing firms in housing provision. Due to institutional constraints and resistance from the developers, these movements have by no means attained their aims. However, the introduction of limited-price housing could be seen as a kind of policy response to these initiatives.

Migrant workers have long been excluded from social security. While they are now eligible to apply for social rental housing or Economic Housing in several cities, accessibility is overall still a big problem. Most local governments lack the resources to provide enough social rental housing even for the officially recognized urban poor, let alone this marginalized social group (Wang 2004). Nonetheless, it is risky to neglect the social needs of such a large group, comprising more than 130 million people, particularly Chinese youth who have a long tradition of playing a significant role in socio-political movements (Johnson, Johnson-Pynn and Pynn 2007). There has also been a profound change in values. Material wealth has become a mark of individual success (Wanxue and Hanwei 2004) and individual rights and interests are increasingly valued. Recent strikes and riots in the coastal areas show the acute tensions which exist between migrants and local people, and that unequal treatment of migrants and their exclusion from the benefits of economic growth are no longer tolerated as before. The authorities have implicitly admitted that unequal treatment, insufficient social and public services, neglect of the rights of migrants and mismanagement are major reasons for the social unrest (Liu 2011a).

Discussion and conclusion: challenging state capacity and governance systems

Neoliberalized housing development and housing policy in China has changed fundamentally the housing distribution mechanism and housing benefits among different sectors and individuals. It has not only led to severe marginalization of the urban poor and housing segregation but has also generated serious housing affordability problems for young people. As this chapter has shown, these problems even encompass the young middle class, represented by the privileged social group of civil servants. This has multiple implications. First, it indicates that housing reform in China has achieved one of its goals, of transforming the in-kind welfare housing distribution system based on administrative ranks into a market-oriented housing system based on affordability and competitiveness in the housing market. Second, the essence of the housing problem has changed from one of absolute housing shortage and unequal distribution among work units and individuals before the reform, to one of housing affordability and housing inequality resulting mainly from the new income distribution. In particular, housing monetarization reform has generated a distinctive unequal distribution of housing assets, leading to a further disparity in household wealth, between cohorts of so-called 'old people' and 'new people'. Third, although housing conditions for the majority of urban citizens have improved considerably and the real estate sector has contributed substantially to the economy, housing problems in China have accumulated and might well harm the stability of the regime without a fundamental change in the policy paradigm.

Housing problems in China result partly from the misperception of decision-makers that, once the housing reform has been completed and a market-oriented system established, the housing market will solve all kinds of housing problems without any government intervention. It was because of this illusion that the government placed undue reliance on housing marketization and the development of the real estate sector, and neglected its responsibilities in housing provision and regulation. It has also underestimated the differential housing benefits for the 'old' and 'new' people. And thus far, apart from the capped-priced housing, there are no tailor-made housing policies aimed at young people.

To address the housing problems for young people in China represents a significant challenge to state capacity and public governance. Despite the increasing extractive capacity of the central government since the mid-1990s, there has been no clear institutional separation of responsibility between the central and local governments in terms of finance and administration of social welfare and social services. Generally speaking, local governments in the centre and west lack sufficient resources to fulfil the task of providing the social policy goods which the central government has promised. The currently poor implementation in public rental housing construction is a good example. By the end of May 2011, only one third of the target of ten million square metres of public rental housing had been started.

In parallel with profound changes in demographic structure and social values, homeownership, seen as a symbol of individual success and social status, has become a Chinese dream for young people, including both college graduates and migrant workers. Their aspirations for a decent home have created strong pressures on the government and challenged the governance and capability of the party state. Hence, housing has become a thorny issue. In the coming years the Chinese government will be striving to strike a balance between social equality, economic growth and political stability. Without properly tackling the housing problems of young people, there could be a major social crisis.

Acknowledgment

This research is supported by 211 project and 985 project of Sun Yat-sen University and is also part of the research project Interests, Institutions and Housing Policy Process.

Notes

1 This was especially the case in Beijing. Most young civil servants refused to take the housing allowance, claiming for in-kind housing from work units, instead. In fact, to some extent, welfare housing distribution has not stopped in the ministries.
2 Here the salary refers to the basic salary, which excludes all kinds of allowances and subsidies, hence their real income is much higher than their salary.
3 This figure comes from the *Guangzhou Statistical Yearbook 2008* (Guangzhou Statistical Bureau 2008).
4 From an interview with officials in the Bureau of State Land and Housing Administration, Guangzhou City, on 14 December 2008.
5 Including 'old people' entitled to receive a lump-sum amount of housing subsidy.
6 A compulsory saving scheme aimed at improving affordability and the housing situation for participants. Both employees and employers in China are required to contribute a proportion of employees' salary (no less than 5 per cent) to the scheme. It was conceived as a key component of housing security in China, also as one key strategy in monetarizing housing provision in 1998. The government can use the funds to build social rental housing or Economic Housing.

References

Adams, B. (2009) 'Macroeconomic implications of China Urban Housing Privatization, 1998–1999', *Journal of Contemporary China*, 18(62): 881–888.

Bian, Y., J.R. Logan, H. Lu, Y. Pan and Y. Guan. (1996) 'Work units and commodification of housing', *Sociology Research (Shehuixue yanjiu)*, 1: 28–35.

Cheng, X. (1998) 'Guangzhoushi ceding ahufang butie biaozhun de silu' (On the rationale of setting housing allowance standard in Guangzhou City), *Housing and Real Estate* 5(39): 5–7.

Guangzhou People's Municipal Government (1998)'guan yu guangzhou shi zhi shu ji guan shi ye dan wei zhu fang fen pei huo bi hua de shi shi fang an' (Implementation plan for housing monetarization in governmental departments and institutions), *Housing and Real Estate*, 38(5): 24–27.

Guangzhou Statistical Bureau (2001–2008) *Guangzhou Statistical Yearbook 2001–2008*. Guangzhou: Guangzhou Statistical Bureau. Available at: http://data.gzstats.gov.cn/gzStat1/chaxun/njsj.jsp (accessed May 19, 2012).

Huang, Y. (2009) 'qi ba cheng shi min mai bu qi fang, fu ting liang ge yue gong zi mai bu dao yi fang' (70 to 80 per cent of local residents cannot afford to buy flat, even deputy Bureau level officials cannot buy one square metre with two months' salary), *New Express Daily (Xinkuai bao)*, Guangzhou, p. A04.

Johnson, L.R., J.S. Johnson-Pynn, and T.M. Pynn (2007) 'Youth civic engagement in China: results from a program promoting environmental activism', *Journal of Adolescent Research*, 22(4): 355–386.

Lee, J. and Y.-p. Zhu. (2006) 'Urban governance, neoliberalism and housing reform in China', *The Pacific Review*, 19(1): 39–61.

Liao, J. (2001) '2000 nian Guangzhou shi ju min ju zhu tiao jian jin yi bu gai shan', *Nanfang fangdichang (South China Real Estate)*, 4(191): 14.

Liu, K. (2011a) 'Zhang Guang ning shou tan Xintang ju zhong zi shi shi jian, geng ben yuan yin shi she hui guan li zhi hou' (Zhang Guangning attributes riots in Xitang to lagging social management), *Southern Daily*, Guangzhou. Available at: http://politics.people.com.cn/GB/14562/14976388.html (accessed May 19, 2012).

Liu, S. (2011b) 'bao zhang fang da yue jin yu liu zhijun' (Housing security great leap forward and Liu Zhijun). Available at: http://opinion.caixin.cn/2011-11-23/100330698.html (accessed November 21, 2011).

Logan, J.R., Y. Bian and F. Bian. (1999) 'Housing inequality in urban China in the 1990s', *International Journal of Urban and Regional Research,* 23(1): 7–25.

Mertha, A. (2009) 'Fragmented authoritarianism 2.0? Political pluralization in the Chinese policy process', *The China Quarterly,* 200(1): 995–1012.

Ouyang, H. (2011) 'zhongguo da zhong chengshi qingnian juzhu qing kuang diao cha' (Survey of residential conditions of Chinese youth in major and medium cities), *Xiaokang (Insight China),* 6: 32–36.

Saich, T. (2000) 'Negotiating the state: the development of social organizations in China', *China Quarterly,* 161: 124–141.

State Statistical Bureau of the People's Republic of China (2010) '2009 nian nongmin gong jiance diaocha baogao' (Surveillant and investigative report on migrant workers in 2009). Beijing: State Statistical Bureau of the People's Republic of China.

Tomba, L. (2004) 'Creating an urban middle class: social engineering in Beijing', *The China Journal,* 51: 1–26.

Wang, Y. (2000) 'Housing reform and its impacts on the urban poor in China', *Housing Studies,* 15(6): 845–864.

Wang, Y.P. (2004) *Urban Poverty, Housing and Social Change in China,* London: Routledge.

Wang, Y.P. and A. Murie. (2000) 'Social and spatial implications of housing reform in China', *International Journal of Urban and Regional Research,* 24(2): 397–417.

Wanxue, Q. and T. Hanwei (2004) 'The social and cultural background of contemporary moral education in China', *Journal of Moral Education,* 33(4): 465–480.

World Bank (1992) *China: Implementation Options for Urban Housing Reform,* Washington, DC, USA: World Bank.

Yi, X. (2004) 'jing ti fang di chan yao xie zhong guo jing ji' (Be alert to the kidnapping of China's economy by the real estate sector), *guo ji jing rong bao (International Finance News),* 30 July. Available at: http://finance.sina.com.cn/roll/20040730/0313912177.shtml (accessed May 21, 2012).

Zhu, Y. (2009) 'Struggling among economic efficiency, social equality and social stability: housing monetarization reform in China', pp.253–284 in *Changing Governance and Public Policy in East Asia,* edited by K.-H. Mok and R. Forrest. Abingdon: Routledge.

Zhu, Y. (2010) 'Target groups' views and policy implementation: lessons from Guiyang's housing monetarization reform', *Politics & Policy,* 38(4): 817–841.

Zhu, Y. and J.Y.S. Cheng (2011) 'The emergence of cyber society and the transformation of the public policy agenda-building process in China', *The China Review,* 11(2): 153–182.

PART III

Economic change and generational fractures

9

HOUSING AND GENERATIONAL FRACTURES IN JAPAN

Yosuke Hirayama

Introduction

Over the past few decades, many developed countries oriented towards home ownership have undergone increasingly unstable socio-economic and policy conditions (Doling and Ford, 2003; Forrest, 2008; Forrest and Yip, 2011; Horsewood and Neuteboom, 2006; Kurz and Blossfeld, 2004; Ronald and Elsinga, 2012). This has resulted in different housing situations for different generations. Unlike older cohort households, which were supported by high-speed economic development and government subsidies in entering owner-occupied housing markets, younger cohort households are experiencing more volatile economic circumstances and diminishing government support in accessing home ownership. There has thus been an obvious decay in the cycle in which successive generations follow conventional housing paths to property ownership. This creates new challenges in the sustainability of 'homeowner societies'.

Japan serves as a prime exemplar with regard to the decline in young people's housing opportunities. The housing system in postwar Japan has been focused on the formation of a 'social mainstream' by expanding middle-class home ownership (Hirayama, 2003, 2007). In line with this, many households have led conventional life-courses in terms of ascending the housing ladder towards property ownership. Since the 1990s, however, a more insecure economy combined with the retreat of the government from housing subsidy schemes has increasingly excluded younger people from routes up the owner-occupied housing ladder (Hirayama, 2010, 2011a). There has been a notable increase in young, unmarried adults who live in their parents' homes indefinitely, while increasing numbers of single-person households have remained in the rented housing sector with few prospects of entering the owner-occupied sector. Even in cases where young families purchase housing, they have been confronted with heavier mortgage burdens for houses whose values as assets have become more uncertain. Along with a decrease in young people's moves towards home ownership, the mechanisms for maintaining the social mainstream have begun to disintegrate.

Moreover, it has been argued that changes in the housing circumstances of younger cohorts have a significant effect on low fertility rates (Mulder, 2006; Mulder and Billari, 2010). The total population of Japan, which has one of the lowest fertility rates in the world, began to decrease in 2004. According to a 2006 estimate by the National Institute of Population and Social Security Research, the population, 128 million in 2005, will decrease to 90 million by 2055. This will be accompanied by an inevitable decrease in the workforce and an accelerated increase in the proportion of older people. The percentage of people aged 65 or more, 20.2 per cent in 2005, is forecast to increase to as much as 40.5 per cent by 2055. There are various factors accounting for low fertility, but it is evident that the exacerbation of housing constraints discourages young people from establishing their own independent families. In this sense, housing provision is a significant policy issue not only in terms of shelter but also in respect of overall social sustainability.

In this chapter, we explore generational fractures in Japan's home-owning society, placing particular emphasis on the growing centrality of young people's shifting housing opportunities in understanding contemporary social transformations. Empirical evidence was obtained by recalculating micro-data from the Housing and Land Survey and the Population Census as well as various other statistics. We begin by exploring how the decline in the social mainstream has led to generational differentiation in housing and life-course patterns. This will be followed by an investigation into housing pathway divergence within younger groups. We then move on to highlight the fragmentation of urban space in relation to changes in young people's life-courses, and conclude with a look at the implications of generational differences for homeowner societies.

Young people and the social mainstream

Inside or outside

Japan's home-ownership-oriented housing system has operated in tandem with employment and family systems to nurture the creation of a social mainstream (Hirayama, 2003). Within this framework, many people have led a conventional life-course by securing a job, establishing a family and acquiring an owner-occupied home. Over the past two decades, however, socio-economic and policy transformations have affected the housing conditions of younger people, thus provoking generational fractures in the homeowner society. In this section, we explore changes in the employment, family and housing systems to look at young people's housing situations within the context of decline in the social mainstream.

As shown in Figure 9.1, mainstream society was originally organized around a 'social flow' of people moving from the 'outside' to the 'inside'. This 'inside' was primarily made up of middle-class family households who acquired owner-

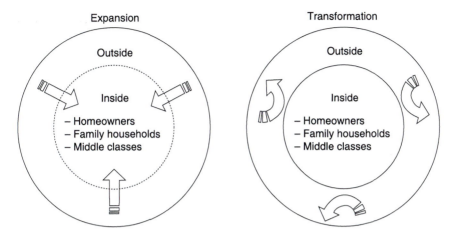

FIGURE 9.1 Changes in the 'social mainstream'.

occupied housing (Hirayama, 2007). Many people were encouraged to ascend the housing ladder from a rented dwelling to an owner-occupied dwelling, and the consequent aggregation of mobility up the ladder enlarged the homeowner society. The private ownership of housing provided a material basis for securing homes and accumulating wealth. The physical condition of owner-occupied housing in terms of amenities and floor area was much better than rented housing. Owning a home meant the accumulation of property assets, whereas rent payment was regarded as a waste. Further, owner-occupied housing was not only defined in a material sense but also represented the new social status of its owners (Hirayama, 2003). It symbolized a 'family space', middle or high-level income and ownership of a real estate asset. Owner-occupation was bound with an image of autonomy and control, and homeowners were expected to be responsible for order in society. Residential property ownership has thus been symbolic of the 'inside' – that is, belonging to mainstream society.

Since the 1990s, however, as a consequence of socio-economic and policy changes, the 'social flow' of moves towards the 'inside' has become stagnant, with a decrease in people climbing the owner-occupied housing ladder (see Figure 9.1). This has increasingly differentiated life-course patterns between generations and significantly undermined young people's housing opportunities. Economic decline has undoubtedly been responsible for the erosion of the social mainstream. Immediately after the 'bubble economy' collapsed at the beginning of the 1990s, Japan entered a prolonged period of recession, characterized by minimal or negative real growth in GDP, rising unemployment rates and reduced real incomes. While the Japanese economy eventually began recovering in 2002, the economic upturn did not translate into an improved household economy. Moreover, Japan reentered a severe recession in 2008, after becoming entangled in the global financial crisis triggered by the U.S. subprime mortgage meltdown. Subsequently, an additional strong blow was dealt to the nation's weakened economy by the major earthquake in Tohoku in 2011. Thus, since the early 1990s, economic insecurity has come to be perceived as 'normal' rather than 'abnormal'. Meanwhile, in response to the post-bubble recession, and within the context of pervasive neoliberalism, the government has moved sharply towards accentuating the role of the market in formulating policy (Forrest and Hirayama, 2009). This has been especially noticeable in the areas of housing and employment. The government deregulated the market economy and substantially reduced various public subsidies. The impact of economic changes and neoliberal policy on people's life-courses has not been equal across generations, but concentrated on younger generations. Young people are now experiencing a narrowing of the routes to the 'inside' of mainstream society and are facing difficulties in following conventional life paths towards home ownership.

Labour market reorganization

Until recently, Japan was often described as a 'company society' in which the government supported employment security and ensured corporate-based welfare with regulatory measures and tax incentives. The system of 'company as a community' underpinned the foundation of the home-ownership-based society. Major corporations implemented in-house systems to aid their employees in securing housing, which reinforced the strength of the housing ladder (Sato, 2007). Low-rent employee dwellings and rental subsidies were supplied for young employees, while employees at higher rungs of the ladder had access to a company loan system for home purchases. Within the framework of the company society, many companies adopted a lifelong employment system and a seniority system for wages and promotion. This enabled employees to assume a steady increase in income and consequent financial stability in housing purchases.

However, the post-bubble recession eroded the economic pillar of the company society, encouraging the 'casualization' of the labour force. Increasing numbers of corporations began abandoning the system of lifelong employment and introduced a performance-based system to replace the seniority system. In alignment with neoliberal policy, the government, which had placed importance on protecting employment security, began to deregulate employment practices. Major amendments to the Dispatched Labour Law (governing employees recruited from agencies) in 1999 and 2003 played a significant role in promoting casual employment. The labour market has thus been reoriented around declining stability in employment with associated sharp increases in the number of short-term contracts, part-time workers and temporary employees.

Changes in the labour market have particularly affected younger generations. While the company society system has been relatively well maintained for older cohorts, neoliberal policies have exacerbated employment conditions for younger ones (Genda, 2001). It has consequently become more difficult for young people to secure employment and thus housing. According to the Employment Status Survey, between 1987 and 2007, the rate of non-regular employees (part-time, temporary and dispatched employees) aged 20–24 increased sharply from 15.2 to

43.2 per cent. Some of this can be explained by an increase in the numbers of university students in casual employment. During the same period, however, the figure rose from 11.3 to 28.2 per cent for the 25–29 age group, and from 13.1 to 25.9 per cent for the 30–34 age group. This can be attributed to neoliberal labour policy and the consequent casualization of the employment market.

Changes in family formation

There has been a close link between establishing a family and acquiring an owner-occupied home in Japan's postwar mainstream society. Within the framework of family-oriented public policy, housing policy has concentrated on encouraging conventional family households to achieve home ownership (Hirayama and Izuhara, 2008). Tax and social security systems, which have corresponded to the proliferation of the 'male breadwinner family' model, have provided explicit advantages to households including a homemaker wife (Nagase and Murao, 2005; Yokoyama, 2002). The system of corporate-based welfare has also provided a variety of benefits to male employees with dependent family members. Various public policy measures have thus advantaged family households while mostly excluding unmarried people.

Nevertheless, there has been a noticeable increase in younger people who have delayed marriage and the establishment of their own families. In Japan, where owner-occupied housing represents 'family space', most people do not purchase a house until marriage. The increase in unmarried individuals has therefore translated into a decline in housing purchases. According to the Population Census, between 1980 and 2005, the percentage of unmarried people in the 30–34 age group rose from 21.5 to 47.1 per cent for men and from 9.1 to 32.0 per cent for women. Unlike many Western societies, cohabitation by non-married couples is uncommon in Japan, although such couples are on the increase. The unmarried rate is higher for men than for women for all age groups. In addition, the percentage of never-married people at the age of 50, who are defined as 'lifelong never-married persons' in Japanese statistics, increased to 15.4 per cent for men and 6.8 per cent for women by 2005. This figure is expected to further increase to 29.5 per cent for men and 22.5 per cent for women by 2030.

Moreover, worsening economic conditions have increasingly deprived young individuals of the opportunity to get married and establish their own families. The formation of families in Japan has mostly been based on the 'male breadwinner family' model. This is reflected in the clear correlation between the unmarried rate and economic status, particularly among men. The Employment Status Survey in 2002 revealed that the percentage of unmarried men aged 30–34 in regular employment was 41 per cent, while the figure for those in non-regular employment was substantially higher, at 70 per cent. Changes in people's attitudes towards marriage have led to young people delaying the start of independent households. According to a survey periodically conducted by the NHK Broadcasting Culture Research Institute (2004), the rate of those who answered 'it is a matter of course to get married' decreased from 45 per cent in 1993 to 36 per cent in 2003. The younger the respondents were, the lower the figure. In addition, many young people are spending a longer time in university and are thus forming households later. It is, however, necessary to look at not only the change in people's attitudes towards marriage but also the apparent tendency of young people with a lower employment status to more often remain unmarried. Regardless of young people's attitudes towards marriage, it is difficult for male non-regular employees with low wages to choose to get married.

Housing market volatility

The level of home ownership has been maintained at approximately 60 per cent since the 1960s, reflecting its position as the dominant housing tenure. Together with socio-economic and policy transformations, however, the level of owner-occupied housing has dropped significantly among younger households, implying a decline in the cycle of successive moves towards home ownership that have sustained the social mainstream. Between 1983 and 2008, the percentage of owner occupation decreased from 24.9 to 11.7 per cent for households with a head aged 25–29, and from 60.1 to 46.5 per cent for those aged 35–39 (see Figure 9.2). Despite the drop in the level of home ownership for younger households, the average level of home ownership for all households has largely been stationary. This is due to an increase in the proportion of the older population having higher home ownership levels.

Since the bubble burst, the Japanese housing economy has been substantially reorganized, resulting in a decrease in the number of young homeowners. The

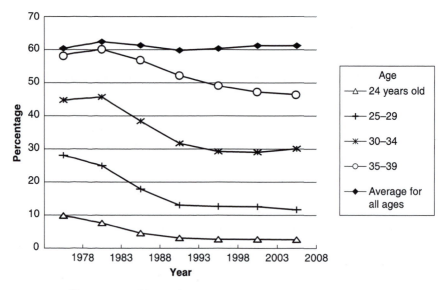

FIGURE 9.2 Home ownership rate by age.
   Source: Housing Survey of Japan and Housing and Land Survey of Japan

economic burdens imposed by accessing and maintaining home ownership have become heavier (Hirayama, 2010). Although the collapse of the bubble led to deflation in housing prices, a decrease in incomes has translated into smaller deposits and therefore larger mortgage liabilities. Consequently, despite the drop in house prices, the burdens of mortgage repayments have increased. Younger households with lower incomes have been plunged into particularly disadvantageous economic conditions in terms of purchasing a house. According to the National Survey of Family Income and Expenditure, of owner-occupier households with a head aged 34 or less, the percentage of those whose mortgage repayments represented 20 per cent or more of their disposable income increased from 14.8 per cent in 1989 to 33.0 per cent in 2004 (Hirayama, 2010).

Before the bubble collapsed, the system of home ownership expansion was implicated in the capital gain-based economy, in which owning a house was a primary mechanism of accumulating assets. Renters entering the home ownership market as first-time buyers were able to expect an appreciation in the real value of properties they were purchasing, while those owning a house had the prospect of moving to a better house using the current property as a stepping stone. Indeed, capital gains fuelled the system of propelling people towards the top of the property ladder. Since the bubble collapsed, however, most residential properties have continued to fall in value, with an increase in capital losses (Hirayama, 2011b). This has meant a substantial shift in the economic aspects of home ownership, with the tendency for owner-occupied housing to generate capital losses coming to be perceived as 'normal' rather than 'abnormal'. The asset conditions of homeowners have worsened, with an increase in outstanding mortgage debts and a decrease in the values of residential properties. As a result, approximately a quarter of young homeowners became trapped in negative housing equity by the mid-2000s (Hirayama, 2011b). There has been an increase in owner-occupiers with heavier mortgage liabilities who have retained properties whose values have continued to drop.

Post-bubble stagnation has encouraged the reorientation of housing policy. Since the immediate postwar period, the government has driven the growth of middle-class home ownership (Hirayama, 2003, 2007). The Government Housing Loan Corporation (GHLC), established in 1951 as a state agency, provided middle-class households with low-interest mortgages to acquire or construct their own homes. Of the various measures available through housing policy, the supply of GHLC loans was especially emphasized to facilitate home ownership. In the mid-1990s, however, the government began to direct housing policy towards a more neoliberal course. The 2007 abolition of the GHLC, which had been the core of traditional housing measures, was a particularly significant watershed in the history of Japanese housing policy and occasioned a dramatic expansion of the private mortgage market. This reorganization of housing policy measures has inevitably affected the housing conditions of younger cohort households. Older generations have moved up the housing ladder towards home ownership, supported by public subsidies. Younger generations will not be provided with the same level of support.

Divergence in housing trajectories

Delay in transitions

Social, economic and policy transformations have brought about divergence in housing conditions, not only between different generations but also within younger generations. The focus of this section is on young people's housing pathway divergence between 'parental home dwellers', 'single people' and 'family formers'. Here, 'parental home dwellers' are defined as unmarried individuals living in their parents' home where their parent is the head (main earner) of the household; 'single people' are unmarried individuals who form one-person households; and 'family-formers' are defined as married individuals establishing their own independent households who are either the head of their household or the spouse of the head.

It has long been assumed that, in the conventional life-course, young individuals change from being parental home dwellers to independent singles and then to family-formers, or from parental home dwellers directly to family-formers. However, as shown in Table 9.1, which was prepared from a combination of various data from the Population Census, parental home dwellers and single people – parental home dwellers in particular – have been increasing in number, while family-formers have been declining. This is primarily due to the rising number of unmarried people. Between 1980 and 2005, the percentage of parental home dwellers and single people rose from 24.0 per cent and 12.1 per cent to 41.3 per cent and 19.3 per cent, respectively, for the 25–29 age group. Even among older individuals, aged 35–39, during the same period the rate of parental home dwelling rose from 2.9 to 16.0 per cent, and that of single people from 3.4 to 8.9 per cent. Conversely, the ratios of family-formers continuously dropped to 28.1 per cent for the 25–29 age group, and 50.3 per cent for the 30–34 age group by 2005. This apparent stagnation in transitions into becoming family-formers means a decline in conventional life-course patterns. The category of 'Others' in the table includes married individuals, sometimes with children, who live in parental homes to form extended family households. The percentage of married individuals living in parents' houses decreased to 11.4 per cent for the 30–34 age group by 2005. The number of people in this category is much lower in large cities than in provincial cities.

There are differences in the ways households are established between men and women. The number of family-formers is higher for women than for men. This corresponds to the fact that there are more unmarried men than unmarried women. The 2005 percentage of family-formers among those aged 30–34 was 44.8 per cent for men and 55.8 per cent for women. Of unmarried individuals, women are more likely to be parental home dwellers compared to men. In 2005, among those aged 30–34, there were 1.6 times as many men living in the parental home as there were single men, while for women the multiplier was 2.4. This means that unmarried women tend to continue to live in their parents' homes and that they do not tend to leave home to become independent singles, but rather when they get married.

TABLE 9.1 Changes in household type by age.

Year	Parental home dwellers (%)	Single people (%)	Family-formers (%)	Others (%)	Total (%)
Age 25–29					
1980	24.0	12.1	46.0	17.9	100
1985	29.0	13.5	40.5	16.9	100
1990	34.2	15.7	36.9	13.2	100
1995	37.8	17.1	34.5	10.6	100
2000	40.6	17.6	31.6	10.2	100
2005	41.3	19.3	28.1	11.2	100
Age 30–34					
1980	8.2	5.6	68.5	17.8	100
1985	10.8	7.0	62.8	19.4	100
1990	14.0	8.1	59.7	18.2	100
1995	17.6	10.1	57.4	14.9	100
2000	21.5	12.3	54.1	12.1	100
2005	24.8	13.5	50.3	11.4	100
Age 35–39					
1980	2.9	3.4	80.4	13.3	100
1985	5.1	4.6	74.2	16.1	100
1990	6.9	5.6	70.1	17.4	100
1995	9.3	6.5	66.7	17.4	100
2000	12.1	7.9	64.9	15.1	100
2005	16.0	8.9	61.8	13.2	100

Source: Author's calculations from Population Census of Japan

In addition to post-bubble economic stagnation, the organization of housing policy has been responsible for changes in young people's household formation. The government has characteristically operated a tenure-discriminatory housing system, with explicit emphasis on promoting middle-class home ownership. There has been little assistance for the improvement of private rental housing and absolutely no provision of rental subsidies. Public housing has been allocated to low-income households and public corporations have constructed rental housing for urban middle-income households. The direct supply of rental housing by the public sector, however, has been positioned as a residual measure. The housing system, which has neglected the rented housing sector, has produced a delaying effect on young people's transition to become family-formers. It is most likely that young individuals who wish to leave home to form their own households need adequate, affordable rental housing before entering the home ownership market. However, the limited number of public rental dwellings available for young households, the low quality of private rental housing in terms of floor size and amenities, and high rents for privately rented housing have effectively combined to discourage young people from establishing their own independent families. Further, the reorientation of housing policy in a more neoliberal direction has meant fewer public subsidies for young households to secure housing.

Parental home dwellers

In the following argument, we examine the differences in housing situations according to the type of household, drawing on recalculations of the micro-data obtained from the 2003 Housing and Land Survey. A novel phenomenon relating to younger generations is the rapid increase in parental home dwellers. Until the mid-1990s, the aftermath of the bubble generated an image that young adults living in parental homes indulged themselves in the consumption of luxury goods without having to incur housing costs or food expenses. Yamada (1999), who called parental home dwellers 'parasite singles', explicitly pointed out young people's dependent attitudes. This catchy term provided a trigger, provoking a 'parasite-bashing' phenomenon in popular discourses, in which the dependent behaviour of young adults was severely criticized (Kitamura, 2001). Since the late 1990s, however, with the post-bubble recession as a backdrop, many researchers have begun to focus on the economic instability of younger cohorts, and various surveys on young individuals have found that many parental home dwellers are non-regular employees who do not have sufficient income to leave home to establish an independent household (Iwagami, 1999; Kitamura, 2001; Nagase, 2002; Miyamoto, 2004; Ohishi, 2004; Shirahase, 2005). It is thus reasonable to regard the increase in parental home dwellers not as a phenomenon reflecting young people's dependent attitudes but as a consequence of economically rational behaviour in terms of securing places to live.

The increase in parental home dwellers was made possible by a particular form of intergenerational relationship or family reciprocity. According to the 2003 data, more than four-fifths of parental home dwellers were living in owner-occupied housing. Most owners of owner-occupied houses can reasonably be assumed to be parents. The sustained promotion of home ownership has encouraged the current parents' generation to acquire their own spacious homes, which has enabled the younger generation to live with them. It can be assumed that most parental home dwellers occupy their own private rooms in the house.

There is a tacit assumption that neoliberal policy and the consequent deregulation of the market economy promote individualization in welfare provision by weakening the role of the family system (Beck, 1992). Nevertheless, the increase in parental home dwellers has implied that parent generations have increasingly supported offspring generations with more precarious employment conditions, in terms of securing housing (Forrest and Hirayama, 2009). Indeed, the owner-occupation-based family system of protecting younger people has underlain and underpinned the implementation of neoliberal labour policy. Transformations in the labour market, towards an increase in non-regular workers, particularly among younger cohorts, have been perceived to be a potential factor for social destabilization. However, the new form of intergenerational relations which has produced 'parasite singles' has arguably functioned as a buffer against a decline in social stability. An increasing number of young, unmarried people have continued to live in parents' houses for long periods. In addition, there has also been an increase in 'returners' who once left home to become independent singles but could not continue to be independent due to reduced incomes or job losses, and then returned to their parents' houses. The exacerbation of instability in employment circumstances has encouraged a number of single people to return to parental homes, if they are able to choose to do so. Parental housing has thus played a role in harbouring both those who have continued to be parental home dwellers and 'returners'.

The high level of owner-occupied housing for parental home dwellers implies relatively stable housing conditions. However, it is noticeable that the household incomes of older dwellers in parental homes are lower than those of younger parental home dwellers. This is mostly caused by the parents' retirement. Regardless of whether or not parental home dwellers are 'parasitic', their parents' incomes, which they may rely on, decrease with advancing age. If parental home dwellers are in secure employment, an increase in their own incomes with advancing age is likely to compensate for the decrease in their parents' incomes. However, many parental home dwellers are casual workers with low wages.

Single people

The rising number of those who remain unmarried is reflected not only in the increase in parental home dwellers but also that of one-person households. Most single people who leave home have been living in private rental housing. The rate of private renting for single dwellers aged 25–29 is very high; approximately four out of five. The figures among older age groups are lower than among younger age groups but remain high: about seven in ten of those aged 35–39. The annual incomes of single people increase with advancing age but remain relatively low. People who continue to be single can therefore hardly acquire an owner-occupied dwelling. The older they are, the higher their level of home ownership is. However, the home ownership rates for those aged 35–39 are low, at around one in five.

It is important to note that there are gender-based differences in terms of single people's housing situations. Single women's incomes are considerably lower than those of men. Women have been and continue to be discriminated against in the labour market, which brings about the noticeable income gap. However, women tend to live in rental housing with higher rents compared to men. This suggests differences in housing preferences between men and women. Single women in urban areas placed particular importance on short commuting times and thus central locations, anti-crime environments and high-quality amenities (Yui, 2004). This arguably accounts for single women's more expensive rent payments. As discussed earlier, compared to unmarried men, unmarried women are more likely to be parental home dwellers. This is partly because they desire high-cost housing despite their lower incomes.

Housing paths experienced by single people have completely diverged from those for family households. This is not a 'natural' phenomenon but has been socially produced by various public policies. Housing policy has assisted family households in securing housing while mostly excluding one-person households. The GHLC did not provide mortgages for one-person households until 1981. Of single-person households, GHLC mortgages were only available to those aged 40 or over until 1988 and then to those aged 35 or over, before the age restriction was removed in 1993. Public corporations provided rental housing mainly to family households, with a very limited number of dwellings for single-person households. The public housing system for low-income people excluded one-person households. Elderly singles qualified for public housing in 1980, but non-elderly single households are still excluded from public housing. Taxation, social security and corporate-based welfare systems have also given an advantage to 'male breadwinner families' and disadvantaged single households. Moreover, neoliberal policy has particularly influenced the housing conditions of single households. The dissolution of the GHLC has made it unavoidable for home buyers to obtain bank mortgages. Unlike government housing policy, the mortgage market does not discriminate against single people. However, marital status is clearly correlated with economic status in Japan. Family households who largely belong to middle- to high-income groups are able to access the mortgage market, whereas it is difficult or impossible for an increasing number of single people in unstable employment to procure housing loans.

Family-formers

Unlike parental home dwellers and single people, family-formers have ascended the housing ladder to become homeowners relatively nimbly. According to the 2003 data, while the percentage of private rental housing is high for family-formers aged 25–29, at 56.6 per cent, the figure is low for those aged 35–39, at 27.5 per cent. Alternatively, the level of home ownership is much higher at 58.7 per cent for the 35–39 age group compared to 23.0 per cent for the 25–29 age group. Family-formers have experienced a continual increase in their incomes, which has buttressed their moves up the property ladder. Moreover, housing policy measures have prioritized the improvement of housing conditions for conventional family households. Nevertheless, as has been argued, the number of family-formers has been decreasing significantly, meaning a decline in the social mainstream.

Family-formers at younger ages are also more likely to live in public rental housing compared to parental home dwellers and single people. The percentage of public housing (including both public housing for those with low incomes and public corporation housing) in 2003 was 16.2 per cent for the 20–24 age group and 10.3 per cent for the 25–29 age group. Parental home dwellers hardly ever need public rental housing to move into since they can live in their parents' houses. The public rental housing system has also excluded young one-person households. These factors have differentiated the rates of public rental housing among young people according to the type of household. Public rental housing has provided a foothold on the lower rungs of the housing ladder, but this has only been provided to households including married couples.

Divisions in urban residential spaces

Divergence in young people's life-courses has increasingly accelerated divisions in urban space. In this section, we look at differences in residential locations between parental home dwellers, single people and family-formers in the Tokyo metropolitan area, including the prefectures of Tokyo, Kanagawa, Chiba and Saitama.

In postwar Japan, as in many other societies, urban planning policy revolved around the 'male breadwinner family' model and encouraged the development of suburban residential estates. Within the framework of a housing system oriented towards home ownership, it was assumed that young people would form a nuclear household and aim for the top of the housing ladder, namely single-family housing in a suburb. During the period of high-speed economic growth, particular life-course patterns were idealized and landscapes of suburban single-family housing were indeed symbolic of postwar mainstream society. As has been discussed, however, young people's life-courses have begun to change, with a decrease in traditional family households and a countering increase in those who have remained unmarried. This has led to the fragmentation of urban space, weakening the foundation of postwar urban planning policy aimed at developing suburban estates.

Figures 9.3–9.5, prepared by re-calculating micro-data taken from the 2005 Population Census, show the geographical distribution in the Tokyo metropolitan area of individuals aged 25–34 according to the type of household. The percentage of parental home dwellers is particularly high for fringe areas (see Figure 9.3). In the fringes, employment opportunities and rental housing properties are scarce, while owner-occupied homes acquired by the current parents' generation are spacious. This has accounted for high rates of parental home dwellers in peripheral areas. In various 'parasite bashing' discourses, unmarried adults living in parental homes were assumed to be the best customers for trendy boutiques and expensive restaurants, since they were considered able to spend all their earnings on themselves. However, such discourses were not based on fact. For example, many parental home dwellers are casual workers with low incomes. In addition, in fringe areas with an increasing number of parental home dwellers, there are almost no fashionable districts, but instead rather boring landscapes dotted with cheap shops.

Although both single people and parental home dwellers are unmarried individuals, their residential locations are completely different, leading to divisions in the urban space. Unlike parental home dwellers, who tend to live in peripheral areas, many singles live in the central districts of Tokyo (see Figure 9.4). The extent to which residential locations concentrate on specific areas is much higher for singles than for parental home dwellers. Most young singles place importance on convenience and short commutes when making residential choices, and thus concentrate on central areas. There are many studio flats and various rental dwellings in the central districts, which have absorbed increasing numbers of single people.

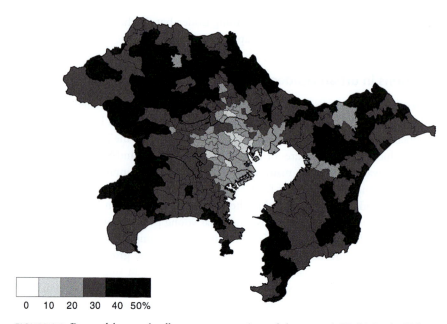

0 10 20 30 40 50%

FIGURE 9.3 Parental home dwellers as a proportion of those aged 25–34 in the Tokyo metropolitan area, 2005.
Source: Author's calculations from micro-data from the 2005 Population Census of Japan

As has been noted, female singles, who aspire to central locations as well as secure neighbourhoods, tend to bear high rents in order to live in the city centre, despite low earnings.

Young singles have not necessarily been readily accepted by long-term inhabitants, who are firmly established in local neighbourhoods. In Tokyo, an increasing number of ward municipalities have begun to impose restrictions on the development of studio flats in terms of floor area and amenity standards, with the intention of controlling the supply of dwellings to single people. Behind this restrictive policy are explicit or implicit prejudices against single-person households. Dwellers in studio flats are often considered irresponsible in terms of community activities like controlling noise and litter. Many local municipalities also prefer owner-occupier families rather than single renters with regard to creating a quiet community. Nevertheless, there has been a continual increase in singles moving into central city neighbourhoods. Although the new development of studio flats is being restricted, a large number of existing rental properties are accepting single dwellers.

The percentage of family-formers is high in the suburbs, which form concentric circles between inner-city areas and the fringes (see Figure 9.5). During the era of high-speed economic expansion, many young people established their own independent families and climbed the housing ladder to acquire their own homes, which resulted in the expansion of the suburbs. As has been discussed, however,

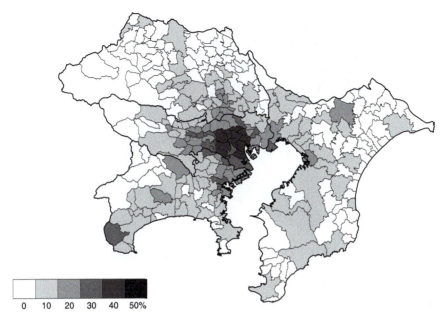

FIGURE 9.4 Single people as a proportion of those aged 25–34 in the Tokyo metropolitan area, 2005.
Source: Author's calculations from micro-data from the 2005 Population Census of Japan

there has been a decrease in family-formers. This has meant a decline in young people's moves to the suburbs and the accelerated ageing of suburban communities. While the proportion of elderly people is increasing throughout the Tokyo metropolitan area, the rate of increase is much higher in the suburbs. It has been assumed that Japanese people, historically and culturally, prefer single-family housing to multi-family housing. There is a new tendency, however, for younger generation households not necessarily to prefer living in single-family housing. This is further reducing the demand for suburban houses. According to a survey on housing preferences carried out by the government in 2004, the proportion of respondents who prefer single-family housing was 85.5 per cent for those aged 60 or more and 60.8 per cent for those aged 20–29 (Ministry of Land, Infrastructure and Transport, 2005). Consequently, the extent to which suburban residential estates are symbolic of Japan's postwar mainstream society has begun to decline.

Conclusion

Alongside the development of a housing system focused on the expansion of home ownership, people have experienced a cycle of moving up the property ladder in postwar Japan, which has played a pivotal role in sustaining the 'homeowner society'. In this chapter, however, we have demonstrated that economic decline combined

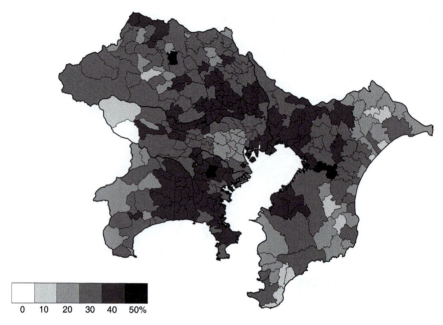

FIGURE 9.5 Family-formers as a proportion of those aged 25–34 in the Tokyo
metropolitan area, 2005.
Source: Author's calculations from micro-data from the 2005 Population
Census of Japan

with the rise of neoliberal policy has made it increasingly difficult for younger
people to follow conventional life-courses in terms of entering the home ownership
sector. The 'social flow' of people moving towards the 'inside' of the 'social mainstream' has consequently been reduced.

Cohort-based differentiation in housing opportunities has begun to erode the
traditional structure of enhanced social integration. During a period when the
economy was considered relatively predictable and followed a clear trajectory, the
system of promoting home ownership provided many people with the 'promise' of
access to mainstream society. Many renters who aimed to purchase a house regarded
themselves as potential homeowners. Young people, who were able to expect a
steady increase in income, had prospects of participating in the home-owning
society. However, socio-economic and policy transformations have increasingly
undermined the link between the housing ladder and social integration. The
younger generation is increasingly failing to realize the 'promise' of postwar home
ownership, and pathways into family formation, occupational careers and housing
acquisition are disintegrating.

Moreover, the unevenness of housing opportunities has been seen not only
between different generations but also within younger generations. Young people's
housing experiences are noticeably different for 'parental home dwellers', 'single
people' and 'family-formers'. Although many family-formers have moved towards

attaining home ownership, overall they have declined in number. At the same time, increasing numbers of parental home dwellers and single people have been almost completely excluded from the housing ladder system. In addition, divergence in young people's housing paths has led to the fragmentation of urban space. There are many parental home dwellers on the fringes while single people concentrate in central city areas. In the suburbs, a decrease in young family-formers is accelerating the ageing of communities.

Finally, it is worth emphasizing that Japan's low fertility rate can, at least partly, be attributed to the decline in young people's housing opportunities. The increase in parental home dwellers and single people will inevitably undermine fertility even more, accelerating a decrease in the total population and consequently in the workforce. Japan's housing system has been significantly geared towards expanding home ownership, but younger generation households are now facing unprecedented economic difficulties in purchasing owner-occupied housing. The government has not improved conditions in the rented housing sector, and the number of adequate, affordable rented houses is further decreasing. These changes in housing circumstances are likely to prompt young people to further delay leaving home and establishing a family. In this context, the housing situation of younger cohorts is a key driver for future social changes. An examination of trends in Japan demonstrates that housing for young people is a significant policy issue not only in itself but also in terms of social sustainability.

References

Beck, U. (1992) *Risk Society*, London: Sage.

Doling, J. and Ford, J. (eds) (2003) *Globalization and Home Ownership: Experiences in Eight Member States of the European Union*, Delft: Delft University Press.

Forrest, R. (2008) Globalisation and the housing asset rich: demographies, geographies and policy convoys, *Global Social Policy*, 8(2): 167–187.

Forrest, R. and Hirayama, Y. (2009) The uneven impact of neo-liberalism on opportunities, *International Journal of Urban and Regional Research*, 33(4): 998–1013.

Forrest, R. and Yip, N.-M. (eds) (2011) *Housing Markets and the Global Financial Crisis: The Uneven Impact on Households*, Cheltenham: Edward Elgar.

Genda, Y. (2001) *Shigoto no Naka no Aimai na Fuan [The Vague Uneasiness of Work]*, Tokyo: Chuo Korou Shinsha.

Hirayama, Y. (2003) Housing and social inequality in Japan, in M. Izuhara (ed) *Comparing Social Policies: Exploring New Perspectives in Britain and Japan*, Bristol: Polity Press, 151–171.

Hirayama, Y. (2007) Reshaping the housing system: home ownership as a catalyst for social transformation, in Y. Hirayama and R. Ronald (eds) *Housing and Social Transition in Japan*, London: Routledge, 15–46.

Hirayama, Y. (2010) Housing pathway divergence in Japan's insecure economy, *Housing Studies*, 25(6): 777–797.

Hirayama, Y. (2011a) The shifting housing opportunities of younger people in Japan's home-owning society, in R. Ronald and M. Elsinga (eds) *Beyond Home Ownership: Housing, Welfare and Society*, London: Routledge, 173–193.

Hirayama, Y. (2011b) Towards a post-homeowner society? Homeownership and economic insecurity in Japan, in R. Forrest and N.-M. Yip (eds) *Housing Markets and the Global Financial Crisis: The Uneven Impact on Households,* Cheltenham: Edward Elgar, 196–213.

Hirayama, Y. and Izuhara, M. (2008) Women and housing assets in the context of Japan's home-owning democracy, *Journal of Social Policy,* 37(4): 641–660.

Horsewood, N. and Neuteboom, P. (eds) (2006) *The Social Limits to Growth: Security and Insecurity Aspects of Home Ownership,* Delft: Delft University Press.

Iwagami, M. (1999) Niju-dai, sanju-dai mikonsha no oya tono dobekkyo kozo [Research into unmarried people in their twenties and thirties co-residing with own parents in Japan], *Jinko Mondai Kenkyu [Journal of Population Problems],* 55(4): 1–15.

Kitamura, A. (2001) Seijin mikonsha no rika to oyako kankei [Unmarried adults, home leaving and family relations], *Life Design Report,* 7: 22–45.

Kurz, K. and Blossfeld, H. (eds) (2004) *Home Ownership and Social Inequality in Comparative Perspective,* Stanford: Stanford University Press.

Ministry of Land, Infrastructure and Transport (2005) *Tochi Hakusho [Government White Paper on Land],* Tokyo: National Printing Bureau.

Miyamoto, M. (2004) *Posuto Seinenki to Oyako Senryaku [Post-Youth Period and Family Strategies],* Tokyo: Keiso Shobo.

Mulder, C.H. (2006) Home-ownership and family formation, *Journal of Housing and the Built Environment,* 21(3): 281–298.

Mulder, C.H. and Billari, F.C. (2010) Homeownership regimes and low fertility, *Housing Studies,* 25(4): 527–541.

Nagase, N. (2002) Jakunenso no koyo no hiseikika to kekkon kodo [Marriage timing and the effect of increase in non-standard employment among the youth in Japan], *Jinko Mondai Kenkyu [Journal of Population Problems],* 58(2): 22–35.

Nagase, N. and Murao, Y. (2005) Shakai hosho ya zeisei tou ha kazoku, kazokukeisei ni eikyo wo ataeruka [Do social security and taxation systems influence family formation?], *Kikan Shakai Hosho Kenkyu [Journal of Social Security Research],* 41(2): 137–149.

NHK Broadcasting Culture Research Institute (2004) *Gendai Nihonjin no Ishiki Kozo [People's Attitudes in Contemporary Japan],* Tokyo: Nihon Hoso Shuppankyoku.

Ohishi, A. (2004) Jakunen shugyo to oya tono doubekyo [Young people's employment and their living arrangements with parents], *Jinko Mondai Kenkyu [Journal Population Problems],* 60(2): 19–31.

Ronald, R. and Elsinga, M. (eds) (2012) *Beyond Home Ownership: Housing, Welfare and Society,* London: Routledge.

Sato, I. (2007) Welfare regime theories and the Japanese housing system, in: Y. Hirayama and R. Ronald (eds) *Housing and Social Transition in Japan,* London: Routledge, 73–93.

Shirahase, S. (2005) *Shoshi Korei Syakai no Mienai Kakusa [Invisible Inequalities in Low Fertility, Aged Society],* Tokyo: Tokyo University Press.

Yamada, M. (1999) *Parasaito Shinguru no Jidai [The Time of Parasite of Singles],* Tokyo: Chikuma Shobo.

Yokoyama, F. (2002) *Sengo Nihon no Josei Seisaku [Public Policy for Women in Postwar Japan],* Tokyo: Keiso Shobo.

Yui, Y. (2004) Daitoshi niokeru shinguru josei no manshon konyu to sono haikei [Condominium purchase by single women in large cities], in Y. Yui, H. Kamiya, Y. Wakabayashi and T. Nakazawa (eds) *Hataraku Josei no Toshi Kukan [Urban Space and Working Women],* Tokyo: Kokin Shoten, 141–168.

10

RESIDENTIAL TRAJECTORIES OF YOUNG FRENCH PEOPLE

The French generational gap

Fanny Bugeja-Bloch

Introduction

In France twenty years ago, questions around residential strategies, residential mobility (at a geographic level), access to home ownership, residential choices and the articulation between family structure and housing were the focus of a substantial amount of research. But nowadays it seems that this issue is of little interest to researchers. In reality, however, this is only an impression, because of the difficulties of setting boundaries and identifying the different aspects of such a subject (Authier *et al.*, 2010). Several aspects of residential trajectories, often linked to economic and political contexts, have been studied for the past 50 years. Before the 1980s, researchers focused on access to social housing. After this, and due to the shift from bricks-and-mortar to personal subsidies at the end of the 70s, questions of access to homeownership and residential choices became progressively more important.[1]

During the 90s, residential trajectories were analysed in relation to family. An initial approach focused on the role of family transmission (of economic, social and symbolic resources) in influencing residential status: tenant or homeowner (Bonvalet and Gotman, 1993; Bonvalet *et al.*, 1999). A second approach emphasised the fundamental need to consider not only residential choices at the level of the household but also at the level of the whole family. From this perspective, residential mobility was not only linked to the nuclear family but also to the extended family ('famille étendue') or family circle ('entourage familial') (Bonvalet, 1997; Bonvalet *et al.*, 1999). If there are multiple definitions of residential trajectories, defining 'young people' also raises several issues. In 1988, Baudelot had already highlighted the difficulties of defining the new youth. How to define the boundaries of youth? How to characterise the transition from adolescence to youth and then the progression to adulthood? Is youth only a question of age? What does the usual category, 18–25 years old, mean? In France, 18 years old is the legal and civic age for majority.

But, others ages such as 16 years old, the minimum age for leaving compulsory education, are also symbolic. Moreover, these boundaries, defined by age criteria, differ by country. So, comprehending youth by this method of age boundaries, i.e. a fixed period, is not relevant (Chanvril *et al.*, 2009). Actually, 'youth' means a period of transition which leads to autonomy or independence (De Singly, 2000). The use of these two terms is not innocent, since it is frequent for a young person to be independent but not self-sufficient. For instance, an increasing number of young people are workers but live in the parental house. In the same way, some live alone but with the financial assistance of their parents. Therefore, the definition of 'youth' is clearly linked to the question of financial and residential independence. In addition, analysing young people implies a need to compare youth over the generations. From this point of view, youth is not a precise age range, and this chapter will expose the extent to which youth, as a life stage, tends to increase from one generation to the next. Given all these considerations, this chapter is intended to analyse residential trajectories of people aged between 15 and 35. Choosing a large range is necessary since 'youth' evolves over the generations.

This chapter reviews the literature on the residential trajectories of young people, outlining the main features of French youth and its evolution over time and through the generations. A brief comparison with the European context is also provided. In this way, all aspects of residential trajectories are analysed. Empirical work, based on the analysis of Insee's *Budget de Famille* surveys from 1985 to 2005 then describes in detail the tenure choices or, perhaps more precisely, tenure constraints of French society and French youth.

Residential trajectories of young people in France: a search through the literature

Since the beginning of the 90s, youth has been characterised by its extension (Galland, 1994; Arnett, 2000; Baudelot and Establet, 2000; Van de Velde, 2008; Chanvril *et al.*, 2009). Galland describes the longer period of transition between the end of study and family formation, which coincides with an extended period of single life. On this issue, sociological debate focuses on the question of a new life stage captured by the term 'emerging adulthood' (Arnett, 2000). According to Arnett, this new life stage is characterised by carefreeness, since this progressive independence is not yet associated with adult responsibilities. But, do these characteristics only concern a particular 'fringe' of youth? Indeed, this definition better describes the upper categories of students than the young people with low education levels who have difficulties entering the labour market (Bourdieu, 1984; Baudelot and Establet, 2000; Chanvril *et al.*, 2009). Galland (1994) explains that the extension of this period of single life may be associated with two contradictory significations: a signification of 'luxury' for the child of upper social categories, who voluntarily delays family commitments, or a signification of 'poverty' for the children of manual workers who do not succeed in entering the labour and marital markets.

The next section explains this debate in three stages. The first stage clarifies this extension of youth. The second analyses the causes of the phenomenon. And, the last examines the social consequences for young people.

Characterisation of the prolongation of youth

In order to analyse the residential trajectories of young people, defining precisely all the operational terms is imperative. Villeneuve-Gokalp (2000) explains clearly the difference between 'decohabitation' and 'residential independence'. Decohabitation is the moment when the child leaves the parental home; while a young person acquires residential independence when parents no longer provide any financial support for lodging. According to these definitions, since the beginning of the 90s, the age of decohabitation has been stable, whereas residential independence is occurring later. The age of access to independence decreased up to the generation born in 1957, then increased for following generations. Consequently, the image of children living in their parents' home until they are 30 years old does not reflect the truth. Moreover, between decohabitation and residential independence, there are many other situations.

> Between the ages of 19 and 24, 56 per cent of men live on a permanent basis with their parents and have never left. At the other extreme, 17 per cent live in their own accommodation and pay the rent themselves. Between these two extreme situations, which mark the beginning and the end of the process, there are also temporary residential conditions: living with parents but being absent most of the time, living in one's own home with parental assistance for the payment of the rent, coming back to the parental home after a leaving.[2]
>
> *Villeneuve-Gokalp 2000: 62*

All these intermediate stages are increasingly frequent and consolidate the idea of an extension of youth. Indeed, the residential trajectories of young people are less and less linear (Galland, 1994; Van de Velde, 2008).

The reasons for this prolongation

Economic impacts

Most macroeconomic factors influence housing behaviours and residential trajectories. Basing her analysis on the length of cohabitation between generations, Bonvalet (1991) has explained this phenomenon. Length of cohabitation (between children and their parents or grandparents) is inextricably linked to economic situation and housing supply. After World War II, the housing shortage led to high levels of family support. And the extended cohabitation of children with their parents is the tangible evidence of this increasing role of family solidarity. Conversely, during the 70s, the decline of cohabitation between generations was the result of a relaxation of the housing market. But since the 80s, with a housing shortage, a rise in unemployment rates which has affected young people particularly[3] and the increasing instability of career paths, children have been living with their parents longer[4] (Bonvalet, 1991).

If changes (economic and demographic) over time significantly shape the evolution of the residential trajectories of young people, the notion of generations is also significant. Chauvel (1998) highlighted the different destinies of different generations. He distinguished three main generations:

- A first, born between 1920 and 1935, has benefited from full employment and the growth of social protection.
- A second, defined as the favoured generation, born between 1936 and 1950, that is to say part of the first baby-boomer generation (1946–74), entered the labour market during a period of economic growth ('les trente glorieuses' – Fourastié, 1979).
- The generation born between 1950 and 1965 is the first which did not experience upward social mobility and faced increases in unemployment rates.

These different destinies of the generations also impact on the residential trajectories of young people. Indeed, new generations of young people are being 'sacrificed': they do not have the same opportunities in the labour and housing markets.

Impact of demographic changes

The lengthened period of cohabitation is correlated not only with housing and economic markets but also with changes in family behaviour.[5] In fact, the average ages at first marriage and at birth of the first child have risen markedly over time. In the same way, the duration of study has increased considerably in France over the last fifty years. Even though it is impossible to determine which aspect is the determinant of the other, demographic changes are clearly linked to the mutation in the residential behaviour of youth.

Impact of institutional factors

While the pattern of a rising age of parenthood is similar in all West European countries, there are strong national differences in the age of the achievement of residential independence. Actually, the boundaries of youth and the date of independence (residential and financial) differ between Nordic, Southern, English-speaking and continental countries. According to Van de Velde (2008), these differences are linked to the type of welfare regime (Esping-Andersen, 1999). In Nordic and social-democratic countries, young people become independent (residentially and financially) more quickly. If the life stage devoted to study is longer than in other European countries, social policies tend to favour courses which enable students to study part-time and work part-time. So, in these countries, residential and financial independence are relatively correlated. In Southern countries, however, where the role of the family is fundamental, cohabitation between children and parents lasts very much longer. Young people wait for the end of their studies to enter the labour and housing markets before leaving the parental house. Since the rental market[6] is virtually nonexistent, young people wait to accumulate enough savings to buy or to build a house. Due to the late departure from the familial home, the two forms of independence are simultaneous and this autonomy also often corresponds with the creation of one's own family. In liberal regimes, the period spent studying is among the shortest of all the European countries. There, the logic is for young people to support themselves as soon as possible. Subsequently, the trajectories of young people are quite short and the access to residential and financial autonomy is concomitant and rapid.

Trajectories of young people living in France and in most corporatist countries are rather more complicated. In France, more time is spent studying. This period is more often financed by parental assistance. And this help (residential or financial) is seen as totally legitimate, since the link between a diploma and the quality of a first job is considered significant. So, increasing numbers of students are independent in terms of housing but not in economic terms. Research undertaken on behalf of Caisse Nationale des Allocations Familiales established a typology of youth trajectories. According to the authors, contemporary youth tends to be more and more characterised by 'independent trajectories', which means that young people leave their parents' home quickly but wait a long time before having a child (Chanvril *et al.*, 2009). So, on the one hand, there are young students who receive financial support from their parents and, on the other, there are all the young people who do not spend a long time studying and are characterised by shorter trajectories only if they succeed in finding a job and renting accommodation.

Social consequences of this change for young people

The increasing role of family support

The extension of youth (Galland, 1994), that is to say the delay of residential independence (Villeneuve-Gokalp, 2000), the lengthening of the period of cohabitation since the 80s (Bonvalet, 1991) and the expansion of 'independent trajectories' among young people (Chanvril *et al.*, 2009) has changed the role of the family. Indeed, the place and the assistance of the family have become more fundamental. Parents can help their children in different ways: through cohabitation, or as a labour force to build housing (this is particularly frequent in southern countries) or help with everyday tasks if children and parents live in the same town or district (Bonvalet, 1997). Some 40 per cent of the interviewees of the survey *Peuplement et dépeuplement* who were living in Paris had obtained their housing with the help of their family (Bonvalet, 1991). Villeneuve-Gokalp (2000: 66) explains that the age at decohabitation did not change between 1992 and 1997 because the development of family financial support allowed an increasing number of children to leave the parental home despite their being still economically dependent.

The degree and the type of help, financial or otherwise, vary considerably with family resources and with social class. For instance, middle or senior managers provide more financial support than manual and office workers. Conversely, non-financial help is more frequent among the latter (Bonvalet, 1997). However, parental financial assistance is a key determinant of access to housing. And this family role is not only a determinant of access to private (Grafmeyer, 1991) but also to the social housing sector (Vervaeke, 1992). In France, private and public landlords ask future tenants for a guarantor. And in the case of young people, it is usually the parents who stand surety for the payment of the rent.

In the same way, banks and other lending institutions request a guarantee of the payment of loan. In France, the main system of credit is the loan on real property with a deposit and fixed interest rate. This system totally differs from mortgage systems such as those in the United Kingdom or Denmark.[7] It is personal credit, which means that eligibility criteria are linked to the income stability and income level of the borrower. So, in France, the poor, students, members of the liberal professions, people with fixed-term contracts and those with precarious contracts have no chance of obtaining a loan: lenders are much more focused on a borrower's income in France than in countries with mortgage systems (where the guarantee is linked to the property) (Jachiet et al., 2004; Bugeja, 2011).

Further, regarding the rental sector, Grafmeyer has highlighted the financial role of parents: 'two-thirds of the accepted files contained a guarantee from close relatives, whereas 70 per cent of the rejected files did not mention any guarantee' (Authier et al., 2010: 29, citing Grafmeyer, 1990).

While family support is increasing, more and more young people also benefit from national assistance through housing allowances. In 1997, 50 per cent of students who did not live with their parents benefited, compared to only 17 per cent five years previously. This policy is, however, not totally efficient and does not permit a reduction in family help since its major impact is to increase rent levels (Fack, 2005).

An accumulation of difficulties

New generations of young people have to face growing difficulties. In addition to difficulties in the housing market, they also experience difficulties in the labour market. The generation born in 1950–55 has been the first to experience downward social mobility. And, among the generation born after 1960, the percentage of those with a lower social position than their parents is rising (Peugny, 2009). Today, these 'descendant mobiles' represent 25 per cent of 35–39-year-olds, compared to 18 per cent 20 years ago. This development is linked to changes in the employment structure, which does not fit with the increasing numbers of young people with high-level qualifications. As a consequence, in this generation, we find numerous victims of a double drop in status: educational, since their qualifications are too high compared to their economic position; and social, since their positions are lower than those of their parents (despite their higher level of qualification).

Two youths?

If the growing place of family means social bonding or solidarity, it also means the return of social inequalities and social reproduction. Taken as a whole, this literature describes an opposition in the destinies of young people, between those who can benefit from parental assistance and others, who try to enter the housing and labour markets. The residential trajectories of the first group are longer than the second, but are to a greater extent the result of choice. Thus, it would seem that the term 'emerging adulthood' (Arnett, 2000) describes the first group better than the second, at least during the period they are studying. With these increasing inequalities among youth, it is important not to ignore the possible extension of social reproduction for these new generations of young people. Indeed, young homeowners are now rather more often the children of homeowners.

An empirical study of 'housing careers'

Before studying the housing careers[8] of young people, it is necessary first to describe the tenure choices of different groups in French society. This first empirical study (with a sample representing the entire population) shows that French society is characterised by strong intergenerational inequalities. Indeed, new generations of young people are increasingly private tenants, whereas households born before or during the 50s achieved unprecedented rates of homeownership. Moreover, access to home ownership (measured by mortgage rates) did not change significantly after 1980. In terms of methodology, this chapter presents both descriptive and explicative (regression) analysis. The latter permits the analysis of homeownership inequalities (or more precisely 'housing careers') and their determinants (see Appendix 10.1 at the end of this chapter). So, the main question is: Does French society produce generational homeownership inequalities because of the structural 'generational shift'?

The second part of the analysis focuses on the 'housing careers' of young people (with a sample representing young households). The primary aims are to explore the reality of the 'two youths' described previously and to highlight intragenerational inequalities in the housing careers of young people. Thus, the first part describes intergenerational inequalities, while the second focuses on intragenerational inequalities in terms of tenure choices.

Housing careers: generational and social inequalities in French society

Home ownership (outright and with a mortgage) has been the dominant form of tenure in France since 1980. It represented about 60 per cent of the housing stock in 2005 (Figure 10.1). Contrary to some liberal models, notably that of the United Kingdom, home ownership without a mortgage is more developed in France than ownership with a mortgage. In terms of the rental sector, there is no real dominant tenure form (in 2005, the private sector represented about 20 per cent of households compared to 14 per cent for the social sector).

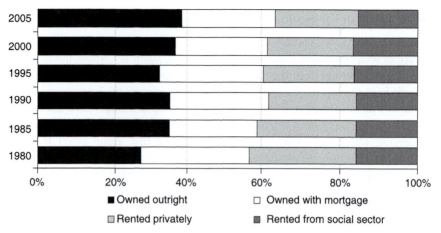

FIGURE 10.1 Tenure distribution in France since 1980.
        Source: Budget de Famille 1979, 1985, 1989, 1995, 2001 and 2006 (Insee)

Figure 10.2 illustrates the French generational gap identified previously, and shows how access to homeownership is becoming more and more difficult for young people. Over the years, successive generations of young people seem to be more and more excluded from this status. Is this the consequence of a generational or age effect?

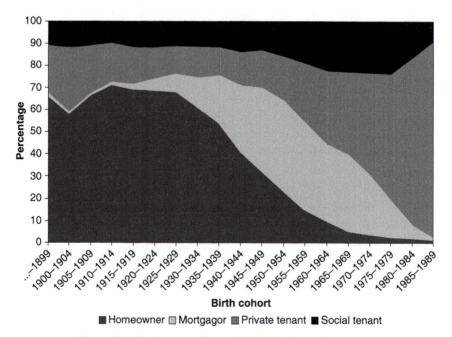

FIGURE 10.2 Tenure distribution according to the birth cohort of the head of household.
        Source: Budget de Famille 1979 to 2006

More and more young private tenants: choice or constraint?

It is important initially to clarify the characteristics of the rental sector. First of all, the practice of flat-sharing with a roommate is unusual in France. In the social rental sector, the share of individual housing has increased significantly (from about 9 per cent in 1985 to about 16.5 per cent in 2005). According to Zittoun (2001), during the 60s and 70s, social housing was built to house the classic French family in larger dwellings (Laferrère *et al.*, 1999). Consequently, in 1980, the main population in this sector was households aged below 35. But since 1990 the proportion of adults under 25 among social tenants has fallen continuously. Indeed, the supply of studios (small apartments) is absent, and this is the type of dwelling best adapted to the needs of this group of young people, characterised by an extended youth. As a consequence, an increasing proportion of young people have had little choice but to seek accommodation in the private rental sector.

Unlike the social sector, the private rental sector is clearly associated with a particular moment of the life cycle: youth (Figure 10.3). The older the household, the less likely it is to be in this sector. This link between youth and private renting has been explained by Arbonville and Bonvalet (2005) and Di Salvo and Ermisch

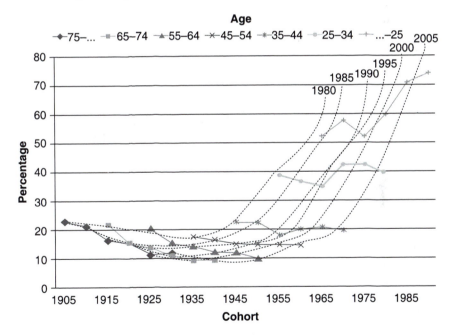

FIGURE 10.3 Proportion of private tenants by cohort.
Source: Budget de Famille 1979 to 2006
Note: The horizontal axis shows birth year, while the different data points represent different age ranges. The year label on each graph line corresponds to the year of survey. For example, 23 per cent of households aged between 35 and 44 years old in 1980 (that is to say, households born from 1945) were private tenants.

TABLE 10.1 Estimation of parameters of multinomial logistic models – probability of being a private tenant rather than a social tenant, a mortgagor rather than a tenant and a homeowner rather than mortgagor in France.

Reference	Model category	Coefficients		
		Private tenant vs social tenant	Mortgagor vs tenant	Homeowner vs mortgagor
Constant		n.s.	−2.68★★★	3.50★★★
Year				
	2005	−1.00★★★	n.s.	1.23★
	2000	−1.14★★★	n.s.	n.s.
	1995	−0.44★	n.s.	n.s.
1985	1990	n.s.	n.s.	n.s.
Age of reference person in 1985				
	...−25	n.s.	n.s.	−4.43★★★
	25–34	n.s.	1.48★★★	−4.40★★★
	35–44	n.s.	2.15★★★	−3.90★★★
	45–54	n.s.	2.35★★★	−3.00★★★
	55–64	−0.46★★	2.03★★★	−2.11★★★
75–...	65–74	−0.31	1.32★★★	−0.95★
Interaction: age and period				
	...−25★2005	1.86★★★	n.s.	n.s.
	25–34★2005	0.93★★★	n.s.	−2.15★★★
	35–44★2005	0.53★	n.s.	−1.86★★
	45–54★2005	0.55★	n.s.	−1.45★★
	55–64★2005	n.s.	n.s.	−1.29★
75–...★1985	65–74★2005	n.s.	n.s.	n.s.

Source: Budget de Famille 1985 to 2006 (Insee) ★ $p < 5\%$, ★★ $p < 1\%$ and ★★★ $p < 0.1\%$ (where p is the probability)

Note: For the interactions, all the years are introduced into the model. 1985 and 2005 only are shown, for ease of reading.

(1996, 1997): young adults are characterised by greater mobility, flexibility and insecurity in the labour market than older households. They prefer to be tenants rather than homeowners, since homeownership is associated with (family and professional) security.

Private tenancy is also linked to cohort effects. Over the last 25 years, increasing proportions of young people have become private tenants (Figure 10.3). Moreover, the likelihood of being a private rather than a social tenant has greatly increased for young people. For households aged less than 25, the likelihood was six times higher in 2005 compared to 1985 (Table 10.1). This is consistent with earlier research by Meron and Courgeau (2004). They pointed to the delay in the age of first entry to homeownership for new generations of young people and explained this phenomenon by the increase in risk in the labour market and the increased period of financial dependence on family among more recent cohorts of young people. Consequently, the revival of private tenancy can be explained by the generational discontinuity identified by Chauvel (1998). The generations born after 1975 have to choose this tenure. Conversely, generations born before 1955 were increasingly able to gain access to homeownership (Figure 10.4 and Table 10.1) since they bene-fited from the growth of the 'trente glorieuses' (Fourastié, 1979).

Does the development of homeownership concern only older households?

Home purchase rates are also clearly associated with age group and concentrated on households aged between 35 and 45. The regression analysis (Table 10.1) illustrates this phenomenon: other things being equal, the French life stage of home ownership access is concentrated between the ages of 35 and 54 years old. This pattern is quite stable over the entire period, despite the changing policy measures in favour of homeownership (Table 10.1). Age and generation also determine outright home ownership rates. Indeed, owning property without a mortgage constitutes the end of the residential trajectory. The older a household, the more likely it is to own a home outright (Table 10.1 and Figure 10.4).

Generational inequalities can be overlain on these age disparities. The generations born before 1940, which benefited from the growing prosperity of the period 1945–75, are systematically more likely to be outright homeowners than previous genera-tions. Conversely, the share of outright homeownership among households aged less

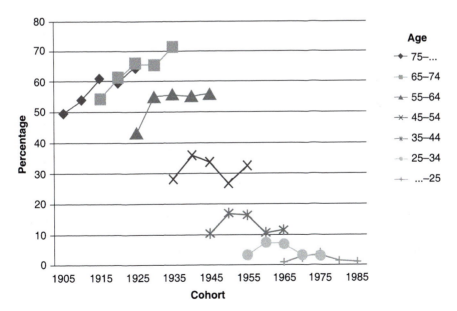

FIGURE 10.4 Proportion of homeowners (without a mortgage) by cohort.
Source: Budget de Famille 1979 to 2006

than 45 has progressively decreased since 1995. Other things being equal, compared to the oldest households (aged 75 or older), the chances of being a home owner rather than a mortgagor have decreased for all younger people since 1985 (Table 10.1).

Finally, intergenerational inequalities in access to homeownership have been particularly acute for young people who experience economic and social difficulties. If home ownership inequalities are linked to individual aspiration, they are also associated with economic and social condition and with institutional and national factors, such as welfare regimes and housing policies.

In France, the weakness of housing policy incentives to increase home purchase rates did not change the French generational gap that favours households born between 1945 and 1955. In the same way, the lack of credit system reform[9] before 2005 did not allow less privileged categories to access home ownership (Appendix 10.2). Further, we should not forget that these young people have also experienced another constraint: not only are more and more young people becoming private tenants, they are also experiencing the greatest constraint in terms of rising housing costs (Accardo and Bugeja, 2009).[10]

'Housing careers' of young French people

The focus now shifts to households less than 35 years old. The analysis draws on surveys from 1985 and concerns all people born after 1950. The methodology remains the same: multinomial logistical regressions which show the probability of being a private rather than a social tenant and the probability of being a mortgagor rather than a private tenant. Because the sample concerns only younger households, it is not possible to analyse the probability of being an outright rather than a mortgaged homeowner, since outright home owners represent less than five per cent of this reduced sample.

Before analysing these regressions, some limitations should be acknowledged. First, these data only allow the analysis of the residential trajectories of young people who do not live with their parents. Indeed, what are referred to here as young people are young households, i.e. households with a young reference person. Consequently, it is not possible to identify young people who live in the parental home since they have not succeeded in finding stable employment and independent accommodation. Second, the occupational scheme does not differentiate students from the unemployed or from economically unoccupied persons. A third limitation concerns professional status and stability of employment position. The data do not provide this information. This constitutes a real limitation, since young people experience job insecurity more often than older people. It is thus important to relativise social position: for example, the status of higher-grade professional may be insecure. Moreover, if the urbanisation dimension is introduced into these models, it does not control for distance from the town centre. But this geographic hierarchy is clearly linked to the level of housing prices and to urban segregation.

As explained earlier, young people have increasingly been excluded from social tenancy. And, over the past 20 years, people less than 22 years old have increasingly been likely to be private rather than social tenants, compared to older households (Table 10.2). Age categories (among young people) are not sufficient to explain the likelihood of being a private rather than a social tenant. But, there has been a significant demographic evolution over the period: more and more younger households are composed of one person. This effectively excludes them from social renting. Consequently, they have to choose private tenancy, an increasingly expensive alternative. Income level and social position combine to make up another determinant of tenancy status. Their influence on the probability of being a private rather than a social tenant is as significant for young people as for the entire population. Only poorer and lower social status young people get into social housing. But this statistical model (Table 10.2) describes the particular effect of social position (i.e. when the effect of income is stable). At constant income, social position reinforces the effect of income.

TABLE 10.2 Estimation of parameters of multinomial logistic models – probability of being a private tenant rather than a social tenant and of being a mortgagor rather than private tenant among French households aged less than 35.

Reference	Model category	Coefficients	
		Private tenant vs social	Mortgagor vs private tenant
Constant		n.s.	−0.80★
Years			
	2005	n.s.	0.79★★
	2000	n.s.	0.58★
	1995	n.s.	n.s.
1985	1990	n.s.	n.s.
Age of reference person in 1985			
	...−22	n.s.	−2.15★★★
	23–25	n.s.	−1.00★★
	26–28	n.s.	−0.61★
	29–31	n.s.	n.s.
34–35	32–33	n.s.	n.s.
Income decile			
	1	−0.71★★	−1.97★★★
	2	−0.89★★★	−2.01★★★
	3	−0.82★★★	−1.61★★★
	4	−0.78★★★	−1.04★★★
	5	−0.84★★★	−1.05★★★
	6	−0.66★★	−0.72★★★
	7	−0.40★	−0.50★★
	8	−0.49★	−0.30★
10	9	n.s.	n.s.

(continued)

TABLE 10.2 *(continued)*

Reference	Model category	Coefficients	
		Private tenant vs social	*Mortgagor vs private tenant*
Occupation of reference person			
	Not occupied (not retired)	0.82★★★	−0.55★
	Farmer	1.25★★	n.s.
	Artisan, shopkeeper, proprietor or manager	1.50★★★	−0.39★
	Higher-grade professional	1.64★★★	−0.54★★★
	Lower-grade professional, technician or foremen	0.52★★★	n.s.
Manual worker	Clerk	0.17★	n.s.
Interaction: age and period			
	...−22★2005	1.02★	n.s.
	23–25★2005	0.70★	n.s.
	26–28★2005	n.s	n.s.
	29–31★2005	n.s	n.s.
34–35★1985	32–33★2005	n.s.	n.s.
Composition of household			
	One person	1.10★★★	n.s.
	Couple without child	0.90★★★	n.s.
	Couple with one child	0.34★★	0.74★★★
	Couple with two children	n.s.	1.33★★★
Others	Couple with three or more children	n.s.	1.36★★★
Degree of urbanisation			
	Rural	0.55★★★	n.s.
	Urban Unit: less than 20,000 inhabitants	n.s.	−0.41★★
	Urban Unit: between 20,000 and 100,000 inhabitants	0.24★	−0.58★★★
Paris and its suburbs	Urban Unit: more than 100,000 inhabitants	n.s.	−0.26★
Dwelling type			
Flat	House	1.48★★★	1.88★★★

Source: Budget de Famille 1985 to 2006 (Insee)

★ $p < 5\%$, ★★ $p < 1\%$ and ★★★ $p < 0.1\%$ (where p is the probability)

When we compare the determinants of the probability of being a mortgagor rather than a private tenant among young households (Table 10.2) with the entire population (Appendix 10.2), they are quite similar. As stated previously, in France, this pattern is strongly associated with age. The reduction of the sample to households aged less than 35 describes the same relationship. Age inequalities as regards access to home ownership are also evident among young people: the younger the household, the weaker its chances of being a mortgagor. For those less than 22 years old, the likelihood of being a home buyer (rather than a private tenant) is eight times lower than for those aged between 34 and 35, (Table 10.2). This pattern is relatively stable over time.

The main difference between the two populations (the entire population and the young population) lies in income level. Indeed, among young people, this factor is more central and the gap between rich and poor households is larger. Does this disparity relate to the greater job insecurity experienced by young people? Another explanation may be the relatively low level of their savings.

Social position can also constitute an important determinant of access to home-ownership. It may be surprising, but, other things being equal, the higher the social status of a younger household, the weaker its chances of being a mortgagor (rather than private tenant). There is, however a simple explanation for this result. Artisans, shopkeepers, proprietors and managers are self-employed persons, and this status often involves taking out a professional loan. And French banks are not in favour of multiple loans (both real estate and professional). Consequently, these upper categories of the self-employed face more difficulty in borrowing to buy a house. As far as higher-grade professionals are concerned, their relative exclusion from homeownership relates to the length of time spent in education. These young people enter the labour market, live in a couple, and form a family at a more advanced age than manual workers who spend less time studying. Thus, they are also likely to delay their first housing purchase. Further, compared with other social classes, the upper categories are more likely to live in town centres where house prices are highest. Consequently, housing purchase involves a longer wait, needed to accumulate enough savings.

Conclusion

Youth in France can be characterised by age inequalities: among young people, the youngest are increasingly excluded from the social rental sector. And youth can also be described in terms of strong intragenerational inequalities: between rich home-owners and poor tenants. This suggests a strengthening pattern of social reproduction: young homeowners are the children of homeowners. Because of limitations in the data, however, we cannot resolve the debate over the implications of the prolongation of youth and on the inequalities between the 'two youths': those who can benefit from family assistance and financial support, and the others . . . . But French society is clearly characterised by strong inter- and intragenerational inequalities in relation to residential choices.

Regarding intergenerational inequalities, the chances of gaining access to home-ownership differ significantly between generations. The generations born before 1940 (and perhaps before 1950) experienced such benign economic and social conditions that they had considerably enhanced opportunities to access home-ownership. Conversely, new generations, characterised by the prolongation of youth and more difficult labour market conditions, have more limited residential choices. Their demographic characteristics exclude them from social tenancy and their economic and social circumstances are an obstacle to homeownership. High income levels have become even more of an imperative, and a crucial criterion for bank lending, than for older age groups. In other words, intragenerational inequalities are particularly marked among young people. Those in higher social categories (when income is controlled for) have to delay their access to homeownership since they have spent more time studying. In this context the question is the extent to which this is a matter of choice or constraint. Then there are the young people at the bottom of the social hierarchy – who enter home ownership relatively quickly … but this tenure status may involve living a long way from a town centre and thus long commuting times. Moreover, home ownership in this context may involve generally poorer living conditions.

Notes

1 Until the reforms of 1977, housing policy was centred on housebuilding. The aim of this interventionist policy was to respond to a universal social need (Zittoun, 2001). Following reform, there has been a partial shift from bricks-and-mortar subsidies ('aide à la pierre') to personal subsidies ('aide à la personne'). Indeed, the main measure was the introduction of housing benefit, which is a means-tested social security benefit intended to help people with low incomes. The second main measure was the expansion of social mortgage financing (Bidou, 1996). But there is no strong political orientation, since new bricks-and-mortar subsidies were established, too.
2 'Entre 19 et 24 ans, 56 per cent des hommes vivent chez leurs parents de manière quasi permanente et n'en sont jamais partis. A l'autre extrémité, 17 per cent résident dans un logement personnel dont ils paient eux-mêmes le loyer. Entre ces deux situations extrêmes, qui marquent le début et la fin du processus, s'intercalent des conditions résidentielles provisoires: habiter chez ses parents tout en s'absentant de chez eux plus de la moitié du temps, vivre dans un autre logement payé par leurs soins, être de retour après un départ provisoire' (Villeneuve-Gokalp 2000: 62).
3 The unemployment rate among people aged less than 25 years old was 22.3 per cent in 1980 compared to 9.2 per cent on average at the end of 2010 (Insee, ministère de l'emploi).
4 The differences between the conclusions of Bonvalet (1991) and Villeneuve-Gokalp (2000) are due to the fact that they are studying different periods of time.
5 If the French birth rate is the highest in Europe (2 children per woman in 2011; Insee), the age at the birth of the first child is also the highest, at 23 years old for the generation born in 1950 and 29 years old for the one born in 1974 (Insee, Etat civil, recensement de la population). Showing a similar trend, the median age of women at marriage was 22.5 years old in 1974 and 31.5 in 2003 (Daguet, 1996 and Eurostats).
6 Indeed, the proportion of homeowners is the highest out of all the European countries and represents more than 85 per cent of the housing stock (Vorms, 2009).
7 In France, the mechanism of mortgage equity withdrawal ('extraction de valeur immobilère') is nonexistent and the renegotiation of the loan is unusual and difficult. The term of the loan is shorter than in countries with mortgage systems (15 years on average in France in 2000, compared to 23 years in the UK in 2002) although this is increasing.
8 The notion of 'housing careers' relates to the idea that there is (arguably) a hierarchy or a linearity of housing tenure. The linearity is linked to life cycle. In this way, young people are tenants, who then access home ownership at the age of 35–45, and this

housing becomes unmortgaged property in their later years. This trajectory is quite typical in French society but not in all societies, notably that of the UK (Bugeja, 2011). If a distinction between private and social sectors is made, the hierarchy of housing tenure can be: social tenant, private tenant, mortgagor and homeowner. In France, social tenancy is not clearly correlated with life cycle since the main criterion for this form of tenure is a low income.

9 In France, a loan on real property ('crédit immobilier') with a deposit and fixed interest rate is usual. There is no possibility of mortgage equity withdrawal ('extraction de valeur immobilère'). Consequently, the French credit system is not as risky as it is in, notably, the UK. The term of the loan was 15 years on average in 2000 and more than 18 years in 2005.

10 For example, for private sector tenant households aged between 25 and 45, who belong to the poorest quarter of the population, the proportion of income spent on housing, for a one-room dwelling, was about 15 per cent in 1985, and 27 per cent in 2005; this compares to a 7 per cent average, overall.

References

Accardo, J. and F. Bugeja, (2009), 'Le poids des dépenses de logement depuis vingt ans', *Insee Références. Cinquante ans de consommation en France*, 33–47.

Arbonville, D. and C. Bonvalet, (2005), 'Famille, logement et urbanisation en France', *cahier INED* 157.

Arnett, J. (2000), 'Emerging adulthood. A theory of development from the late teens through the twenties', *American psychologist* 55, 469–480.

Authier, J., J. Bidet, A. Collet, P. Gilbert and H. Steinmetz (2010), 'Etat des lieux sur les trajectoires résidentielles', Technical report, Plan Urbanisme Construction Architecture, Ministère de l'Ecologie, de l'énergie, du Développement Durable et de la Mer.

Baudelot, C. (1988), 'La jeunesse n'est plus ce qu'elle était: les difficultés d'une description', *Revue économique* 39, 189–224.

Baudelot, C. and R. Establet (2000), *Avoir 30 ans en 1968 et 1998*, Seuil.

Bidou, C. (1996), 'Les rigidités de la ville fordiste, sur les dysfonctionnements dans les banlieues françaises', *Espaces et sociétés* 82–83, 97–118.

Bonvalet, C. (1991), 'La famille et le marché du logement: une logique cachée', in M. Segalen, ed., *Jeux de famille*, Presse du CNRS, pp. 57–77.

Bonvalet, C. (1997), 'Sociologie de la famille, sociologie du logement: un lien à redéfinir', *Sociétés contemporaines* 25, 25–44.

Bonvalet, C. and A. Gotman, (1993), *Le logement, une affaire de famille*, L'Harmattan.

Bonvalet, C., A. Gotman and Y. Grafmeyer (1999), *La famille et ses proches. L'aménagement des territoires*, Presses Universitaires de France – INED.

Bourdieu, P. (1984), 'La jeunesse n'est qu'un mot' in P. Bourdieu, *Questions de sociologie*, Edition de minuit, pp. 143–154.

Bugeja, F. (2011), 'Les inégalités d'accès à la propriété et leurs déterminants institutionnels. Etude comparative France et Royaume-Uni (1980–2005)', *Revue française de sociologie* 52(1), 37–69.

Chanvril, F., A. Cousteaux, V. L. Hay, L. Lesnard, C. Mechinaud and N. Sauger (2009), 'La parentalité en Europe, Analyse séquentielle des trajectoires d'entrée dans l'âge adulte à partir de l'Enquête sociale européenne' (122), Technical report, Caisse d'allocations familiales.

Chauvel, L. (1998), *Le destin des générations. Structure sociale et cohortes en France en XXe siècle*, PUF.

Daguet, F. (1996), 'La parenthèse du baby-boom', *Insee Première* 479, 4.

De Singly, F. (2000), 'Penser autrement la jeunesse', *Lien social et politiques* 43, 9–21.

Di Salvo, P. and J. Ermisch (1997), 'Analysis of the dynamics of housing tenure choice in Britain', *Journal of Urban Economics* 42, 1–17.

Ermisch, J. and P. Di Salvo (1996), 'Surprises and housing tenure decisions in Great Britain', *Journal of Housing Economics* 5, 247–273,

Esping-Andersen, G. (1999), *Les trois mondes de l'Etat-Providence. Essai sur le capitalisme moderne*, PUF.

Fack, G. (2005), 'Pourquoi les ménages pauvres paient-ils des loyers de plus en plus élevés? L'incidence des aides au logement en France (1973–2002)', *Economie et statistique* 381–382, 17–40.

Fourastié, J. (1979), *Les trente glorieuses ou la révolution invisible de 1946 à 1975*, Fayard.

Galland, O. (1994), 'La jeunesse en France, un nouvel âge de la vie', in A. Cavalli and O. Galland, eds, *L'allongement de la jeunesse*, Actes Sud, pp. 529–551.

Grafmeyer, Y. (1990), 'Solidarités intergénérationnelles dans l'accession au parc locatif privé lyonnais' in C. Bonvalet and A.-M. Fribourg, eds, *Stratégies résidentielles*, Ined.

Grafmeyer, Y. (1991), *Habitez Lyon. Milieux et quartiers du centre ville*, Presses Universitaires de Lyon.

Jachiet, N., V. Champagne, P. A. Malleray, J. Bourquard and C. Rostand (2004), 'Rapport d'enquête sur l'hypothèque et le crédit hypothécaire', Technical report, Inspection générale des Finances et Inspection générale des Services Judiciaires.

Laferrère, A., D. L. Blanc and R. Pigois (1999), 'Les effets de l'existence du parc HLM sur les profils de consommation des ménages', *Economie et Statistique* 328, 37–60.

Meron, M. and D. Courgeau (2004), 'Home ownership and social inequality in comparative perspective in France', in K. Kurtz and H.-P. Blossfeld, eds, *Home Ownership and Social Inequality in Comparative Perspective*, Stanford University Press.

Peugny, C. (2009), *Le déclassement*, Grasset.

Van de Velde, C. (2008), *Devenir adulte. Sociologie comparée de la jeunesse en Europe*, Presses Universitaires de France, Le Lien Social.

Vervaeke, M. (1992), 'Les logiques familiales d'accès au logement' in E. Lelièvre and C. Lévy-Vroelant, eds, *La ville en mouvement. Habitat et habitants*, L'Harmattan.

Villeneuve-Gokalp, C. (2000), 'Les jeunes partent toujours au même âge de chez leurs parents', *Economie et statistique* 337–338, 61–80.

Vorms, B. (2009), 'Les accédants à la propriété bousculés par la crise en Europe et en Amérique du Nord, diversité des situations, convergence des remèdes', *Anil habitat actualité*, 1–9.

Zittoun, P. (2001), *La politique du logement 1981–1995. Transformation d'une politique controversée*, L'Harmattan.

Appendix 10.1: Methodology for multinomial logistic regressions

The statistical method used to analyse home ownership inequalities is the multinomial logistic regression. The variable to be examined is categorical. To understand 'housing career', defined as the link between life cycle and residential trajectory, three models were used. The first looks at the probability of being a tenant in the private sector rather than in the social sector; the second, the probability of being a mortgagor rather than a private sector tenant; and the third the probability of being a homeowner rather than a mortgagor.

In Table 10.1 (and Appendix 10.2), the sample is the entire population.

Seven categorical variables are introduced in these models: the period or year of survey (1985, 1990, 1995, 2000 and 2005), the income deciles (with category 1 representing the lowest incomes and category 10 the highest), the age of a reference person (one category for 10 years), the household composition (one person, couple with one child, couple with two children, couple with three or more children and other households), the occupation of a reference person, the type of dwelling (individual house and flat) and the degree of urbanisation (six categories covering Paris and its suburbs, towns defined by population, and rural villages).

Interactions are introduced too, between age and period and between occupation and period. These interactions permit the examination of the impact of period.

The reference categories were 'last income decile', 'more than 75 years old', 'other households', 'manual worker', 'flat', and '1985' and 'Paris and its suburbs'.

In Table 10.2, the sample is reduced to French households less than 35 years old.

Only two models were used, since the sample size was too small to study the category of home owners (without mortgage).

The same categorical variables were introduced in these models, and an interaction between age and period.

Reference categories were 'last income decile', '34 or 35 years old', 'other households', 'manual worker', 'flat', '1985' and 'Paris and its suburbs'.

Appendix 10.2

TABLE 10.A Estimation of parameters of multinomial logistic models – probability of being a private tenant rather than a social tenant, a mortgagor rather than a tenant and a homeowner rather than mortgagor in France.

Reference	Model category	Coefficients		
		Private tenant vs social tenant	Mortgagor vs tenant	Homeowner vs mortgagor
Constant		n.s.	−2.68***	3.50***
Year				
	2005	−1.00***	n.s.	1.23*
	2000	−1.14***	n.s.	n.s.
	1995	−0.44*	n.s.	n.s.
1985	1990	n.s.	n.s.	n.s.
Age of reference person in 1985				
	...–25	n.s.	n.s.	−4.43***
	25–34	n.s.	1.48***	−4.40***
	35–44	n.s.	2.15***	−3.90***
	45–54	n.s.	2.35***	−3.00***
	55–64	−0.46**	2.03***	−2.11***
75–...	65–74	−0.31	1.32***	−0.95*

Reference	*Model category*	*Coefficients*		
		Private tenant vs social tenant	*Mortgagor vs tenant*	*Homeowner vs mortgagor*
Income decile				
	1	−0.77★★★	−1.75★★★	0.71★★★
	2	−0.89★★★	−1.79★★★	0.49★★★
	3	−0.89★★★	−1.42★★★	0.31★★★
	4	−0.83★★★	−1.04★★★	n.s.
	5	−0.79★★★	−0.87★★★	n.s.
	6	−0.65★★★	−0.64★★★	n.s.
	7	−0.53★★★	−0.47★★★	n.s.
	8	−0.48★★★	−0.34★★★	n.s.
10	9	−0.26★	−0.17★	n.s.
Occupation of reference person				
	No occupation (not retired)	n.s.	−0.61★	0.93★★★
	Farmer	1.94★★★	n.s.	0.95★★★
	Artisan, shopkeeper, proprietor, manager	1.25★★★	n.s.	0.34★
	Higher-grade professional	1.34★★★	n.s.	n.s.
	Lower-grade professional, technician, foreman	0.30★★	n.s.	n.s.
Manual worker	Clerk	0.14	n.s.	−0.21★
Interaction: age and period				
	...−25★2005	1.86★★★	n.s.	n.s.
	25–34★2005	0.93★★★	n.s.	−2.15★★★
	35–44★2005	0.53★	n.s.	−1.86★★
	45–54★2005	0.55★	n.s.	−1.45★★
	55–64★2005	n.s.	n.s.	−1.29★
75–...★1985	65–74★2005	n.s.	n.s.	n.s.
Interaction: occupation and period				
	No occupation (not retired)★2005	n.s.	n.s.	n.s.
	Farmer★2005	n.s.	−0.81★	n.s.
	Artisan, shopkeeper, proprietor ★2005	n.s.	n.s.	n.s.
	Higher-grade professional★2005	n.s.	0.50★★	n.s.
	Lower-grade professional ★2005	0.52★★★	n.s.	n.s.
Manual worker★1985	Clerk★2005	n.s.	n.s.	0.37★

Source: Budget de Famille 1985 to 2006 (Insee)

★ $p < 5\%$, ★★ $p < 1\%$ and ★★★ $p < 0.1\%$ (where p is the probability)

Note: For the interactions, all the years are introduced into the model. 1985 and 2005 only are shown, for ease of reading. Three control variables are used: household composition, dwelling type and degree of urbanisation.

11

YOUNG PEOPLE'S TRAJECTORIES THROUGH IRISH HOUSING BOOMS AND BUSTS

Headship, housing and labour market access among the under 30s since the late 1960s

Michelle Norris and Nessa Winston

Introduction

The economic, social and demographic history of the Republic of Ireland since World War II is distinctive in western European terms. While many of her neighbours experienced strong economic and population growth during the post-war decades, resulting in unprecedented prosperity for the generation born during the post-war baby boom, Ireland experienced economic stagnation and population decline during the 1950s, punctuated by a period of growth in the 1960s and early 1970s, until the traditional pattern of economic stagnation was reinstated in the 1980s (Kennedy *et al.* 1988). This longstanding pattern of economic underperformance changed in the mid-1990s with the advent of the 'Celtic tiger' economic boom. During the decade which followed, Ireland's economic growth caught up with and then surpassed the western European average, employment and household disposable income grew radically and the Irish population expanded by 20 per cent (Clinch *et al.* 2002). However, this boom came to a shuddering halt in 2007. GNP contracted by 20 per cent during the two years which followed and in November 2010 the Irish government was forced to accept an emergency loan from the International Monetary Fund (IMF) and the EU, to finance public spending and a bank recapitalization programme (Norris and Coates 2010).

The concurrent history of Irish housing policy, tenure patterns and housing finance markets is more uniform and reflective of norms in other Anglophone countries. Irish home ownership rates were comparatively high in the 1950s (54 per cent of households lived in this tenure in 1951) and they grew steadily during the following decades to a high of 80 per cent in 1991, before contracting slightly to 77 per cent by 2006 (Central Statistics Office, various years). Until the 1990s, home ownership was facilitated by generous and universalist public subsidies, non-profit sector (building societies and local government) provision of most mortgage credit and strict government regulation of mortgage lenders (Baker and O'Brien 1979). These public subsidies were rolled back steadily from the mid-1980s and during this period the mortgage finance system was almost entirely marketized and deregulated (Murphy 1994). Alongside the Celtic tiger boom, Ireland also experienced unprecedented mortgage credit growth and house price inflation, which has recently ended in a price correction of close to 50 per cent in nominal terms (Norris and Coates 2010).

This chapter examines the implications of these developments for housing access rates among young people, as indicated by variations in headship rates among the 20–29 years age cohort since the 1970s. Headship rates refer to the percentage of all people in an age group who are household heads. The rates are important because of their effect on housing demand, which is related to the propensity of young adults to establish their own households rather than live with parents, other relatives or friends (Carliner 2003). This chapter reveals that the Irish equivalent of the US and western European 'baby boomer' generation – the cohort which was under 30 years old during the 1960s and early 1970s – experienced dramatic growth in headship rates during these decades. By contrast, headship rates for this age group remained static during the 1980s and 1990s, but then increased again during the Celtic tiger boom. These historic trends in youth headship patterns are related to different patterns of intergenerational inequality in housing access, labour market and educational participation, and occupational segregation during different decades.

The analysis of these issues presented here is organized chronologically and periodized with reference to the four socio-economic phases in modern Irish history. The next section considers intergenerational variations in headship rates, education access, occupational groups and housing access during a sustained period of economic and population growth in the late 1960s and the 1970s. This is followed by three sections which examine the prolonged economic stagnation of the 1980s and early 1990s, the Celtic tiger boom between 1996 and 2006 and the economic bust post-2007. The conclusions to this chapter outline the key changes in intergenerational inequalities in housing access in Ireland.

The 1960s and 1970s

The 1960s and 1970s were a period of radical economic change in Ireland. The hitherto protected and largely agricultural economy was opened up to competition, international trade and industrialization. As a result, the century-long pattern of economic stagnation and population decline was at last arrested. GNP almost doubled between the late 1950s and early 1970s, population and employment grew and living standards improved markedly (Kennedy et al. 1988). Table 11.1 demonstrates that this period was also distinguished by sharply rising headship rates among young people. In 1966 only 7 per cent of 20–24-year-olds were household heads; by 1971 this had risen to 9 per cent and by 1979 it had risen further, to 15 per cent (Central Statistics Office, various years). A similar pattern is evident among the 25–44 years age group. Headship rates among this section of the population

TABLE 11.1 Headship rates by age cohort, 1966–2006.

Age cohort	1966	1971	1979	1981	1991	2002	2006
	%	%	%	%	%	%	%
20–24	6.8	9.4	15.0	15.8	14.0	18.9	19.3
25–29	31.0	33.8	31.3	32.5	29.8	31.2	33.8
30–34			40.1	41.7	42.8	42.9	45.0
35–39			43.3	45.2	47.6	47.8	49.2
40–44			45.7	47.0	49.6	50.8	51.3
45–64	51.1	51.3	52.2	53.0	54.8	54.2	55.3
65+	45.7	55.2	59.0	57.4	61.1	61.9	62.6

Source: Central Statistics Office, various years

increased from 31 per cent in 1966 to 34 per cent in 1971, to 40 per cent in 1979. Conversely, headship rates among the older population remained almost static – 51 per cent in 1966, 51 per cent in 1971 and 52 per cent in 1979.

The drivers of rising youth headship rates are not obvious from the labour market, educational and occupational data presented in Table 11.2 below. These

TABLE 11.2 Paid employment, university/college education, professional and unskilled manual employment by age cohort, 1966–2006.

Category	Age cohort	1966	1971	1981	1991	2002	2006
		%	%	%	%	%	%
Men in paid employment	20–24	84.6	83.1	77.1	62.7	63.4	64.2
	25–29	92.6	91.7	84.9	78.4	84.9	86.6
	30–34	93.8	92.9	86.1	80.6		
	35–39	93.3	92.5	86.9	80.2	85.8	87.6
	40–44	92.7	91.8	86.3	78.3		
	45–64	87.4	86.3	78.3	68.5	72.3	74.5
	65+	46.6	41.1	23.1	16.5	11.3	12.0
Women in paid employment	20–24	64.8	62.9	65.0	61.7	56.3	55.7
	25–29	34.6	29.9	42.2	62.2	71.2	75.1
	30–34	21.5	20.8	25.1	47.6		
	35–39	18.4	18.3	21.7	37.0	58.8	64.9
	40–44	17.3	18.5	23.0	31.8		
	45–64	20.3	20.3	20.8	24.2	42.5	51.2
	65+	7.9	9.5	4.7	3.3	2.5	3.5

Category	Age cohort	1966	1971	1981	1991	2002	2006
		%	%	%	%	%	%
University/college education	20–24	4.0	4.9	8.0	17.0	31.6	31.8
	25–29	7.0	7.8	11.7	20.0	45.9	48.4
	30–34	6.3	7.2	10.6	16.4	38.3	47.1
	35–39	5.5	6.0	8.8	13.6	30.7	37.9
	40–44	4.5	5.2	7.1	10.9	25.5	31.1
	45–64	4.0	3.8	4.8	8.1	18.2	22.2
	65+	1.8	2.4	3.2	4.0	9.0	11.5
Professional occupation	20–24	Nav	10.1	11.4	10.1	16.5	15.8
	25–29	Nav	11.8	14.5	13.3	23.6	24.2
	30–34	Nav	10.8	13.2	13.8		
	35–39	Nav	10.1	12.5	14.2	18.9	20.1
	40–44	Nav	7.8	11.2	13.0		
	45–64	Nav	6.7	11.9	10.7	17.4	18.3
	65+	Nav		8.9	7.5	14.7	16.7
Unskilled manual occupation	20–24	Nav	8.2	6.1	5.7	5.2	4.9
	25–29	Nav	8.3	7.0	6.0	4.4	4.0
	30–34	Nav	8.5	7.3	6.6		
	35–39	Nav	9.4	6.6	7.0	5.3	6.9
	40–44	Nav	9.6	7.0	7.4		
	45–64	Nav	10.3	8.4	7.3	7.4	5.6
	65+	Nav		9.4	7.6	11.6	7.6

Source: Central Statistics Office, various years
Note: 'Nav' means not available

indicate that the proportions of 20–24 and 25–29 year old males in paid employment fell slightly between 1966 and 1971 (female labour force participation rates were very low concurrently).

The proportion of young people who had completed university or college level education was relatively low and remained almost static during this period (7 per cent and 8 per cent among 25–29 year olds in 1966 and 1971 respectively) and only slightly higher than the university/college completion rates of older age cohorts at this time (5 per cent of 40–44 year olds had completed university or college education in 1966 compared to 5 per cent in 1971). Consequently, in 1971 both professional jobs and unskilled manual employment were relatively evenly distributed across age cohorts. Thus during the early 1970s at least, the socio-economic context of static youth employment, participation in university or college education and access to professional (and presumably higher-paid) employment does

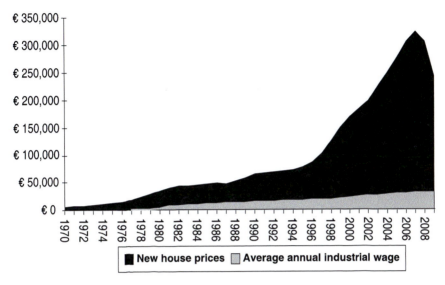

FIGURE 11.1 New house prices and average annual industrial wage, 1970–2009.
  Source: Department of the Environment, Heritage and Local Government,
  various years, and data provided by the Central Statistics Office
  Note: Data are in current prices

not appear conducive to rising independent household formation among the younger age cohorts.

The data presented in Figures 11.1 and 11.2 indicate that developments in housing and mortgage markets and in social housing provision were more important drivers of youth headship rates in the late 1960s and 1970s than employment or education levels. For instance, they demonstrate that house price affordability improved markedly during the 1970s. In 1970 average new house prices were 7 times average industrial earnings but, despite marked house price inflation, this declined to 5 times by 1977 because general price inflation and wages grew even faster. This meant that in practice recipients of the average industrial wage who had purchased an average-priced new home in 1970 would have found that their mortgage debt was only two times their income in 1975, *solely* as a result of wage inflation.

Mortgage finance availability also improved during the 1970s. Only 12,471 new mortgages were drawn down in 1970, compared to 24,540 in 1977 (Department of the Environment, Heritage and Local Government, various years). The vast majority of these mortgages were provided by non-profit lenders. Lending to lower income groups was dominated by the local government sector (which provided 30 per cent of mortgages by value in the 1970s), while lending to middle to higher income households was dominated by building societies (which provided around 65 per cent of mortgage loans by value during the 1970s) (Fahey *et al.* 2004; Murphy 1994). Although local government lenders were characterized by higher

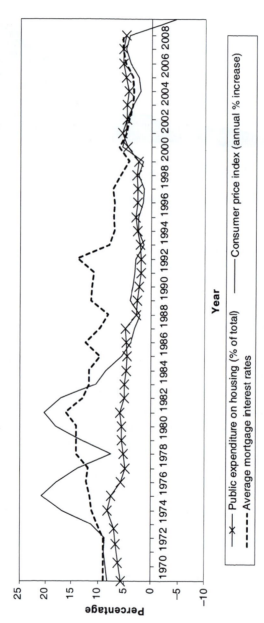

FIGURE 11.2 Consumer price inflation, mortgage interest rates and percentage of public expenditure devoted to housing, 1970–2009.

Source: Data provided by the Central Statistics Office; Baker and O'Brien, 1979

Note: All interest rate data refer to December of the relevant year, with the exception of 2008 (March) and 1970–1976 (annual average) loan-to-value ratios and more flexible qualification criteria, the maximum loans available were strictly constrained by government order at around three times borrowers' incomes, and were significantly below average contemporaneous house prices (Baker and O'Brien 1979). Baker and O'Brien's examination of building societies in the 1970s concluded that they 'tended to set fairly stiff criteria with regard to the size of the deposit required, the minimum income in relation to the size of the loan and the type of property involved . . . generally it is impossible to get a loan greater than two and a half times income' (1979: 41). They also report that both local authorities and building societies generally lend 'only two-thirds or at most four-fifths of the value of the house' (1979: 42–43).

Accumulating such a substantial deposit proved challenging, particularly for households just above the income limit for access to social housing and, for those who had successfully secured a mortgage, interest rates were very high by contemporary standards – they rose from 9 per cent to 12 per cent between 1970 and 1975 (see Figure 11.2) (Baker and O'Brien 1979). However, direct government support for home ownership, including grants for first-time buyers and indirect support in the form of the absence of capital gains taxes on principal private residences, as well as the tax deductibility of mortgage interest, also reduced the need to borrow (O'Connell 2005).

Figure 11.2 demonstrates that public expenditure on housing was significant during the 1970s. It accounted for 8 per cent of total (direct and indirect) public spending in 1975. Furthermore, a substantial proportion of this was devoted to support for home buyers, the total value of which equated to 23 per cent of the total costs of servicing the average building society mortgage in that year (National Economic and Social Council 1977). In the context of requirements for large deposits, generous government subsidies, a modest ratio of average house prices to earnings, high consumer prices, and wage inflation which quickly eroded the value of debt, the rate of mortgage-holding was low and only one third of homeowners had mortgages in the 1970s (Fahey et al. 2004; Kelly and Everett 2004). Thus for those who could manage to access home ownership the funding context was benign, but barriers to entry were substantial.

Youth headship rates were further increased in the 1970s by the relative ease of access to social housing – the vast majority of which was provided at the time by local authorities. Social housing output increased from 3767 units in 1970 to a peak of 8794 units in 1975, and output constituted 1.8 units per 1000 inhabitants in 1979, which is more than four times the equivalent figure for 2002 (Department of the Environment, Heritage and Local Government, various years). In addition, those who gained access to a local authority tenancy also gained the right to buy their dwelling at a substantial discount (about 30 per cent) on the market value. The right to purchase was extended to urban local authority tenants in 1966, but had been available to their rural counterparts since the mid-1930s (Norris and Fahey 2011). As a result, in 1971, 10 per cent of households were former social tenants who were purchasing their home from their landlord (Central Statistics Office, various years).

The 1980s to early 1990s

The Irish economy accumulated a variety of structural problems during the 1970s which, combined with the effects of the second oil crash in 1979, resulted in a large public deficit, rising national debt (which peaked at 1.5 times GNP in 1986), recession (GNP fell by 0.3 per cent between 1979 and 1986) and unemployment (which stood at around 20 per cent of the workforce during the first half of the 1980s). This resulted in a re-emergence of the traditional Irish 'safety valve' of emigration, with the number of emigrants exceeding new births by the middle of the decade (Kennedy *et al.* 1988).

In contrast to the previous decade, headship rates among the younger age cohorts declined during the 1980s. In 1981, 16 per cent of 20–24-year-olds were heads of household but this fell to 14 per cent by 1991; headship rates among 25–29 year olds declined from 33 to 30 per cent concurrently. However, headship rates among older age cohorts increased during this period. Also, in contrast to the preceding decade, during the 1980s youth headship rates were shaped by both housing-related and broader socio-economic factors.

The decline in youth headship rates is rather surprising, in view of the radical increase in the proportion of the young population with university or college education during the 1980s. The proportion of 20–24-year-olds in this category increased from 8 to 17 per cent between 1981 and 1991 and the equivalent figures for 25–29 year olds are 12 and 20 per cent (see Table 11.2). This reflected the outcome of growing investment in education during the late 1960s, as a result of a number of radical decisions made by the pioneering education minister, Donogh O'Malley, including the abolition of fees for second-level education, the introduction of means-tested grants for university and college students (fees remained payable by non-grant recipients), and the establishment of new Regional Technical Colleges (similar to polytechnics in the UK) to provide vocational tertiary education. However, at least during the 1980s, students moving out of their parents' home to university towns and cities did not increase youth headship rates. The data presented in Table 11.2 reveal that one of the primary reasons for this was the decline in the proportion of young people in the workforce during this period. The proportion of 20–24-year-olds in paid employment fell from 77 per cent in 1981 to 63 per cent in 1991 and at the same time the proportion of 25–29-year-olds in employment fell from 85 to 78 per cent. This development was due principally to rising unemployment among these age cohorts, rather than rising university and college education, and it is likely to have severely impeded their ability to form independent households.

Declining social housing availability almost certainly made a further contribution to reducing young people's opportunities for independent household formation. Between 1980 and 1986, social housing output continued at the same rate as in the 1970s – around 7000 units per year, or 1.6 units per 1000 inhabitants in 1986 (Department of the Environment, Heritage and Local Government, various years). However, the social rented sector bore the brunt of swingeing public expenditure reductions introduced in the mid-1980s. Output fell to just over 1000 units per annum between 1987 and 1991, or just 0.3 units per 1000 inhabitants in the latter year. The proportion of households living in the sector contracted from 13 to 10 per cent between 1981 and 1991 (Central Statistics Office, various years), which impeded independent household formation on the part of young people in need of accommodation in this tenure.

The role which the housing market played in declining youth headship rates during the 1980s is more complex. Barriers to entry to this sector were significant, particularly for low-income households, due to rising unemployment and falling disposable incomes in the face of rising taxes. The number of mortgages provided by local government, the traditional source of finance for low-income buyers, was radically reduced, to 2 per cent of new mortgages in the mid-1980s, because these counted as part of the public debt, which the government was anxious to shrink (Blackwell 1988). Local government lending has remained at this rate since then, and, due to falling social house building and residualization of this tenure, sales of dwellings to tenants have also fallen significantly since the 1980s – thereby restricting a key route to home ownership for low-income households (Central Statistics Office, various years). Tax subsidies for building societies were also withdrawn in the mid-1980s and, in response, banks, which traditionally played a minor role in mortgage lending in Ireland, increased their percentage of new mortgage loans from 8 per cent in 1985 to 37 per cent in 1987. This development increased competition in the sector but, according to Murphy (1994), did not diminish lending standards, and a deposit of 10 per cent remained a requirement for access to mortgages. In the context of high unemployment, accumulating a deposit of this size would have proved a significant challenge for many young people.

However, for households who were in the type of employment that would enable them to accumulate a deposit and secure a mortgage (or who had done so in earlier decades) the situation was much more positive in the 1980s. House prices declined in real terms during the early part of this decade, while wages did not. Consequently, average new house prices were 5.5 times average industrial earnings in 1980, but this declined to 4.0 times by 1986 (see Figure 11.1). Although interest rates were volatile during the 1980s (ranging from a high of 16.3 per cent in 1980 to a low of 8.3 per cent in 1988) and remained well below general price inflation, mortgage holders continued to enjoy very generous tax relief on their mortgage interest. This was payable at the highest rate of income tax (for households in this tax bracket) over the entire lifetime of the mortgage. Blackwell (1988) estimates that in 1988 households paying the top rate of income tax paid an actual mortgage interest rate of 8.8 per cent but an effective interest rate of 4.2 per cent. Furthermore, he points out that in 1987 the mortgage interest relief and direct grants for home buyers cost 2.3 times the entire social housing budget (□572.6 million compared to □246.8 million). In this context, new mortgages drawn down increased from 29,485 to 37,058 between 1981 and 1991 and the percentage of the population accommodated in the owner-occupied sector increased from 67 to 74 per cent concurrently (Central Statistics Office, various years).

The late 1990s to mid-2000s

Irish economic growth and the public finances began to improve in the late 1980s but this was not reflected in jobs growth until the mid-1990s. Between then and mid-2000, Ireland experienced an unprecedented period of economic, employment, income and population growth (Barry 2002). GDP per capita increased from 15 per cent below the EU15 average in 1995 to 48 per cent above in 2006, and concurrently the unemployment rate fell from 10 per cent above the EU15 average to 45 per cent below (Eurostat, various years). This economic transformation had significant social implications. For instance, between 1996 and 2006 the Irish population rose by 17 per cent and the number of households expanded by 14 per cent (Central Statistics Office, various years).

This period was also distinguished by a significant increase in headship among under-30-year-olds. Table 11.1 demonstrates that the proportion of 20–24-year-olds who were heads of household increased from 14.0 per cent in 1991 to 19 per cent in 2002, to 19 per cent in 2006, while headship rates among 25–29-year-olds increased from 30 to 31 to 34 per cent concurrently. Headship rates also increased among the older age cohorts during this period but only marginally.

The data presented in Table 11.2 indicate that the rising youth headship was related to rising labour market participation among under-35-year-olds, their higher levels of education and their greater representation in professional (and presumably better remunerated) employment compared to older age groups. Between 1991 and 2006 the proportion of 20–24-year-old men in paid employment rose from 63 to 64 per cent and the equivalent figures for those in the 25–34 age group are 80 and 87 per cent. Notably, during this period the traditionally low labour market participation rates of Irish women also ended. Only 55 per cent of 25–34-year-old females were in paid employment in 1991 but by 2006 this had risen to 75 per cent. University and college education completion rates among younger people also increased steadily during the 1990s and early 2000s, to the extent that 48 per cent of 25–29-year-olds had university or college education in 2006, compared to only 22 per cent of 45–64-year-olds. Significantly, from the perspective of the discussion at hand, the steady rise in university and college education participation among young people during the preceding decades began to feed into high levels of professional employment by the early 2000s. In 2006, 24 per cent of 25–34-year-olds were in professional employment compared to 18 per cent of 45–64-year-olds. Thus in the late 1990s and early 2000s, the rising proportion of dual income households and professional jobs improved housing affordability and eased independent household formation for younger households. For lower earning young people seeking social housing, the situation was not so positive. Output continued to decline in relative terms during the Celtic tiger period, from 1.02 units per 1000 inhabitants in 1996 to 0.12 per 1000 in 2006 (Department of the Environment, Heritage and Local Government, various years). Sales of social housing to tenants fell further during this period, thereby cutting off a potential route to home ownership for low-income households (Central Statistics Office, various years).

Aspirant home owners also faced galloping price inflation during the Celtic tiger period (see Figure 11.1). House price inflation jumped from 2.1 per cent per annum between 1990 and 1993 to 23.4 per cent per annum between 1995 and 2000, and continued to rise, albeit at a lower rate (12.7 per cent per annum), until late 2007. As a result house prices increased by a total of 314 per cent in nominal terms between 1995 and 2007.

In addition to rising demand created by economic, employment and income-related factors, rising house prices were driven, at least initially, by a slow supply response. Total housing output grew from 33,725 new dwellings in 1996 to 49,812 dwellings in 2000, but from the latter year output expanded radically to a high of 93,419 dwellings in 2006 (Department of the Environment, Heritage and Local Government, various years). To place these output rates in context, in 2006 the UK built just over twice the number of dwellings Ireland did (209,000 units) for a population 15 times greater (60 million, compared to 4 million) (European Mortgage Federation, various years). As supply restrictions were addressed, the latter phase of the Celtic tiger house price boom was driven principally by growing credit availability. Table 11.3 demonstrates that between 2000 and 2008 mortgage credit outstanding in Ireland rose by 388 per cent and from 31 to 80 per cent of GDP. Although mortgage lending and private sector credit increased across the EU and most developed countries concurrently, this trend was especially pronounced in Ireland (Doyle 2009). Between 2000 and 2007 outstanding mortgage credit in Ireland expanded by four times the rate of growth in the 27 current EU members (80 per cent). Consequently, in the latter year, the Irish mortgage debt to GDP ratio was over one third higher than the EU27 average (European Mortgage Federation, various years).

The growth in mortgage credit outstanding was due to both an increase in the number of mortgages granted and in the size of these loans (see Table 11.3). Table 11.3 also reveals that the number of mortgages granted per annum rose from 74,300 in 2000 to a peak of 111,300 in 2006. However, residential mortgage debt per capita rose even faster – from €8620 to €29,290. Loans of over €250,000 increased from 2.3 per cent of new mortgages in 2000 to 41 per cent in 2008. One hundred per cent mortgages first became available around 2004 and between then and 2008 rose from 4 to 12 per cent of new mortgages granted. Furthermore, mortgages with terms of 30 years plus increased from 10 to 39 per cent of mortgages drawn down, and interest-only mortgages also increased significantly during this period.

Detailed analysis of the data presented in Table 11.3 indicates that very large mortgages were taken out mainly by first-time buyers based in Dublin (Department of the Environment, Heritage and Local Government, various years). In 2006 74 per cent of this group drew down mortgages of over €250,000, compared to 38 per cent of first-time buyers in the country as a whole. In the same year 64 per cent of repeat home buyers and property investors in Dublin also borrowed on this scale. Also in 2006, 31 per cent of first-time buyers in Dublin took on 100 per cent mortgages, compared to 34 per cent of first-time buyers in the country at large and just 5 per cent of repeat buyers and investors in Dublin. In the same year, 70 per

TABLE 11.3 Trends in mortgage debt and new lending, 1996–2010.

	1996	1998	2000	2002	2004	2006	2008	2010
Mortgage credit outstanding (€m)	Nav	Nav	29,474	43,416	73,120	110,602	114,290	108,282[1]
Mortgage debt to GDP ratio (%)	Nav	Nav	31.1	36.3	55.2	70.1	80.0	Nav
New mortgages (N)	56,000	61,400	74,300	79,300	98,700	111,300	53,600	Nav
Mortgage debt per capita (€)	3830	5650	8620	12,110	19,120	29,290	33,750	Nav
% of average income required to service a mortgage on an average-priced dwelling[2]	23	35	36	34	25	31	29	Nav
% of outstanding mortgages which are:								
for principal private residences	Nav	Nav	Nav	Nav	80.0	73.7	71.9	72.8[3]
for buy-to-let dwellings	Nav	Nav	Nav	Nav	18.8	25.1	26.9	26.1[3]
for holiday/second homes	Nav	Nav	Nav	Nav	1.1	1.2	1.2	1.1[3]
% of new mortgages which are:								
>€250,000	Nav	Nav	2.3	5.9	18.0	37.0	41.0	Nav
100% loans	Nav	Nav	Nav	Nav	4.0	14.0	12.0	Nav
>30 year term	Nav	Nav	Nav	Nav	10.0	31.0	39.0	Nav
interest only	Nav	Nav	2.4	2.7	5.7	12.6	Nav	Nav

Source: Central Bank, various years; Central Statistics Office, various years; Department of the Environment, Heritage and Local Government, various years

Note: All monetary data are at current prices. 'Nav' means not available

1 Includes first 11 months only

2 Data refer to two-earner, married households, whose income = average industrial wage + average non-industrial wage. Mortgage payments are on a 20-year mortgage for 90 per cent of the average new house price for that year, repaid at average mortgage rates for that year

3 Includes the first 6 months only

cent of the mortgages drawn down by first-time buyers in Dublin had terms of over 30 years, compared to 20 per cent of loans granted to repeat buyers and investors in the city and 61 per cent of those granted to first-time buyers in the country as a whole. As the average age of a first-time home buyer was 30 in 2005, and 84 per cent of first-time buyers in this year were under 35, it is reasonable to assume that the vast majority of first-time home buyers during the Celtic tiger boom were in the younger age cohort (Duffy and Quail 2005).

Mortgage interest tax relief was radically reduced in value during the decade under examination. From 1997 it was made payable only at the standard rather than the higher rate of income tax and in 2009 its availability was further restricted to the first seven years of a mortgage. However, Figure 11.2 demonstrates that average mortgage interest rates declined steadily from 13.9 per cent in 1992 to 3.9 per cent in 2006. This development played a key role in enabling the radical growth in mortgage lending because it reduced average mortgage servicing costs from 36 to 31 per cent of the average income of a dual-earner household between 2000 and 2006 (see Table 11.3), despite the marked concurrent house price growth. Therefore, young home owners during the Celtic tiger period paid a similar effective interest rate to their counterparts in the 1980s (National Economic and Social Council 2004). In common with several other peripheral EU members, such as Greece, Italy, Spain and Portugal, this decline in nominal interest rates is related to Ireland's entry into the European Monetary Union in 1999, and the resultant transfer of interest rate setting powers from the Irish Central Bank to the European Central Bank (European Central Bank 2009). However, unusually intense competition in the Irish mortgage market, particularly after 2003, also played a key role in driving down interest rates and in liberalizing lending standards, which contributed to the growth in both the number and size of mortgages described above (European Central Bank 2009). Between 2000 and 2010 the number of major mortgage lenders operating in the Irish market (i.e. registered with the Irish Central Bank) increased from 12 to 17 (Central Bank, various years a). The development was driven by the entry of some Irish banks into the mortgage market for the first time, the establishment of specialist mortgage lending subsidiaries by existing Irish mortgage lenders and the entry of a number of foreign lenders into the Irish market (such as Bank of Scotland and Danske Bank A/S). In 2007 these foreign lenders accounted for approximately 30 per cent of mortgage loans advanced in Ireland – a level of market penetration which is unusual in Europe (European Central Bank 2009). These lenders offered lower interest rates than domestic institutions (which traditionally charged a higher yield on loans) and pioneered products such as interest-only and 100 per cent mortgages, as well as mortgage equity withdrawal products. However, in the context of intensive competition, domestic lenders felt obliged to follow suit and the number of these products on offer increased radically from 2004 (Hogan and O'Sullivan 2007; McElligott 2007; Doyle 2009). Thus, unlike in the United States, the Irish housing boom was associated with a decline in lending standards among mainstream lenders, rather than with the growth of a specialist sub-prime sector. Although four sub-prime lenders entered the Irish market between 2004 and 2007, they accounted for only 0.5 per cent of mortgage lending by value in the latter year (Coates 2008).

As well as driving increased indebtedness among the younger households who could access mortgages, the marked rise in the house price to average industrial earnings ratio during the boom (from four times average industrial earnings in 1995 to ten times in 2007) also priced a large number of younger households out of the owner-occupied sector. Home owners held 80 per cent of outstanding mortgages in 2004 but only 73 per cent in 2006, while investor activity rose during this period (see Table 11.3). As a result, the private rented sector expanded between 1991 and 2002, after many decades of sustained decline (Central Statistics Office, various years).

2007 to date

Ireland's house price boom started to falter in early 2007, and the data presented in Figure 11.1 indicate that prices nationally fell by 25 per cent between this date and 2009. However, most commentators agree that these official data underestimate the true extent of price decline, which is closer to 45–50 per cent to date (see Duffy 2009). The economic collapse slightly lagged the housing market crash. GNP grew by 5.7 per cent in 2007, but it declined by 5.0 per cent in 2008 and by 15.2 per cent in 2009. Employment fell by 8.3 per cent between 2007 and 2009 and the exchequer balance fell sharply to −8.2 per cent of GNP in 2008 and to −18.8 per cent in 2009 (Central Statistics Office, various years). In addition, an acute banking and credit availability crisis developed in 2008 as, following the collapse of Lehman Brothers in the United States, Irish banks and building societies found themselves unable to raise money on wholesale money markets (International Monetary Fund 2010).

The housing market bust made a central contribution to the economic, fiscal and banking bust and the latter subsequently helped to reinforce the former. The decline in gross value added (GVA) from construction accounted for 27.3 per cent of the decline in GNP between 2007 and 2009. Falling construction employment accounted for 65 per cent of the decline in employment. Falling revenue from residential property market related taxes accounted for 35 per cent of the contraction in total tax revenue between 2007 and 2008 (Norris and Coates 2010). Concerns about the overexposure of Irish banks and building societies to the property sector and the implications of this for their profitability and the health of their loan books were the key causes of their funding crisis in 2008 (International Monetary Fund 2010). Lending for property development and mortgages made up 37 per cent of their total lending in 2000 but this rose to 72 per cent by 2006 and was up to 90 per cent in some institutions (Kearns and Woods 2006). As Table 11.3 demonstrates, new lending fell dramatically in the wake of this funding crisis, which helped to drive down house prices.

Falling house prices have also had a very severe impact on household wealth. Duffy (2009) estimates that 9 per cent of mortgage holders were in negative equity by the end of 2008, rising to 18 per cent by the end of 2009 and 30 per cent by the end of 2010. In the US, 10 per cent of mortgages in single-family dwellings were in negative equity in 2008 while in the UK 7 to 11 per cent of owner-occupier mortgages were in this situation in that year (Hellebrandt et al. 2009; Ellis 2008). However, Duffy's (2009) estimates do not include mortgage top-ups or interest-only mortgages, and they are based on conservative estimates of the scale of house price decline (in the region of 30 per cent between 2007 and 2009), which indicates that negative equity is more widespread than he suggests.

Rapidly rising unemployment coupled with falling incomes among those in work, due to tax increases and in many cases cuts in pay and/or working hours, combined with interest rate increases have effected a marked rise in mortgage arrears among home owners as well as arrears on other loans and utility bills (Russell et al. 2011). Comprehensive mortgage arrears data are only available from the third quarter of 2009. These reveal that 3 per cent of mortgages were in arrears of over 90 days in Q3 2009, this increased to 4 per cent in Q1 2010 and to 6 per cent in Q4 2010. Additional data on restructured mortgages to enable the borrower to reduce their repayments are also available for Q4 2010. These indicate that an additional 35,205 mortgage loans (accounting for 5 per cent of all mortgages) had been restructured by the end of this quarter but were not categorized as in arrears (Central Bank, various years b). In view of the very high proportion of mortgages in arrears or subject to restructuring, levels of repossessions have remained surprisingly low to date. In Q4 2009, 110 residences were repossessed on foot of a court order or voluntarily surrendered or abandoned, and the equivalent figure for Q4 2010 is 106. The rate of repossessions in the UK during 2010 was seven times higher (Mortgage Arrears and Personal Debt Expert Group 2010). The modest repossession rates in Ireland are due primarily to an agreement between the government and lenders that the latter would not initiate repossession proceedings for twelve months after the first missed mortgage payment. In the absence of this measure, Goldman Sachs Global Economics (2010:5) estimate that Irish repossession rates would be four times higher.

While no data are available on the distribution of distressed mortgages and negative equity between different age cohorts, the available evidence indicates that young people are likely to have been affected. This is because, as mentioned above, most first-time buyers during the housing boom were young people, and Duffy (2009) estimates that rates of negative equity are significantly higher among this category of borrower because they generally had less equity in their dwellings than older borrowers prior to the bust. Furthermore, as was outlined in the preceding analysis, most very large mortgages, 100 per cent mortgages and mortgages with an above average repayment period were taken out by first-time buyers, the vast majority of whom are under 35 years of age. This means that young people are at higher risk of both negative equity and mortgage arrears. Finally, young people have been more negatively affected by falling employment during the bust than the older age groups. Total employment fell by 11.3 per cent between Q4 2008 and Q4 2010, but employment among 20–24-year-olds fell by 35.6 per cent, while the equivalent figure for 24–29-year-olds is 12.4 per cent (Central Statistics Office 2011). This phenomenon is due primarily to the concentration of young people, particularly young men, in construction employment. According to the 2006 census, 16 per cent of 20–24-year-olds and 12 per cent of 25–29-year-olds worked in this sector (Central Statistics Office, various years).

Conclusions

This chapter has examined the importance of both labour market and housing market factors in the formation of independent households among the under-30 age group in the Republic of Ireland since the late 1960s. It highlights significant differences in the experiences of this age cohort in this regard.

In the 1970s, headship rates among young people increased, largely due to a benign housing market situation but also to the ready availability of social housing. During this period, the labour market situation was also relatively favourable and certainly not a serious barrier to independent household formation.

In the 1980s, headship rates among young people declined due to economic recession and dismal labour market conditions. However, there were also a range of other barriers to independent household formation during this period including: high interest rates, limited credit, high deposit requirements from lenders and a lack of social housing.

During the Celtic tiger boom of the late 1990s and early 2000s, headship rates for younger people increased as the labour market context, in particular, improved. Young people in this period had very high rates of participation in university and college education compared to their counterparts in previous decades. Therefore, during this economic boom they enjoyed easy labour market access and easier access to professional jobs, and therefore higher earnings than older households. In this period, the under 30s experienced great difficulty in accessing social housing and galloping house price inflation. However, mortgage credit was more widely available and was cheaper, as interest rates were negative for much of the early 2000s. Therefore, those who could afford to do so overcame these housing market barriers by taking on very large debts to purchase a home. Thus although the young 'Celtic tiger' cubs faced lower threshold barriers to independent household formation compared to young people during the 1970s and in particular the 1980s, they faced much higher long-term payment barriers. Young people in the 1970s faced significant challenges in saving a deposit and raising a mortgage, but once they did purchase a home their debt was eroded by inflation and rising earnings and was generally paid off after 20 years. For this reason, the vast majority of Irish home owners aged 50 years plus are mortgage free. In the late 1990s and early 2000s, young people borrowed much larger amounts compared to their incomes and commonly took on 100 per cent mortgages, with repayment terms of 30 years or longer. Although the cost of servicing this debt was generally affordable during the Celtic tiger boom, in the face of the sharp contraction in the Irish economy since 2007, this is no longer the case for many households. Furthermore, due to higher borrowings and low inflation, even those households who can meet their repayment costs face much higher lifetime debt-servicing costs than previous generations.

References

Baker, T. and O'Brien, L. (1979) *The Irish Housing System: A Critical Overview*, Dublin: Economic and Social Research Institute.

Blackwell, J. (1988) *A Review of Housing Policy*, Dublin: National Economic and Social Council.

Barry, F. (2002) 'The Celtic Tiger era: delayed convergence or regional boom?', *ESRI Quarterly Economic Commentary*, Summer: 36–42.

Carliner, M. (2003) 'Headship rates and housing demand', *Housing Economics*, June: 8–12.

Central Bank (various years a) *Quarterly Review*, Dublin: Central Bank.

Central Bank (various years b), *Residential Mortgage Arrears and Repossessions Statistics*, Dublin: Central Bank.

Central Statistics Office (various years) *Census of Population of Ireland*, Dublin: Stationery Office.

Central Statistics Office (2011) *Quarterly National Household Survey, Quarter 4 2010*, Dublin: Central Statistics Office.

Clinch, P., Convery, F. and Walsh, B. (2002) *After the Celtic Tiger: Challenges Ahead*, Dublin: O'Brien Press.

Coates, D. (2008) 'The Irish sub-prime residential mortgage sector: international lessons for an emerging market', *Journal of Housing and the Built Environment*, 23(2): 131–144.

Department of the Environment, Heritage and Local Government (various years) *Annual Housing Statistics Bulletin*, Dublin: Department of the Environment, Heritage and Local Government.

Doyle, N. (2009) 'Housing finance developments in Ireland', *Central Bank Quarterly Bulletin*, 09(04): 75–88.

Duffy, D. (2009) *Negative Equity in the Irish Housing Market*, Dublin: Economic and Social Research Institute Working Paper No. 319.

Duffy, D. and Quail, A. (2005) *First-Time Buyers in the Irish Housing Market*, Dublin: Economic and Social Research Institute.

Ellis, L. (2008) 'How many in negative equity? The role of mortgage contract characteristics', *Bank of International Settlements, Quarterly Review*, December: 81–90.

European Central Bank (2009) *Housing Finance in the Euro Area*, Frankfurt: European Central Bank.

European Mortgage Federation (various years) *Hypostat*, Brussels: European Mortgage Federation.

Eurostat (various years) *Population and Social Conditions Database: Employment and Social Conditions Theme*, Luxembourg: Eurostat.

Fahey, T., Nolan, B. and Mâitre, B. (2004) *Housing, Poverty and Wealth in Ireland*, Dublin: Institute of Public Administration.

Goldman Sachs Global Economics (2010) *European Weekly Analyst Issue No: 10/40*, London: Goldman Sachs.

Hellebrandt, T., Kawar, S. and Waldron, M. (2009) 'The economics and estimation of negative equity', *Bank of England Quarterly Review*, Quarter Two: 110–121.

Hogan, V. and O'Sullivan, P. (2007) 'Consumption and house prices in Ireland', *Quarterly Economic Commentary*, 2007(3): 46–61.

International Monetary Fund (2010) *Cross-Cutting Themes in Economies with Large Banking Systems*, New York: IMF.

Kearns, A. and Woods, M. (2006) 'The concentration in property-related lending – a financial stability perspective', *Central Bank Financial Stability Report, 2006*, Dublin: Central Bank.

Kelly, J. and Everett, M. (2004) 'Financial liberalisation and economic growth in Ireland', *Central Bank Quarterly Bulletin*, 04(03): 91–112.

Kennedy, K., Giblin, T. and McHugh, D. (1988) *The Economic Development of Ireland in the Twentieth Century*, London: Routledge.

McElligott, R. (2007) 'Irish retail interest rates: why do they differ from the rest of Europe?' *Central Bank Quarterly Bulletin*, 07(01): 137–252.

Mortgage Arrears and Personal Debt Expert Group (2010) *Final Report*, Dublin: Mortgage Arrears and Personal Debt Expert Group.

Murphy, L. (1994) 'The downside of home ownership: housing change and mortgage arrears in the Republic of Ireland', *Housing Studies*, 9(2): 183–198.

National Economic and Social Council (2004) *Housing in Ireland: Performance and Policy*, Dublin: National Economic and Social Council.

National Economic and Social Council (1977) *Report on Housing Subsidies*, Dublin: National Economic and Social Council.

Norris, M. and Coates, D. (2010) 'How housing killed the Celtic Tiger: anatomy, consequences and lessons of Ireland's mortgage boom and bust, 2000–2009', paper presented to the Cambridge Centre for Housing and Planning Research Conference – Housing: the next 20 years, 16–17 September.

Norris, M. and Fahey, T. (2011) 'From asset based welfare to welfare housing: the changing meaning of social housing in Ireland', *Housing Studies*, 26(3): 459–469.

O'Connell, C. (2005) 'The housing market and owner occupation in Ireland', in M. Norris and D. Redmond (eds) *Housing Contemporary Ireland: Policy, Society and Shelter*, Dublin: Institute of Public Administration.

Russell, H., Mâitre, B. and Donnelly, N. (2011) *Financial Exclusion and Over-indebtedness in Irish Households*, Dublin: Department of Community, Equality & Gaeltacht Affairs and ESRI.

12

THE LIVED EXPERIENCE OF HOUSING AMONG YOUNG PEOPLE IN RUSSIA

Jane Zavisca

Introduction

After the Soviet government collapsed in Russia in 1992, the new government introduced the Housing Sector Reform Project, which aimed to transform the housing sector into a market. A joint project of the Russian and American governments, the HSRP conceived of markets according to the American model of private ownership and securitized mortgage finance. Elements of a market did emerge: mass privatization of socialist housing created a nation of homeowners, and the legal and financial infrastructure for market transactions and mortgage lending now exists. However, privatization was much more successful than marketization, creating a housing system I call "property without markets," in which housing is privately owned but not fully commodified. Limited rental and mortgage markets render housing wealth illiquid and make it difficult to convert earnings at work into better conditions at home.

This new housing order creates acute difficulties for young people. Older Russians, who controlled the process of privatizing Soviet apartments, retain de facto control over property rights they often legally share with their children. Many young people, shut out of unaffordable housing markets yet without hope of government assistance, live with parents or in-laws well into adulthood, awaiting a gift or inheritance from extended family. A 2011 survey asked urban youth aged 18–29 to list the issues that most complicate their lives. The so-called "housing question" was selected by 42 percent, ranking behind only low incomes and unemployment. Half said they were dissatisfied with their housing conditions, but few felt in control of their housing destinies. The survey researchers conclude, "To purchase their own housing is nearly impossible even for those urban youth who may be considered middle class based on their incomes" (Gudkov *et al.* 2011: 37–38).

The scholarly literature on housing in Russia is paltry, given the issue's social significance. Most existing literature focuses on the macro-economy, tracking statistical indicators of housing construction and affordability, mortgage lending and securitization, and legal developments. This chapter analyzes the "lived experience" of housing from the perspective of young adults.

I borrow the concept of "lived experience" from cultural studies of class (for example Thompson 1978; Sewell Jr. 1980; Willis 1990). Although this literature concentrates on class experiences at work, class is also experienced, and even constituted, at home. John Rex (1968: 214–15), in a study of the United Kingdom, observed that people with the same status at work may have unequal access to housing, due to state subsidies or family inheritances. His concept of "housing class" builds on Max Weber's definition of class as shared market position to elucidate the distinctive stratifying properties of housing (c.f. Saunders 1984). The concept has been applied to socialist societies (Szelényi 1983) and post-socialist Russia (Burawoy et al. 1999). Russia today presents an extreme case of mismatch between labor market position and living conditions, making housing status a key dimension of the stratification order.

To articulate the lived experience of property without markets, I present a qualitative portrait of suffering among young people whose housing conditions fall short of Russian notions of normalcy, and whose constraints limit their sense of control over their housing destinies. These experiences in turn produce an "immanent critique" of housing markets, derived from the gap between market ideology and everyday reality.

My analysis draws on a qualitative interview study with Russians aged 21–35 in 2009. Three Russian sociologists, under my supervision, conducted 130 semi-structured interviews about respondents' housing histories, current conditions, future aspirations, and attitudes toward housing policy. The interviews were conducted in Kaluga, a city 200 kilometers from Moscow in which I have been conducting field studies for a decade. As of 2009, Kaluga's housing stock, unemployment rate, average wages, and income inequality were typical of Central Russia, excluding Moscow, Russia's wealthiest and most unequal city.

The case studies presented in this chapter neither represent the population nor describe the full range of experiences across housing classes. Rather, they illustrate how Russians with unsatisfactory housing navigate the new order. For extensive analysis of the full qualitative dataset, as well as statistical analyses of national surveys, see my book, *Housing the New Russia* (2012).

Before I present qualitative evidence on lived experience, I will briefly compare Russia's socialist and post-socialist housing regimes, that is, the political and ideological apparatuses that shape the lived experience of housing.[1] To conceptualize regimes of housing distribution, I turn to Karl Polanyi's (1957 [1944]) typology of modes of economic organization: market exchange, state redistribution, reciprocity within social networks, and household self-provisioning. Market exchange dominates in capitalist regimes and state redistribution dominates in socialist regimes, but the various modes of distribution can coexist. For instance, in capitalist economies, young people typically purchase housing through mortgage markets, but extended family often help with down payments (reciprocity), while tax credits may subsidize mortgages (redistribution). The particular mix of allocating mechanisms in any society characterizes its regime of distribution.

The Soviet housing regime: redistribution and reciprocity

In 1957, Nikita Khrushchev launched the largest public housing initiative in history. The goal was to house every Soviet nuclear family in its own apartment within two decades. These so-called "separate apartments" were to replace "communal apartments," a unique form of socialist housing in which multiple families were forced to share apartments expropriated by the revolutionary state. The urban housing stock more than doubled and half the Soviet population was rehoused from 1955–1970; 40 percent of households moved into new apartments between 1970 and 1985. By the 1980s, the party state owned over 80 per cent of the urban housing stock. This feat was accomplished through standardized production using prefabricated materials, and emphasizing quantity over quality. This first generation of mass Soviet housing—known as *khrushchevkas*—was shoddy by Western standards. Still, in 1960s Russia, amenities such as a private kitchen, central heating, and indoor plumbing were luxuries.

Despite the pace of construction, demand always exceeded supply. Apartments were allocated via queues: people who qualified could join waiting lists at their workplaces or through their municipalities. Eligible persons included those with less than nine square meters of space per capita, households composed of more than two generations, families with multiple children, and residents of communal apartments and hostels.

State redistribution mattered most, but other modes of distribution also existed. Reciprocity took two forms. First, people helped each other through the informal economy of favors. Personal connections to administrators of housing queues enabled jumping ahead in the line. Second, families passed resources across generations, as residency rights were lifelong and transferable to descendants. A quasi-market also existed: people could swap residency rights at will, often accompanied by illegal side payments. Finally, in rural areas, where the state owned only one-third of housing, many families built their own ramshackle houses.

Although standardized designs limited inequality—most apartments had from one to three rooms—significant inequalities persisted in waiting time and the quality of apartments received. Some differences were a function of family structure and generation. Those who became eligible to queue in later decades received better apartments, since design improved over time. Although later Soviet apartments had larger rooms and more "auxiliary space" (bathroom, kitchen, hallway), few had more than three rooms; most had one or two.[2]

Other inequalities were less happenstance. Official ideology held that basic housing was a right for all, but good housing was a right for work. In fact, status and connections mattered more than personal productivity. White-collar professionals and party members were better housed, although socialist ideology glorified manual workers. Economic sectors favored by central planners received more resources for housing construction. Within enterprises, people with personal connections often jumped ahead in queues that were supposed to be ordered by need and seniority.

Despite these problems, the separate apartment had transformed from a newfound luxury to a commonplace expectation. To live in a separate apartment was to "live normally." Soviet people came to view a separate apartment as both a gift and a right. Although legal ownership remained with the state, Soviet citizens experienced the dwellings they inhabited as their own.

The post-Soviet housing regime: reciprocity and redistribution amidst market failure

After the Soviet Union collapsed, the new government tried to transform the socialist housing sector into an American-style market. To jumpstart the market, residents were allowed to privatize for free the housing units in which they were officially registered in 1992 (or subsequent state housing they might receive through residual housing queues).[3] Privatization created the chief source of household wealth in the new economy. However, those without decent housing at the time, who were disproportionately young, lost out. Twenty per cent of the population had been queuing for improved housing, while another 25 per cent were hoping to become eligible to join queues. But queues barely moved, since state construction and distribution plummeted.

The architects of housing reform expected the market to provide for those who missed out on the great giveaway of 1992. Financing would be provided by "a Russian copy of the American secondary mortgage market system" (Mints 2000: 50). Nevertheless, a mortgage market failed to emerge, for complex reasons explained in Zavisca (2012: Chapters 2 and 3). After a decade of retrenchment, the state reinvested in the housing sector through subsidies targeted to stimulate mortgage markets, as well as the declining birthrate. The centerpiece of the new initiative is "Maternity Capital," $10,000 vouchers for all Russian women who gave birth to a second child after 2007. The vouchers can only be applied toward housing, education, or the mother's pension. Related policies include downpayment assistance for young families, mortgage lending by state-sponsored banks, and subsidies for constructing economy housing.

These policies were accompanied by an intensive social marketing campaign. National leaders touted mortgages as the route to a civilized market; related advertisements appeared on billboards and public transportation. Figure 12.1 shows such an ad. A family of four clutches a maternity capital certificate, a new apartment building behind them. The caption reads: "Maternity Capital: pay down your housing loan by 312,000 rubles."

Yet when the fledgling market peaked in 2008, Russian mortgage debt stood at just 3 percent of GDP, compared to 50 percent in the European Union and 80 percent in the United States. The emerging market was decimated by an economic

FIGURE 12.1 Government advertisement for Maternity Capital. The caption reads: "Maternity Capital: pay down your housing loan by 312,000 rubles." *Source*: Pension Fund of the Russian Federation

crisis in 2009. As of 2010, fewer than 3 per cent of Russians had ever had a mortgage. Most could not qualify for a loan, even with Maternity Capital. Interest rates of about 12 percent are part of the problem—but similar interest rates prevailed internationally until the 1990s. The main issues are unstable salaries and high prices relative to incomes.

Restricted credit also impeded construction. Builders targeted a small luxury market for luxury buyers who could pay cash. Figure 12.2 depicts a typical *khrushchevka* building in Kaluga. In the background is a new apartment building, purchasable only by those who could pay a high price in full. The epitome of post-Soviet luxury housing, however, is the detached modern home. Figure 12.3 depicts two elite houses in Kaluga, built just behind a modest prewar house. These new houses, which comprise a tiny portion of the housing stock, are visible reminders of the drastic growth in inequality.

Most Russians continue to live in the Soviet housing stock. Ninety per cent of existing housing was constructed before 1995. In the Kaluga region, about one-third of apartment buildings date to the Khrushchev housing campaign, and half to the Soviet period after 1970. Another 5 per cent are pre-World War II (Rosstat 2011). Many of these apartments are in bad shape, with poor insulation, decaying pipes, and problems with moisture and mold (UNECE 2004).

This privatized Soviet property does recirculate on a secondary housing market. Yet half of official transactions involve inheritances or gifts, not sales, and many informal transfers among relatives do not get officially recorded. Even access to cash-only markets is conditioned on redistribution—access to privatized government housing—and reciprocity—transfers of privatized housing within the extended family. These are the defining features of the regime of property without markets.

FIGURE 12.2 Apartment buildings in Kaluga. The building in the foreground is a *khruschhevka* from the 1960s; the building in the background was built during the post-Soviet period.
Source: Photograph by Anastasia Smirnova

The lived experience of property without markets

A successful market transition should have made earnings in labor markets a path to housing mobility. However, two decades after the collapse of socialism, labor markets play a limited role in determining housing chances. In an analysis of the Russian Longitudinal Monitoring Survey (RLMS),[4] I found scant association between housing mobility and standard measures of market position such as wages, occupation, and education (Zavisca 2012: Chapter 4). Nevertheless, the housing order is not completely static. By the age of 40, over half of Russians do obtain a place of their own. For young people, housing chances now depend most of all on reciprocity—gifts of privatized property from the extended family.

Young Russians are thus sharply stratified into two housing classes: those with and without secure housing of their own. Consistent with local understandings, I classify young adults as "owners" if they live in a residence in which at least one member of the household either holds title or retains the right to privatize, and in which the household is comprised only of members of the nuclear family, i.e. self, spouse, and/or minor children. As of 2009 only one-third of urban Russians aged 21–40 had such housing. Half were living with extended family; the rest were renting or living in hostels.

Young Russians also differ in the physical qualities of the apartments in which they live. Renovation (*remont*) is a national pastime, as Soviet apartments require

FIGURE 12.3 Detached homes in Kaluga. The modest house in the foreground was built before World War II. The luxury homes in the background were built within the past five years.
Source: Photograph by Anastasia Smirnova

constant repair. At the same time, markets provide new opportunities to upgrade interiors, given sufficient income. Some structural aspects of quality such as size, however, cannot be improved by renovating. According to the RLMS of 2009, just one in four urban Russians age 21–40 lived in dwellings with at least one room per person. One in three lived in homes with fewer rooms than there were generations in the household, forcing multiple generations to sleep in the same room.

Qualitative evidence is consistent with these statistical trends. In the Kaluga interview study, most respondents with homes of their own had received a gift or inheritance of privatized Soviet housing. For example, Sergei, a 26-year-old construction worker, lived with his wife in an apartment his mother inherited from her sister. The two-room apartment, built in the 1970s, had "everything a modern person needs—a large kitchen, isolated rooms, separate toilet and bathroom, a telephone, internet, everything." Although the apartment still technically belonged to Sergei's mother, who was living in a village not far from Kaluga, she promised to transfer title to him, and he described the apartment as his own.

Starting capital for housing purchases can usually be traced back to an inheritance or gift from extended family. For instance Marianna, director of a local company, was able to buy a new apartment only with help from family. She lived with her mother-in-law in a two-room *khrushchevka* until her husband inherited an apartment in another city from his grandmother. With proceeds from selling that apartment, plus their own savings and cash gifts from both sides of the family, they purchased a three-room apartment.

Young people without their own places often devise housing strategies around expected inheritances. Extended families try to distribute inheritance rights so as to provide for all young adults if possible. For example, Max lived with his wife Vera's grandparents, whose apartment she expected to inherit. Living with Vera's grandparents was the only arrangement among extended family that would provide them with their own room. Vera's parents only had a one-room apartment; spare rooms in Max's parents' apartment were already occupied by his brother's family of three. Although Max owns a one-quarter share of that apartment, he expected his brother to remain there long-term.

Vera's grandparents promised to bequeath their apartment to Vera, in implicit exchange for her helping them in their old age. Vera's grandparents will likely die before Max's parents do, meaning Max will have his own place before his brother does. However, there is a trade-off in quality and security. His future apartment is much older and smaller than his parents' apartment, which was constructed in the 1980s. Max is also at greater risk than his brother in case of divorce. Families are usually careful to exclude in-laws from potential property claims. When young people who have moved in with spouses must leave, they may have already missed their chance to inherit from their own relatives.

Reliance on intergenerational transfers creates family tensions and conflict. Young adults often urge their parents to exchange their apartments for two smaller ones, which may leave parents in poor conditions for the rest of their lives. Grandparents also fear losing control before they die. Raisa's story illustrates such tensions. Raisa was living with her husband Peter and their son in a tiny room in a workers' hostel. They rented the room for a pittance from Peter's great-aunt, who told them they could stay there until her grandson turned eighteen.

Their housing woes suddenly seemed solved when her grandmother decided to move to her childhood village to live with her own sister. She offered Raisa her apartment, as long as she could keep a room there for when she came to town. However, the plan fell through, leaving Raisa despondent: "We helped her renovate that apartment. We put a lot of energy and money into it and we felt at home there. But then she decided she didn't like living in the village, and she brought her sister here to live with her. So far she hasn't put us on the deed. Also now she says we need to split our inheritance with our cousin in Kazakhstan, so she wants us to buy out his share, which of course we can't afford to do."

Others with multiple siblings and/or no extended family had no hope of a gift or inheritance. Diana lived with her parents and brother in a one-room apartment, which they had partitioned into tiny sleeping areas. Miserable as her conditions were, she could not afford to rent, let alone buy her own place. Marriage was her only exit strategy. Her parents half-jokingly encouraged her and her brother to only date people who had their own apartments.

All these strategies—awaiting inheritance, cajoling elders, getting married—rely on familial reciprocity, not labor market earnings. There was little talk of working to buy an apartment. Young people without inheritances felt shut out of markets. As Oksana, who lived with her husband and child in her parents' three-room apartment, explained:

> Only people who already have property can buy housing. Because even with a good salary by Kaluga standards, you won't be able to buy an apartment. You've got to have starting capital, for example a grandmother. I have a friend who got her own apartment when her grandmother died. They sold it and borrowed money from their parents to buy a better apartment.

However, affordability is not the entire story—many young people who could afford to rent or borrow choose to live with extended family instead. This disposition derives from the distinction young Russians draw between autonomy and security when evaluating housing options.

The meaning of ownership: autonomy and security

When the Russian government tried to import the American housing system, it transplanted formal institutions, but did not successfully transplant the cultural understandings of ownership that legitimate mortgages in the U.S. As in China after privatization, property rights in Russia involve "bundles of meanings embedded in the institutions of family and kinship, the party-state, and the market" (Davis 2004: 290). In the United States, owning versus renting is the primary distinction people use to categorize housing tenure. Russians by contrast employ two principles of classification—autonomy and security—to interpret property rights. Autonomy means living separately from extended family (*otdel'no*) as the master of one's own domain (*khoziain*). Security entails affordable and permanent control over property rights.

Figure 12.4 below illustrates these differences in classification schema. In the United States, living with one's parents beyond high school or college is rare, an incomplete transition to adulthood. By contrast many Russians live with extended family well into adulthood, making autonomy a key criterion for evaluating housing

Tenure	United States	Russia
live with parents	not adult	not autonomous but secure
renter	on one's own	autonomous but not secure
mortgagor	homeowner	
titleholder without mortgage		separate and secure

FIGURE 12.4 Cultural classifications of housing tenure.

conditions. The two cultures also cognitively collapse different forms of tenure. In the US, titleholders with and without mortgages share the status of "homeowners." Russians rarely use the word homeowner (*sobstvennik*), except when discussing legal matters. They also do not equate mortgages with ownership. Mortgagors in Russia have more in common with renters than do unconditional owners, because both mortgages and rentals violate the key criteria for security—affordability and permanent property rights.

Ownership as autonomy

Nearly ninety per cent of urban Russians aged 21–35 were living in "owner-occupied" homes in 2009,[5] the highest proportion across both Western and Eastern Europe.[6] However, two-thirds of these were living with extended family such as parents, grandparents, and in-laws. Even married couples were nearly as likely to live with extended family as on their own. In Western Europe and the United States, by contrast, intergenerational households and living at home after marriage are rare (Ruggles 2007). Other former Soviet countries, including new EU member states, also stand out for their high rates of multigenerational households (Billari *et al.* 2001; Mandic 2008).

Post-Soviet societies resemble Southern Europe, which also combines high homeownership rates with late leaving of the parental home (Schwartz and Seabrooke 2008). This tendency in Italy, Spain, and Greece has been attributed to traditional family values as well as constrained housing markets. However, traditional values do not keep young Russians living with their parents. In focus groups commissioned by the Russian government, respondents identified the need for separate apartments as the key housing problem facing young families. A national survey asked respondents about the best living arrangement for a young family of two spouses under age 30. Among respondents aged 18–35, 86 percent asserted that young couples should live separately from their parents; 80 percent of older people concurred (FOM 2007).

Most interviewees in Kaluga echoed this sentiment. Oksana, for example, disliked living with her parents. Oksana owned a one-third share of her family's privatized apartment. Nevertheless, she perceived the apartment as belonging to her parents and longed to have her own place where she could "hang her own curtains." She also noted the problem of "two women in the kitchen," shorthand for inter-generational conflicts between women over how to organize the household. When the interviewer asked her to what extent she is satisfied with her living conditions, she replied:

> Of course some people have it worse. But I long to live separately. But there is no way we could afford to buy a place. Therefore we try to satisfy ourselves with what we have.

Interviewer   And what would you like to change about the apartment you are living in?

| *Oksana* | Well we just want to live someplace else! Because "fathers and sons" living together leads to conflicts between generations. |
| *Interviewer* | Yes, everyone knows that. |

A young woman named Alya attributed her recent divorce in part to the stress of living with in-laws. But upon moving back in with her mother and grandmother, she remained an unwanted extra woman in the kitchen. Her mother and grandmother bickered constantly over how to organize the household, and rarely consulted Alya on their decisions. Having little hope of moving on her sales clerk's salary, she viewed living separately as a basic human need and right: "Everyone has the right to some kind of housing of their own. When you live alone, you can solve your own problems between your own walls, without parents, and found a normal, healthy family."

Max, the young man living with his wife's grandparents, also longed for independence. "Lots of people are stuck living with their parents," he noted. "With grandparents, it's even worse! They are nice people, but they are old and have a different lifestyle." The extended family of four shared a two-room apartment, the young couple in the smaller room, the older couple in the larger one. The couple helped their grandparents renovate soon after moving in: they replaced the flooring and most of the pipes, and installed a metal security door. Nevertheless, the apartment is poorly insulated, cold in winter and stuffy in summer. So far funds have not sufficed to replace appliances and fixtures. Even the apartment's smell irritates Max: "The apartment reeks of old age. It's a Soviet relic."

Max and Vera strove to carve a sense of personal space (at least, personal for the couple—personal space for individuals was out of the question). They removed the carpets from the walls, a prototypically Soviet style of décor that doubles as insulation. They bought two computer desks with laptops, on which they spend most of their waking hours at home. Between the desks on one wall and a sofabed and wardrobe on the other, their narrow room is stuffed with furniture. They will have to remove the desks eventually to make room for a crib and play corner for the child they hope to have.

Max at least had a separate room. Others were less fortunate. Martha, a single mother and seamstress, shared a two-room apartment with three generations—her child, adult brother, and grandmother. (Her parents had moved to their rundown dacha but visited frequently to cook and shower.) Martha's brother slept in one room, and Martha shared the other with her grandmother and son. Three beds and a TV stand took up the entire room. "We are crammed in there like illegal migrants," she exclaimed.

The building and apartment needed major repairs. The top-floor apartment suffered constant ceiling leaks and mold, as well as occasional burst pipes.[7] The apartment was also very drafty. The city renovated the building's balconies for fear they would fall off. However Martha was still afraid to use it, or to replace the windows. When a neighbor removed an old window to install a new one, the entire wall crumbled.

Martha fixed up the room she shared with her grandmother and son—she put up new wallpaper, upgraded the furniture, and installed better flooring. She also constructed a makeshift hallway so she would not have to walk through her brother's room to get to hers (making the small rooms even smaller). As for the shared areas of the apartment, "Why should I borrow money to do costly renovations, when no matter what I do living here will continue to be a nightmare?" Instead, she took out a loan each summer to escape to an economy resort in the south of Russia with her son.

In such conditions, Martha was ashamed to invite guests to what she called her "family dormitory." She only felt happy when everyone else was out of the apartment. "If I lived here only with my son, I would fix things up and scrub every corner clean," she said. "If only this was all mine."

Martha's story illustrates how property rights influence experiences of housing quality. Many young Russians will only put effort into renovations, even cosmetic ones, if they feel a sense of practical possession of the space (or the expectation of future possession). Sergei, for example, recalled his pleasure at fixing up his inherited apartment. "I loved the process. I didn't mind the running around or the expense. We bought all the things we never bothered to buy before: new furniture, dishes, pictures for the walls." Costly capital renovations were going slower, but he enjoyed doing it himself.

Quality problems also seem more tolerable in a place of one's own. Veronica, just 21 years old, inherited a *khrushchevka* from her deceased father, who had left the family when she was young and whom she barely knew. She had been living there for two years with her husband and was expecting a child. The infrastructure was as decrepit as Martha's, since they could not yet afford repairs. Nevertheless, when asked how satisfied she is with her housing conditions, she replied:

	It's wonderful in these times to have a two-room apartment. We are absolutely satisfied. We don't complain.
Interviewer	You mentioned problems with pipes and heating and such. Do those things bother you?
Veronica	Those are little things. It's normal. What's important is that I got my own apartment.

Ownership as security

Most young Russians believe that to live separately is to live normally. If living with parents and grandparents is so difficult, why don't more young Russians rent or take out mortgages? Some cannot afford to. Others, given a choice between autonomy and security, choose security. Many respondents named renters when asked to describe the worst housing conditions among people they know. The conditions are often decrepit, Max claimed, since "as everyone knows, as soon as an apartment becomes a rental, maintenance completely stops. You have to fix everything yourself and pay for it, yet it still won't be yours." Likewise, Oksana declared: "Renting is worst of all options. You pay money to some stranger and never know when you will have to leave."

A fraction of young urban Russians do rent—about 8 per cent of urban young adults as of 2009. The Kaluga interview study included 40 renters to get a better sense of their motivations and experiences. Most had no property and no local family with whom they could live. Some had migrated from other places; others' families had asked them to leave due to overcrowding; and still others were escaping violent, abusive homes. Some, mainly affluent and highly educated, could have lived with extended family but chose to rent instead.

Most renters prized their autonomy, saying "it's good to be one's own boss." Nevertheless, even those renting by choice were deeply dissatisfied with their housing conditions due to cost and instability. Few renters have a formal rental contract, causing them to worry constantly about eviction. Several renters suggested that renting made them feel like *bomzhi*, an acronym for persons without a registered address, which also means "bum." Varvara, a doctor with one child, said she would not bring another "homeless" child into the world in a rental apartment. If not for rent, she said, they could have a normal family life: she could take maternity leave and afford a second child.

Although renting provided privacy from parents, many renters complained they could not feel at home in a stranger's apartment. Most Russian landlords are proprietors of only one or two apartments, which they commonly use as storage for everything from old furniture and appliances to books and clothing. One respondent contrasted Russian rentals with her understanding of renting in the West: "In the West, if you rent an apartment, you can make yourself at home. But here you feel like you've come to stay with some auntie and you're underfoot. She's given you permission to stay with her, and charges a fortune for the privilege."

Renters routinely remarked that they were unwilling to fix up someone else's space, even cosmetically, both because it wasn't theirs, and because they feared a rent increase or eviction. One renter, an interior decorator by trade, had done nothing to fix up her rental because she worried her landlord would notice and evict her on the pretense that a relative of his needed housing. Even Raisa, who was renting from a distant relative, refrained from making improvements to her apartment:

> We've been living here for four years. We were on the verge of fixing it up several times, but we understood we'd be investing money in someone else's apartment, which we'd be better off saving. Naturally everyone wants to make their surroundings more comfortable, and no one will be opposed if you do. But when the owners see that you've made their apartment valuable, they will find renters who can pay more and say to you: "Goodbye, go live someplace else."

Mortgages solve some of these issues by providing control over the interior and more stable property rights, given consistent loan payments. Oksana, unhappy living with her parents, thought a mortgage would be better than renting: "In either case you pay a lot. But with a mortgage, after twenty years of paying, at last you'll own a home." However living at home was preferable to either option, she said. Several respondents living with family looked into mortgages when advertisements began appearing around Kaluga, but were turned off by the terms. Max was shocked by the "astronomical overpayment" in interest. "Within five years you will have paid the original cost of the apartment, yet you have to keep paying another five or ten years. What's the point? You go into debt for two apartments, and you don't even own the first one until you've paid for the fictitious second one as well!" Likewise, Alya ruled out mortgages after looking into them: "You've got to have a completely stable salary for twenty years. Our country is in crisis, and you want to speak about mortgages. Today you are working, but what about tomorrow? They can take away the apartment, and leave you with a *kabala* for the rest of your life."

Kabala, which means debt bondage, was the most common metaphor for mortgages across the interviews, framing them as an exploitative, lifelong burden. As Varvara, a renter, put it: "I would never put myself in such an unstable position. How could I be sure nothing would happen to me or my husband or to our jobs? Who would pay then? Our children? They'd be thrown out of the apartment along with us, and we'd live on the street. No. It's a twenty-year *kabala*."

Mortgagors had come to a different conclusion about the relative merits of mortgages versus renting or living with parents. Several interviewees with mortgages had no extended family in Kaluga; others were escaping extreme crowding. Maria, a museum curator, had been living in a two-room apartment with her parents, her boyfriend, and her sister's family of three. She managed to get a highly subsidized loan through a "mortgage demonstration project." Despite her 30 per cent subsidy, the mortgage was a family endeavor. Her parents and sister cosigned for the loan so she could qualify, and all were pitching in on payments. Likewise, Kirill had been living with his wife and mother-in-law in a one-room apartment. After their son was born, the crowding became intolerable. He landed a high-paying job and decided a mortgage was preferable to renting.

Like renters, mortgagors highlighted their autonomy from extended family. Kirill was happy to have "separate housing where we are in control. We can do what we like, without parents and without landlords." Yet the risk of foreclosure and extraordinary expense mean that mortgages do not satisfy Russians' criteria for ownership, which require security as well as autonomy. Ten of the twelve mortgagors in the Kaluga study did not call themselves owners, although they held title to their homes. Kirill, for example, said his mortgaged apartment belonged to the bank: "We've got to pay 17,000 rubles a month for 30 years. When we finish paying, the apartment will finally become our property."

The cost of monthly payments also made it difficult for some mortgagors to renovate their dearly purchased homes. Maria could only afford a one-room *khrushchevka* on the outskirts of town. She was slowly fixing it up, but doing most of the work herself or with help from family. Kirill by contrast hired professionals to gut the three-room Soviet apartment he had mortgaged. He took out an addition loan for "Euro-standard" renovations, including knocking out interior walls to create an open-design kitchen and living area. However, the extra debt left him feeling even less like an owner. His earnings declined in the wake of the recent economic crisis, and he began to call his mortgage a *kabala* and a yoke around his neck.

In sum, conceptualizing property rights in locally meaningful terms—autonomy and security—illuminates the lived experience of housing in a way that conventional statistics on housing tenure, which tend to focus on homeownership rates, cannot. If we overlook autonomy, we will overstate the degree to which young Russians living in "owner-occupied housing" experience that housing as their own. And if we ignore the premium Russians place on security, we will fail to understand why so many Russians prefer to live with extended family versus renting or borrowing.

Immanent critique of the post-Soviet housing regime

In their study of factories in the U.S. and Hungary, Burawoy and Lukacs conclude that consent to domination at work is the result of hegemonic organization, such that the ideological system "does not stand out from lived experience." In contrast, within state socialist regimes, domination is despotic and transparent, leading workers to notice gaps between the promises and lived experience of socialism, generating an "immanent critique" of these gaps (1992: 127). Post-Soviet domination, at home as well as at work, is also more ideological than hegemonic. This is evidenced by young Russians' critiques of the new housing regime, which are grounded in lived experience.

Most young Russians perceive the manifest gap between the ideology of market justice and the arbitrary reality of housing inequality. Capitalist ideology holds that a just market is open to all and rewards hard work (Lane 1986). Surveys on perceptions of fairness suggest that Russians evaluate the legitimacy of markets in terms of their distributive justice (Kluegel and Mason 2004). Inheritance strikes most Russians as an unfair principle for determining the haves and have-nots. Experiences with housing, perhaps more than any other commodity, thus give rise to immanent critique.

Responses to questions on the possibility of earning housing reveal the logic of this critique. Respondents were asked which of the following statements they thought better described the situation in Kaluga: (A) "If a person is capable and works hard, he can earn an apartment," or (B) "No matter how hard a person works, he will not be able to afford an apartment." Responses were about evenly divided between the two options. However, follow-up probes on why respondents chose a given option revealed extreme ambivalence and contradictory discourses, reflecting the contradictions of the housing order itself. It turned out that most respondents who chose option (A) were either describing a remote possibility for an elite class, or endorsed the ideal of merit-based distribution but denied its reality. For example, Alya, who lives with family, initially said "Of course it's possible to earn an apartment; anyone can achieve anything if they set a goal and work intensively toward it." But she quickly backed away from this position:

In our parents' time, it was easier to set a goal of earning an apartment, because people knew what they were working toward. If they worked long enough at a given enterprise, they would eventually receive an apartment. Today, an average person could never save enough to buy an apartment because there is no proportionality between wages and housing prices. Before, work made you middle class. Now there are only rich and poor. I'm not even middle class, even though I'm a store manager, because I can't earn my own apartment. I don't know who manages to buy apartments now—probably only thieves and businessmen.

Even mortgagors did not necessarily agree that it was possible to earn an apartment. Yuri was fairly satisfied with his mortgage, as his earnings were high and he was paying it down quickly. But in response to the question on earning housing, he noted that people who work a lot in today's Russia do not necessarily earn a lot. All the people he knows who had bought new apartments had an inheritance as starting capital. Likewise, he does not think that mortgages make housing more affordable; he personally got lucky with timing and prices. Yuri, like most respondents, thinks that in principle it would be better to be able to earn an apartment through the market than to wait in a Soviet queue. "But the conditions would have to be normal. Serious people are prepared to work, but of course they are afraid to take out a loan. You've got to deny yourself everything and risk everything, in hopes that you will finally live normally after you retire."

The perception that it was easier to earn an apartment in the Soviet system than today is widespread. This perception directly contradicts the promise of market reform that the value of labor would determine who got what. Most would not want to revert to the Soviet epoch in general. As Oksana put it: "In Soviet times, it was possible to earn an apartment by the age of 35. Now it's possible for few. Of course, one needs to live in the present. Nevertheless, it would be fairer if the government would at least give one-room apartments to young people whose grandmothers didn't already give them something."

Likewise, 90 percent of national survey respondents in 2007 agreed the government should help families who need to improve their housing. Nearly as many, when asked an open-ended question about how to improve housing conditions, said that the government should control prices, either by selling housing "for what it actually costs," or at least by establishing a "fair relationship between cost and price" (FOM 2007). In the Kaluga survey, proposals for how to help young families were couched in the language of market justice, but defied the market ideology of prices set by supply and demand. Raisa turned the government's campaign to promote mortgages on its head:

They say "We've got to help young families," but only offer us these useless mortgage vouchers and do nothing about astronomical prices relative to incomes. They complain that we don't want to have children, and we don't want to work in factories. People did unpleasant factory jobs before because there was a stimulus—you would get an apartment. Lots of people would be happy to work in factories if they would guarantee housing. And they would have one child after another. We're prepared to pay for housing out of our wages, but give us the conditions to make that a realistic goal.

Critiques of the status quo go beyond accusations of an unfair relationship between work and housing outcomes. As we have seen, critiques also emerge from the gap between Russian understandings of ownership and the tenure options that American-style markets produce. The two main forms of tenure in such markets—mortgages and rentals—fail to resonate with the dual values of autonomy and security embedded in Russian understandings of ownership.

In conclusion, Russians judge their housing conditions according to their perceptions of how things used to be under socialism, and how they should be under capitalism. The gap between expectations for a normal life and actual conditions, between government promises and lived experiences, produces a pervasive sense of personal suffering and a collective sense of a housing system in crisis. To be sure, some young Russians live in satisfactory conditions, and a few have managed to achieve housing mobility through labor markets, either by purchasing new housing or renovating old housing. Nevertheless, even those with high housing class positions are aware of the role of luck in their own housing trajectories and the difficulties others face. Dependence on family and limited opportunities to earn autonomous and secure housing leads young Russians to experience the post-Soviet housing order as arbitrary and unfair.

Notes

1 For supporting evidence and citations for claims made in this section, see Zavisca 2012, Chapters 1–3.
2 Note that Russians count the total number of rooms in an apartment, not the total number of bedrooms, as rooms typically serve multiple functions.
3 Each person could privatize only once in their lifetimes. The right to privatize did not have to be exercised immediately and the deadline to do so has been extended until 2013.
4 Russia Longitudinal Monitoring Survey, RLMS-HSE, conducted by the Higher School of Economics and ZAO "Demoscope," together with the Carolina Population Center, University of North Carolina at Chapel Hill and the Institute of Sociology RAS. http://www.cpc.unc.edu/projects/rlms-hse
5 Note that, unlike many other analysts, I classify people who have not yet privatized but are eligible to do so "owner occupiers," because their de facto property rights are tantamount to ownership.
6 Based on my analysis of the *European Quality of Life Survey, 2007* (European Foundation for the Improvement of Living and Working Conditions 2009); statistical results are available upon request.
7 For qualitative accounts of plumbing issues and neighborly relations, see Hendley (2011)

References

Billari, F.C., Philipov, D. and Baizán, P. (2001) 'Leaving Home in Europe: The Experience of Cohorts Born Around 1960,' *International Journal of Population Geography* 7: 339–356.

Burawoy, M. and Lucaks, J. (1992) *The Radiant Past: Ideology and Reality in Hungary's Road to Capitalism*, Chicago: University of Chicago Press.

Burawoy, M., Krotov, P. and Lytkina, T. (1999) *Ot dereviannogo Parizhe k panel'noi orbite: model'-zhilishchnykh klassov Syktyvkara*, Syktyvkar: Institut regional'nykh sotsial'nykh issledovanii Respubliki Komi.

Davis, D.S. (2004) Talking about Property in the New Chinese Domestic Property Regime. In *The Sociology of the Economy* (ed. Dobbin, F.), New York: Russell Sage, pp. 288–307.

European Foundation for the Improvement of Living and Working Conditions (2009) *European Quality of Life Survey, 2007* [computer file], Colchester, Essex: UK Data Archive [distributor], October 2009.

FOM (2007) *Zhil'e dlia molodykh semei.* May 31. http://bd.fom.ru/report/map/d072223 (accessed May 15, 2012).

Gudkov, L.D., Dubin, B.V. and Zorkaia, N.A. (2011) *Molodezh' Rossii*, Moscow: Moskovskaia shkola politicheskikh issledovanii.

Hendley, K. (2011) 'Resolving Problems among Neighbors in Post-Soviet Russia: Uncovering the Norms of the Pod"ezd', *Law and Social Inquiry* 36: 388–418.

Kluegel, J.R. and Mason, D.S. (2004) 'Fairness Matters: Social Justice and Political Legitimacy in Post-Communist Europe', *Europe-Asia Studies* 56: 813–834.

Lane, R.E. (1986) 'Market Justice, Political Justice', *American Political Science Review* 80: 383–402.

Mandic, S. (2008) "Home-Leaving and Its Structural Determinants in Western and Eastern Europe: An Exploratory Study," *Housing Studies* 23(4): 615–637.

Mints, V. (2000) 'Selecting a Housing Finance System for Russia', *Housing Finance International*, 15: 49–57.

Polanyi, K. (1957 [1944]) *The Great Transformation*, Boston: Beacon Press.

Rex, J.A. (1968) The Sociology of a Zone of Transition. In *Readings in Urban Sociology* (ed. Pahl, R.), London: Permagon Press, pp. 211–231.

Rosstat (2011) *Zhilishchnoe khoziaistvo i bytovoe obsluzhivanie naseleniia v Rossii: 2010.* http://www.gks.ru/bgd/regl/b10_62/Main.htm (accessed May 15, 2012).

Ruggles, S. (2007) "The Decline of Intergenerational Coresidence in the United States, 1850 to 2000," *American Sociological Review* 72: 964–989.

Saunders, P. (1984) "Beyond Housing Classes: The Sociological Significance of Private Property Rights in Means of Consumption," *International Journal of Urban and Regional Research*, 8: 202–227.

Schwartz, H. and Seabrooke, L. (2008) "Varieties of Residential Capitalism in the International Political Economy: Old Welfare States and the New Politics of Housing," *Comparative European Politics* 6(3): 237–261. Available at: http://dx.doi.org/10.1057/cep.2008.10 (accessed May 21, 2012).

Sewell Jr., W. (1980) *Work and Revolution in France: The Language of Labor from the Old Regime to 1948*, Cambridge: Cambridge University Press.

Szelényi, I. (1983) *Urban Inequalities under State Socialism*, Oxford: Oxford University Press.

Thompson, E.P. (1978) "Eighteenth-Century English Society: Class Struggle without Class?," *Social History* 3: 133–165.

UNECE (2004) *Country Profile on the Housing Sector: Russian Federation.* http://www.unece.org/hlm/prgm/cph/countries/russia/welcome.html (accessed May 15, 2012).

Willis, P. (1990) *Common Culture: Symbolic Work at Play in the Everyday Cultures of the Young*, Boulder, CO: Westview.

Zavisca, J. (2012) *Housing the New Russia*, Ithaca, NY: Cornell University Press.

INDEX

Note: Figures are indicated by *italic page numbers*, Tables by **emboldened numbers**, and notes by suffix 'n' (e.g. "38n4" means "page 38, note 4")